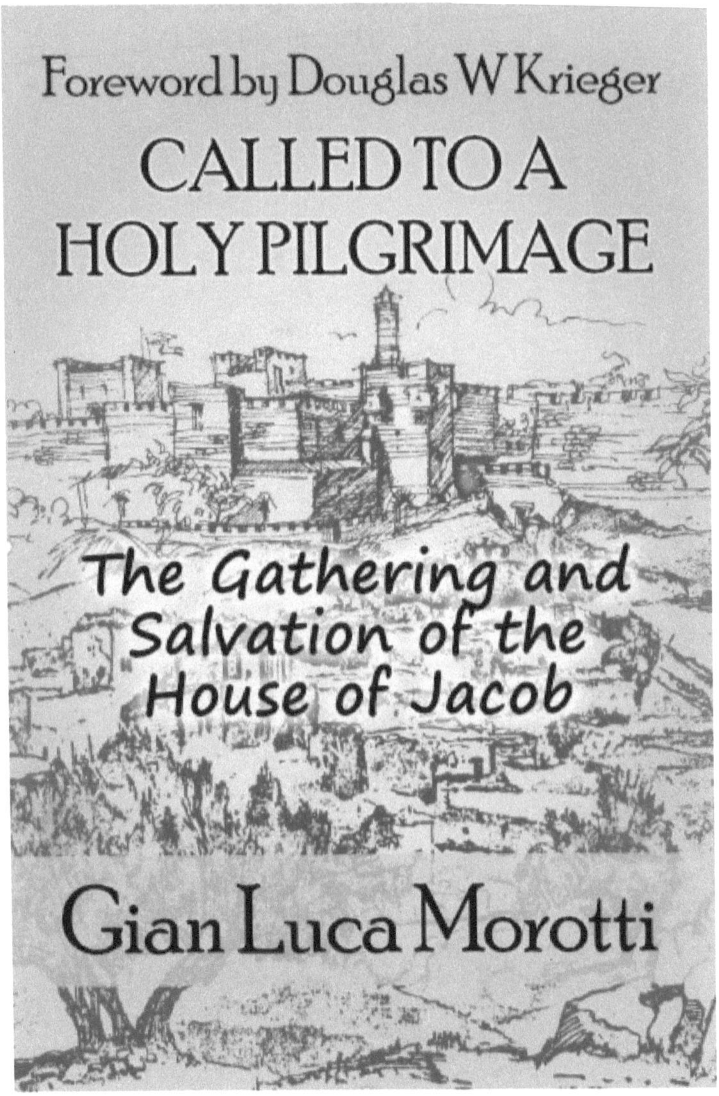

Foreword by Douglas W Krieger

CALLED TO A HOLY PILGRIMAGE

The Gathering and Salvation of the House of Jacob

Gian Luca Morotti

"The glory of this Latter Temple shall be greater than the former"
(Haggai 2:9 NKJV).

Figure 1 - Joshua Crossing the Jordan River

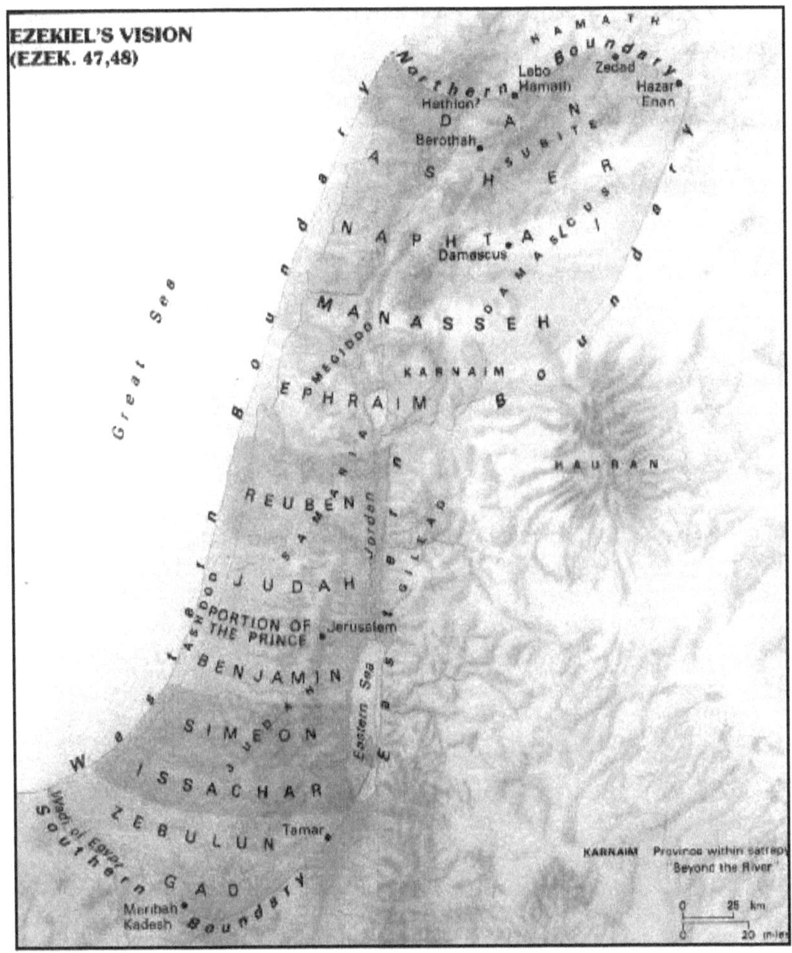

Figure 2 - Ezekiel's Tribes of Israel - Allocations

"'They shall have an inheritance with you
among the tribes of Israel. And it shall be
that in whatever tribe the stranger dwells,
there you shall give him his inheritance,'
says the LORD GOD... 'and the name of the city
*from that day shall be: **THE LORD IS THERE . . .***
YAHWEH SHAMMAH'"
(Ezekiel 47:22-23; 48:35 NKJV).

Called to a Holy Pilgrimage...The Gathering and Salvation of the House of Jacob
By Gian Luca Morotti
Foreword by Douglas W. Krieger

Copyright © 2020 by Gian Luca Morotti,
Phoenix, AZ, USA

ISBN- 979-8-9855176-6-8

Printed in the United States of America
Publication House: Commonwealth of Israel Foundation
info@commonwealthofisrael.org
Phoenix, AZ
In Cooperation with:
Tribnet Publications, Sacramento, CA
https://www.facebook.com/TribnetPublications/

Cover Design by Chris Steinle of the Commonwealth of Israel Foundation – Phoenix, AZ

Ordering Information:
Special discounts are available on quantity purchases by corporations, associations, educators, and others. Contact the publisher or distributor for details.

info@commonwealthofisrael.org
Commonwealth of Israel Foundation
P.O. Box 31007
Phoenix, AZ 85046
U.S. trade bookstores and wholesalers: Please contact the distributor.

CALLED to a Holy PILGRIMAGE

The Gathering and Salvation of the House of Jacob

Oh that the salvation of Israel would come out of
Zion! When God brings back the captivity of His
people, let Jacob rejoice and Israel be glad.
(Psalms 53:6)

By

Gian Luca Morotti

Foreword by Douglas W. Krieger

Commonwealth of Israel Foundation

PHOENIX, ARIZONA

Table of Contents

Figure 3 - Ezekiel's Valley of Dry Bones

Table of Figures

Dedication & Acknowledgements

Dedication

To my wife Michela, the love of my life, and to all those who have believed that the time to favor Zion has come and have given themselves unreservedly to the cause of the Jewish people and their return to the promised land of Israel. Their unlimited commitment validates and brings honor to the prophetic Scriptures.

Acknowledgements

In our personal walk God brings us in contact with people who definitely make an important contribution in determining the final product of the multicolored tapestry of our lives. One of these is Dr. Michael Lake for whom I have insufficient words to express my deep gratitude for the years he equipped me through Biblical Life College and Seminary to do the work of the ministry and for instructing me on the dynamics of warfare in the Kingdom of God.

I then would be extremely remiss not to give my deep appreciation to my longstanding mentor, Douglas W. Krieger, for the influence he has added to my understanding of the prophetic sequence of the scriptural events leading up to the unveiling of Yeshua in the seven-year period at the closing of this present age of fulfillment.

Endorsements

We at Restoration Fellowship International are indeed honored to call Gian Luca Morotti a fellow colleague and partner in advancing the prophetic work of Jesus the Messiah in the earth, and especially His prophetic plan for Israel in these last times. For many years, Gian Luca has been networking with numerous like-minded ministries in Italy, Israel and around the world, which shows forth his holy calling. This magnificent book is his next venture in declaring this vision in a clear, systematic prophetic manner, as only an anointed servant of the Lord could do. Get ready to become an inspired partner in this great quest and calling!

Dr. John A. Looper
Executive Director of Restoration Fellowship International
Tennessee, USA

In his book, ***Called to a Holy Pilgrimage...The Gathering and Salvation of the House of Jacob***, Gian Luca Morotti develops a well-balanced, theologically sound eschatological treatment on the gathering of the Jewish people to Israel, and the responsibility of the commonwealth of Israel - saints in the nations - to share in the Lord's work in these days. Buried beneath mountains of supersessionist theology are found God's promises to Abraham, Isaac, and Jacob. Promises being fulfilled before our eyes. As the eyes of Christian brethren are opened to the covenant Lord's plan for the Jewish people, they discover the fullness of their own shared inheritance, identity, and purpose in the economy of God. Gian Luca assists the reader to look again, with new eyes, at the promises fulfilled, and those yet to be fulfilled, as He draws the Jewish people to their Messiah, Yeshua/Jesus, and to Abraham the promise of nations (Genesis 12:3). I encourage everyone with a heart for the Jewish people, Israel, the Messiah to consider carefully *Called to a Holy Pilgrimage.*

Rabbi Dr. Justin D. Elwell
Messiah Congregation
New York, USA

Thank you, Gian Luca for these writings that reflect an in-depth investigation and analysis under prayer. It is going to be an instrument to help us understand with more clarity God's love and faithfulness to the Jewish People.

Enrique D. Porras
Regional Coordinator for Ebenezer in Latin America
Texas – USA

Gian Luca Morotti's book *Called to a Holy Pilgrimage* describes the Lord's call to the Jewish people: back to Israel, to relationship, to Moses (the Word of God), to transformation, to salvation, and to family reunion. Gian Luca brings a wealth of understanding through examining important concepts in the original Hebrew and their derivatives. It is interesting to learn how Bible-believing Christians from the Reformation onwards have understood the prophetic Scriptures regarding the return of the Jews and the restoration of Israel, e.g. the Puritans, Charles and John Wesley, Spurgeon, J.C. Ryle, and Rees Howells. Also, how Christian Zionism interacts with and both influences and is influenced by Jewish Zionism. I found the chapter *Called to Moses* illuminating with the role played by Rabbi Akiva ben Josef in creating Rabbinic Judaism, and the need now for the Jewish people to return to the *Tanach* as the Word of God. The ultimate purpose of the Lord to bring both Jews and Gentiles together in one new man in Yeshua is treated in an excellent manner. The many illustrations give added attraction to the book.

Philip Holmberg
Ebenezer International Prayer Hub, Sweden

It has been a great blessing to know that the revelatory teaching entitled ***The Threefold Plan of God for The Jewish People*** that Gian Luca brought to us in Quito, Ecuador to a wide audience of pastors and leaders from Latin America, USA, and Canada, as part of our 2019 Ebenezer Operation Exodus Summit of the Americas, later on, became in his heart, the trigger that ignited and motivated him write a divinely guided plan for a full expansion of its spiritual content, bringing, as a result, his enlightening compendium entitled *Called to a Holy Pilgrimage.* The reader of this extraordinary book will find how God is now calling us as His elect among the nations to assist the Aliyah (*going up)* of the Jewish people to the Holy Land, so they might have a progressive spiritual maturity by returning (*going up*) in accordance with God's Word, putting as a result in motion their redemption process that will be culminated with the Second Coming of Messiah. After all, and as described in the book, we have a common heritage, which will make all of us (Jews and Gentiles) *going up* one glorious day to Jerusalem, where God will rule in the person of Jesus Christ on the throne of David.

Heriberto Gonzales
Senior Pastor of Centro Cristiano Filadelfia
Monterrey, Mexico

I have had the privilege to know Gian Luca personally since many years in our walk within the Aliyah ministry. His conviction that the church in our days has a call to bless Israel in the process of the worldwide ingathering of Jewish people after almost 2000 years of diaspora has led him to write this book. Sad to say that a topic which should be part of basic Bible study for every believer has become a marginal issue amongst Christians. My prayer is that many believers may be stirred in their Spirit to start to bless Israel.

Johannes Barthel
Regional Coordinator for Ebenezer International
Germany

I do recommend this book because it is not simply a story of Israel going back to its homeland, neither a list of prophecies that have already come to pass and others that will be accomplished in the future, but it gives us a clear revelation of how we, as gentiles, have entered into the Commonwealth of Israel to share all its promises while shedding light into the salvation of the Jews once they have recognized Yeshua as the Messiah! Blessings upon whoever reads this book!

Romolo Giovanardi
Senior Pastor, Fonte di Vita Church
Modena, Italy

My Italian brother has produced, with God's help, a thorough biblical analysis of the ultimate purpose for Jewish Aliyah, and the role of Gentile believers in supporting this prophetic process as we look forward to the return of Yeshua Messiah. Thank you, Gian Luca, for persevering and seeing this much needed project of understanding through to completion. May the Lord be glorified through the vast end-times mission of Aliyah now underway as He draws His ancient covenant people back to their land and unto Himself.

Gary H. Kah
Author of *En Route to Global Occupation*
Executive Director, Hope for the World
EOE Board of Directors

Gian Luca's systematic presentation of the subject of the "Gathering and the Salvation of the House of Jacob," beginning from the legacy of the Old Testament to the calling to engage in this prophetic task is a brilliant and significant work. He writes with a clarity that comes from not only knowing the prophetic scriptures but also carrying the burden to 'help the Church see' how the fulfillment of her destiny is inextricably connected with the restoration of the Jewish people to their land and to their God.

Be prepared to go on a journey of discovering your part in this great end-time regathering of the House of Jacob. Through these pages, your love for God and your whole-hearted commitment to His cause will be constantly stirred empowering you to engage prophetically and practically in this great redemptive work that God Himself is doing with all His heart and all His soul (Jeremiah 32:41). No way to drop this book until much has moved within your soul. You will want to share this book with everyone you know.

Abe Thomas Oomen
Senior Pastor of The Exodus Church
Kerala, India

Called to a Holy Pilgrimage systematically persuades the reader to consider God's Word, to observe history, and then to embrace the living move of the Spirit, which is drawing Christians and Jews to participate in the common cause of fulfilling man's part in the regathering of Israel. Verses such as Jesus' lament over Jerusalem—that *"they were not willing,"* and *"They shall raise up the former desolations . . ."* (Isaiah 61:4), are indicative of man's role in the Gathering. Without spending superfluous time on the errors of prior theologies, Gian Luca passionately bears the torchlight of Pre-Zionism's British and Scottish Restorationists. I pray only that this skillfully constructed work will become a game-changer in Judeo-Christian thought and attitude towards Israel's active and imminent restoration.

Chris Steinle
Author, Christian Philosopher, Former Minister, CPA – RET.
Editor, Commonwealth of Israel Foundation, Board Member,
Phoenix, AZ - USA

The longing for home is something that almost everyone who has been born has experienced. A long journey that has kept us away from the place of our birth or our upbringing. However, what Gian Luca has captured is something that goes much deeper. It is not just an individual longing to be home, but a whole nation of people. How do you explain a phenomenon on this scale? To what can we attribute such a supernatural desire? The call to go "home" extends its hands beyond time and space and has gripped not only the genetical prodigy of Abraham, but also those who can prove no lineage to Israel. Gian Luca has captured the biblical truths and provided solid evidence within a firm theological framework of *why* this is. Thousands of "Jews" are pouring into Israel out from among the diaspora every year. If you want a true biblical understanding of why this "calling home" is taking place and perhaps even find scriptural evidence for your own desire to dwell in "The apple of God's eye" then this is the book for you! A blessing is sure to follow any who should read this book! Get wisdom. And with thy getting, get understanding.

Chad J. Schafer – Author – Podcast: Disputed Lands

An exciting book! Jesus said the generation that sees the budding of the fig tree would not pass away until all was fulfilled. Gian Luca, in *Called to a Holy Pilgrimage*, masterfully brings together many Scriptures and Rabbinic commentaries to reveal the exciting ways in which God is regathering His people and how the story is much bigger than imagined!

Dr. Douglas Hamp, M.A., PhD
Author, Lecturer, Senior Pastor of The Way Congregation
Commonwealth of Israel Foundation, Board Member
Denver, Colorado - USA

Figure 4 - Ebenezer Operation Exodus - Logo

Figure 5 - King of the Universe - There is Only One

Summary

CALLED to a Holy PILGRIMAGE...The Gathering and Salvation of the House of Jacob is a searing vision of the gathering of Jacob's Household in accordance with the promises of the Hebrew prophets of the Bible who saw and proclaimed as certain the regathering of the children of Israel to the Land of promise in the end times. In it, you will learn that the regathering of the House of Jacob is unto salvation and in stages. The first one is in unbelief (Aliyah)—followed by a nationwide progressive return to the God of Abraham, Isaac, and Jacob in expectation of the coming of Messiah (Zechariah 9:9-10). This pilgrimage has been oriented toward a heavenly promise, that is why it is sacred. Between the promise and the fulfillment lies a life journey of transition to its culmination and a reminder that God is faithful to fulfill His promises at its ultimate conclusion.

Along their route to their journey's end, YHVH, their Creator, has always been mindful of their lot . . . the destiny and the place He had prepared for the children of Israel, while looking forward to the consummation of their encounter with their familial relative, their brother Joseph, a type of Messiah, at the time of His unveiling. What a sight it shall be! But there is more to it than you can possibly imagine, as Jacob's final days are marked by a family reunion with their fellow brethren—the Elect from among the Nations (aka, the Gentiles). At long last, the longstanding rift between the two separate houses of Jacob-Israel (viz. Judah and Ephraim) are about to come to an end! Through my inscriptions you will come to appreciate your citizenship in the obscure but awesome reality of the *Commonwealth of Israel,* while being challenged to prophetically engage by defending the rights of the House of Jacob to their homeland and discovering what is your part in this great regathering at the end of days.

Figure 6 - Zechariah's Universal Menorah & Two Olive Trees

Foreword

By Douglas W. Krieger

"The glory of this latter Temple shall be greater than the former."

(Haggai 2:9)

The rather inglorious laying of the foundation of the Second Temple under the governorship of Zerubbabel witnessed the confused weeping and joy of the elders and newbies . . . for the Second Temple (the first having been destroyed by King Nebuchadnezzar cir. 586 BC on the 9th of Av) paled into insignificance to that of Solomon's massive display of Israel's ascendency in her first temple.

Right, *"For who has despised the day of small things?"* (Zechariah 4:10). In some cosmic prophetic sense the Universal Lampstand displayed in Zechariah 4 was some 49 years in its ultimate dedication from the time of the Cyrus Decree in 537 BC (ending Judah's Seventy-year Captivity) until its completion in 482 BC . . . but the ever-quoted perseverance of the task challenges us to the core:

> *"This is the word of the LORD to Zerubbabel: 'Not by might nor by power, but by My Spirit,' Says the LORD of hosts'"* (Zech. 4:6).

Zerubbabel became the Lord's "signet ring" (Haggai 2:23) to accomplish the task of the Second Temple's rebuilding; his accomplishment was undergirded by this fact: *"'I have chosen you,' says the LORD of hosts"* (Haggai 2:23). It is that announcement of "chosen-ness" which ignites a global outcry against divine election in the first place. Today's breakdown of the Judeo-Christian ethic—antithetical to a globalist mindset which after WWI brought us Communism, Nazism, and Fascism—awaits us in America . . . as in what shall America's breakdown bring us?

I do not digress . . . because the absolute Pilgrimage launched by Gian Luca Morotti and his fellow brethren is embedded in that Judeo-Christian ethic with, trust me, the same contrary results which are leading us to *"nation against nation"* (ethnic wars) and *"kingdom against kingdom"* (ideological wars) forecasted by Yeshua as the "beginning of sorrows" or ever-increasing "birth pangs" prior to His Coming and the commencement of the Messianic Kingdom (Matthew 24:7-8).

Now, let us pivot in what appears to be a completely different focus (but it isn't) . . . that being the Second Temple's dedication mentioned in Haggai's account, in comparison to that of King Solomon's extravaganza—well, putting it mildly, it was the "hut vs. the Empire State Building." They offered "10 bulls, 200 rams, 400 hundred lambs, and 12 goats for the number of the tribes of Israel at the Second Temple's dedication (Ezra 6:17) vs. 22,000 bulls and 120,000 sheep at the Solomonic Temple's dedication (2 Chronicles 7:5).

Not comparing ourselves with ourselves here, but one can readily see that Haggai's *"glory of this latter Temple shall be greater than the former"* does not seem to be comparing apples to apples. One of two things is going on with Haggai—he is either delusional or "he sees something we don't!"

Another oddity observed in Ezra's account are the 12 goats representative of the 12 Tribes of Israel, when in blatant fact it was but Judah, Benjamin and some of the Levites who returned to Jerusalem with the other Ten Northern Tribes, going on some 200 years (745-537 BC) of prior captivity and assimilation among the nations (Hosea 8). Judah and Ephraim were hardly joined at the hip by the time of the Second Temple (488 BC) rolled around. Thus, a faint reminder of sorts?

Notwithstanding the Lord made Zerubbabel like a "signet ring" via election to accomplish His purpose; and, simultaneously crowned Joshua as the Priest-King with an *"elaborate tri ple-braided gold-silver crown"* (lit. "crowns"—Zechariah 6:14) with a signet on its frontal bearing the "name of YHWH" which was thence placed for a memorial in the temple of the LORD . . . *"even* [for] *those from afar shall come and build the temple of the LORD . . . Then you shall know that the LORD of hosts has sent Me to you . . . and this shall come to pass if you diligently obey the voice of the LORD your God"* (Zechariah 6:11, 14-15).

Regarding this "memorial crown/crowns" Israel My Glory states:

"Messiah the branch will build the Temple with gifts donated by righteous Gentiles: 'Even those from afar shall come and build the temple of the LORD. Then you shall know that the LORD of hosts has sent me to you' (v. 15). In other words, like the Jewish delegation from Babylon, Gentiles will bring gifts to Jerusalem; and the Messiah will use them to construct the Millennial Temple (Isaiah 2:2–3; 60:5, 9, 11; 61:6)."[1]

Now, allow me in this Foreword to illuminate the dedicated work and effort of Gian Luca Morotti's ***Called to a Holy Pilgrimage – The Gathering and the Salvation of the House of Jacob***, whereby I shall forthwith unscramble what surely appears as a series of disconnected scriptural passages regarding the *"glory of this latter Temple"* being *"greater than the former."* Once the pieces of the puzzle are arranged in place, then the reader will clearly see the panorama of this mystifying Foreword concerning Morotti's work with Ebenezer International—it does make sense, on a prophetic scale!

The movement by these "righteous Gentiles" from afar, who are committed to building in the House of the Lord, His Temple, are awaiting and effectually impacting the day when Messiah shall be crowned with many crowns as our **King-Priest** after, no less, the Order of Melchizedek—*"first being translated*

---

[1] Israel My Glory @ https://israelmyglory.org/article/messiahs-coronation-and-reign/ (Retrieved on 08.08.2020)

'king of righteousness,' and then also king of Salem, meaning 'king of peace' . . . another priest should rise according to the order of Melchizedek . . . For it is evident that our Lord [Yeshua] *arose from **Judah**, of which tribe Moses spoke nothing concerning priesthood* (only that of the Tribe of Levi—Levitical priesthood—*"for under it the people received the law"*). . . *And it is yet far more evident if, in the likeness of Melchizedek, there arises another priest who has come, not according to the law of a fleshly commandment, but according to the power of an endless life"* (Hebrews 7, excerpts).

You see, Gian Luca Morotti and his fellow brethren are involved in the *"glory of this latter Temple"* which Haggai, as well as Zechariah, repeatedly saw—Haggai from the Temple's perspective and Zechariah, as well, from that of the coming of Messiah as King-Priest (Zerubbabel/Joshua). They, like Zerubbabel, have been "elected" for such a time as this. They know full well their Temple's dedication is involved with Daniel 9:24's vision of the Seventieth Week at the end of the age when *"TO ANOINT THE MOST HOLY PLACE . . . To restore and build Jerusalem until Messiah the Prince"* Who shall reign from Zion's Holy Hill in the United Kingdom of David---for *"The scepter shall not depart from Judah, nor a lawgiver from between his feet, until Shiloh comes; and to Him shall be the obedience of the people"* (Genesis 49:10).

Yes, Haggai repeatedly saw the dedication of this "Latter Temple" beyond the Second Temple's dedication—he saw it again and again *"On the twenty-fourth day of the ninth month"* (Kislev 24/25—Haggai 2:10, 15 [from this day forward], 18, 20). Could it possibly be Haggai's adumbrative tone and calendric timing foresaw, as well, the Feast of Dedication in 165 BC, some 323 years beyond the Second Temple's dedication cir. 488 BC . . . how else could the repetition of Kislev 24/25 be explained? And, more so, how can we explain two other Festival of Lights where Yeshua at this Feast of Dedication in John 10 said to the

Jewish people: *"My sheep hear My voice, and I know them, and they follow Me . . . I and My Father are one"* . . . and so it was and still is a "stumbling block" to His brethren according to the flesh, *"because You, being a Man, make Yourself God"* (John 10:26, 29, 33).

But the day is coming when *"the glory of this latter Temple shall be greater than the former"* for His, the Father's House, *shall be a House of Prayer for all people* (Isaiah 56:7; Jeremiah 7:11; Matthew 21:13; Mark 11:17). How will this be? How would the second Feast of Dedication, to which I alluded, come to pass? How will the "many crowns" be placed upon Him Whose Name is BRANCH—for . . .

> *"Behold, the Man whose name is the BRANCH! From His place He shall branch out, and He shall build the temple of the LORD; Yes, He shall build the temple of the LORD . . . He shall bear the glory, and shall sit and rule on His throne; so He shall be a priest on His throne, and the counsel of peace shall be between them both"* (Zechariah 6:12-13).

Indeed, a final Feast of Dedication awaits us all—and those fulfilling this prophetic destiny by hastening that day are described as follows:

> *"Thus says the LORD GOD: 'Behold, I will lift My hand in an oath to the nations, and set up My banner for the peoples; they shall bring your sons in their arms, and your daughters shall be carried on their shoulders . . . all flesh shall know that I, the LORD, am your Savior, and your Redeemer, the Mighty One of Jacob"* (Isaiah 49:22, 26b).

Those so bearing these children joyfully await that day when *"all flesh shall see it together"* – when in the "latter times" . . . Daniel's 70th Week shall be fulfilled:

> *To finish the transgression,*
> *To make an end of sins,*
> *To make reconciliation for iniquity,*

> *To bring in everlasting righteousness,*
> *To seal up vision and prophecy,*
> And **TO ANOINT THE MOST HOLY PLACE**.
> (Daniel 9:24)

That will be the Feast of Dedication at the close of the 45 days of blessing, for *"Blessed is he who waits, and comes to the one thousand three hundred and thirty-five days"* – some 75 days beyond the close of the 70th Week and 45 days beyond the *"days of desolation"* (the 1,290th day). This is when the Savior and Redeemer of Israel, the Lion of Judah, the Son of David, shall take His scepter, His crown, and reign from His Holy Hill over all the earth.

Now, we are engaged in the lead up to that culminating day: TO ANOINT THE MOST HOLY PLACE. That is precisely why the glory of the LATTER TEMPLE will be far surpassing all other temples in glory . . . for we shall see in this **Pilgrimage** back to Zion has in view this LATTER TEMPLE. "Greater" because, even now, we:

> *". . . have come to Mount Zion and to the city of the living God, the heavenly Jerusalem, to an innumerable company of angels, to the general assembly and ekklesia of the firstborn who are registered in heaven, to God the Judge of all, to the spirits of just men made perfect, to Jesus the Mediator of the New Covenant, and to the blood of sprinkling"* (Hebrews 12:22-24).

Why is this so? Because there is a "brotherly attachment" stronger than Judah's estrangement from Ephraim-Israel whereby Jesus would die *"not for that nation (Judah) only, but also that He would **gather together in one** the children of God who were scattered abroad"* (John 11:52).

At the crux of Morotti's engagement, is that we within the Commonwealth of Israel:

> *". . . are no longer strangers and foreigners, but fellow citizens with the saints and members of the household of*

God, having been built on the foundation of the apostles and prophets, Jesus Christ Himself being the chief cornerstone, in whom the whole building, being fitted together, grows into a HOLY TEMPLE in the Lord, in whom you also are being built together for a dwelling place of God in the Spirit" (Ephesians 2:19-22) – this is the *"glory of the Latter Temple."*

This is the PEACE wrought through the Savior and Redeemer of Israel between Jews and Gentile (aka "the nations") in that:

"Therefore remember that you, once Gentiles in the flesh—who are called Uncircumcision by what is called the Circumcision made in the flesh by hands—that at that time you were without Christ [aka Messiah], being aliens from the commonwealth of Israel and strangers from the covenants of promise, having no hope and without God in the world. But now in Christ Jesus you who once were far off have been brought near by the blood of Christ. For He Himself is our PEACE, who has made both one, and has broken down the middle wall of separation . . . to create in Himself ONE NEW MAN from the two, thus MAKING PEACE, and that He might reconcile them both to God in ONE BODY through the cross, thereby putting to death the enmity. And He came and preached PEACE to you who were AFAR OFF and to those who were near. For through Him we both have access by one Spirit to the Father" (Ephesians 2:11-18).

Yes, you will hear of Hebraic terms propelling those holding Judah's sons and daughters in their arms and on their shoulders in that a Greater Exodus culminates in the Latter Temple. Jacob's ladder where the angels ascend and descend are the "GREATER THINGS" seen by Nathanael upon the Son of Man, Son of God . . . the very place Jacob called BETH-EL: The House of God. God is being brought to Man, and Man is being brought to God (John 1:47-51).

This then is the impactful, intensely personal, account given in "***Pilgrimage***"—believers in Yeshua's Person and Work, we Christians, will find Gian Luca Morotti's impressions unusual and theologically invigorating—assisting on a worldwide basis the movement, the Aliyah, of the Jewish people to Eretz Israel. It is time, overtime, for the Ekklesia Jesus is building to come to terms with her scriptural mandate in that "... *if the Gentiles have been partakers of their spiritual things, their duty is also to minister to them in material things*" (Romans 15:27). Their regathering, their awakening to Torah, and finally their encounter with their Deliverer, their Salvation.

The healing of the "breach of Jeroboam" is taking place—we have every opportunity in participating in this Greater Exodus—all the more since we have discovered that we are those "*children of God who were scattered abroad*"—those for whom Yeshua died—not only for Judah but to "*gather together in one*" both Jews and Gentiles—this is "*The glory of this latter Temple*" – it "*shall be greater than the former!*"

Douglas W. Krieger,

Chair, The Commonwealth of Israel Foundation

Preface

Called to a Holy Pilgrimage is a searing vision of the gathering of the House of Jacob in accordance with the promises of the Hebrew prophets of the Bible who saw and proclaimed as certain the regathering of the children of Israel to the Land of promise in the end times. They spoke of a global scattering among the nations as a consequence of their disobedience and their plight in that journey, but with equal clarity and precision, they wrote of their return and of the glorious terminus awaiting the pilgrims on their return. In its complexity, their original exodus began with a call from God and has since been oriented toward a heavenly promise.

Between the promise and the fulfillment lies a life journey marked by trial and uncertainty at times, of faith and vision at other times. It has been a transition to a final destination and a reminder that God is faithful to fulfill His promises at their ultimate destination. During their pilgrimage to a higher level of holiness, the House of Jacob has never been left void of the covering protection and provision of their Creator, YHVH. Along their route to their final destination, He has always been mindful of their immediate lot while keeping in view their destiny—the place He had prepared for them. The history of the Hebrew people in their plodding towards the goal of their ultimate salvation is one of constant tension in the here and now; of the invisible expectation versus the completion of their calling in the visible reality of their future estate in the consummation of their encounter with their family brother, Joseph, a type of Messiah, at the time of His unveiling to them. What a sight! What a grand deliverance and provision!

Personally speaking, I recall the times when, still in my early childhood, the many and various occasions when my mother would come and sit beside me at bedtime to wish me a good night . . . and with a tender voice—that still resounds within me—she would tell me the story of the Exodus of the children of Israel and of their wandering in the desert, in their pilgrimage to the promised land. In particular, I was very much impressed anytime she would put emphasis on the faithfulness of God towards them, stressing that despite their disloyalty to the Covenant He made with them, He would yet be faithful to His Word to restore and save them at the time they turned to Him by calling on His Name.

> *"And the Lord will scatter you among the peoples, and you will be left few in number among the nations where the Lord will drive you. And there you will serve gods, the work of men's hands, wood and stone, which neither see nor hear nor eat nor smell. But from there you will seek the Lord your God, and you will find Him if you seek Him with all your heart and with all your soul. When you are in distress, and all these things come upon you in the latter days, when you turn to the Lord your God and obey His voice (for the Lord your God is a merciful God), He will not forsake you nor destroy you, nor forget the covenant of your fathers which He swore to them"* (Deuteronomy 4:27-31).

Then her story would usually turn to the Last Days whereupon the emphasis would increase to the point where all that was unveiled before my eyes were the attributes of the Lord's faithfulness and mercy towards His own people despite their wanderings from Him, because God keeps Covenant. Yes, He would have remembered His Covenant with Abraham, Isaac, and Jacob and would repent of the evil which He thought to do unto them if only they returned to Him—*Oh, give thanks to the LORD, for He is good! For His mercy endures forever.* The bedtime stories were not about a fable, but simply what she had learned from reading the Bible. Some years passed by and on other occasions my mother would call my attention by pointing me to the moon or the sun out there in the sky at twilight, being amazingly red and larger than usual. I recall these astronomical happenings especially occurring when we were travelling by car. These became special moments to me, so much so that these signs in the heavens made a lasting impression on my mind anytime she would exclaim with a sense of imminence: "Look at the sky. Jesus said that in the last days there would be signs in the heavens, the moon will turn red and the sun will be darkened before the coming of the Lord!" Undoubtedly, these facts were life-changing to me as the Lord was evidently speaking destiny into my life. He was planting in my spiritual DNA a hunger for knowing the times and seasons concerning the return of the Lord, and the regathering of the Jewish people to the land of Israel (Eretz Israel) being an integral part of that scenario as both events are intrinsically connected. The Lord Himself had been faithful and manifested these things to be true in my life as He used His promises and other events to corroborate what was being implanted in me in my early childhood. With regard to this, I have always been impressed by one of the Almighty's divine attributes wherein He declares the end from the beginning and from ancient times things which appear incomplete, saying that His counsel shall stand and that He will fulfill all His good pleasure (Isaiah 46). So, in light of these premises I was drawn by the Lord to meditate on a set of promises which, when combined together, would disclose His purposes for the end-times' agenda. Allow me to frame one of them found in Isaiah 43:5-6: *"Fear not for I am with you: I will bring your descendants from the east, and gather you from the west; I will say to the north, 'Give them up!' And to the south, 'Do not keep them back!' Bring my sons from afar, and my daughters from the ends of the earth."* These words had been so real to me that if someone asked why I believed that God existed, I would answer: "Beyond a shadow of a doubt, because one day I clearly heard His voice talking to me through these very words of Isaiah 43; His voice was like the sound of rushing waters breaking forth in my spirit."

Called to a Holy Pilgrimage, The Gathering and the Salvation of the House of Jacob was written to help those believers who are passionate in their uncompromised love for Israel and the Jews and who have made their voices heard on behalf of truth revealed in the Scriptures, but who are looking for balance after several swings into zeal, excitement, hype, and then to the far side, experiencing rejection, harsh criticism, and avoidance.

Here I believe I have added one last component to their knowledge—the missing link—the facet or part that is needed to be related to the whole about the gathering of the Jewish people UNTO SALVATION—their ultimate DELIVERANCE! After all, their salvation is what it is all about. Hence, I trust that what is contained in this book is a *"truth that is presently coming to you"* (2 Peter 1:12) which I regard as mandatory at this immediate time and season. Yet, that which is presented here represents only a facet of truth—I am not able to consider orchestrating the whole body of truth on the topic at hand . . . albeit there are indeed other portions of truth upon which the Spirit of God is laying emphasis upon my heart. For now, I have been moved to emphasize writing about the importance regarding the return of the Jewish people to their Land of promise as paramount in the plan of God for their final salvation. Still, I do not wish to explore the possibility of this final salvation of the Jews in a scenario which sees them welcoming Yeshua the Messiah outside of Eretz Israel. I realize that many sincere believers in Yeshua, especially among the messianic community, contend there is no biblical mandate for all Jews in the diaspora to go back to *Eretz* Israel for the day of the unveiling of their Messiah, the Deliverer. Others, instead, maintain those Jewish people remaining in the diaspora—those not yet believers in Yeshua—shall, at the time of the second coming of Messiah, be found alive and thus shall be gathered into His kingdom all at once, but not prior to that day. Consequently, my cognitive contribution is addressed to the purposes of God for those He gathers into the land prior to the day when *"The deliverer* (Messiah) *will come out of Zion, and He will turn away ungodliness from Jacob"* (Romans 11:26; Psalms 14:7; Isaiah 59:20-21).

Called to a Holy Pilgrimage, The Gathering and Salvation of the House of Jacob constitutes the expansion of the Bachelor's Essay in Biblical Studies in Hebraic Heritage for Biblical Life College & Seminary, deriving from the teaching that I gave to the leaders of Ebenezer Operation Exodus in Latin America in 2019 in Quito (Ecuador), entitled ***The Threefold Plan of God for The Jewish People***. It came from hearing in Jerusalem a friend of mine (Iris Goldman) repeatedly say that the plan of God for the Jewish people could simply be defined in three words: *Aliyah, Klitah, Yeshua*.

Figure 7 - Rebirth of Eretz Israel - 1948

Figure 8 - The "Journey Home" Today

CALLED to a Holy PILGRIMAGE

The Gathering and Salvation of the House of Jacob

By

Gian Luca Morotti

Figure 9 - All Israel Shall Be Delivered

Chapter 1
Legacy of the Hebrew Scriptures

After seventy years are completed at Babylon, I will visit you and perform My good word toward you, and cause you to return to this place.

(Jeremiah 29:10)

A Restored Message For Our Generation

THE BOOK OF 2 CHRONICLES CONCLUDES WITH A REMARKABLE APPEAL TO MOBILIZATION ON BEHALF OF THE JEWISH PEOPLE REGARDING THEIR captivity in Babylon. We read in chapter 36 that:

"Now in the first year of Cyrus king of Persia, that the word of the LORD by the mouth of Jeremiah might be fulfilled, the LORD stirred up the spirit of Cyrus king of Persia, so that he made a proclamation throughout all his kingdom, and also put it in writing, saying, 'Thus says Cyrus king of Persia: All the kingdoms of the earth the LORD God of heaven has given me. And He has commanded me to build Him a house at Jerusalem which is in Judah. Who is among you of all His people? May the LORD his God be with him, and let him go up!'" (2 Chronicles 36:22-23).[1]

According to the order of Hebrew biblical canon[2] (the 24 books of the Masoretic Text, the Hebrew Bible or 39 "expanded" in most language translations of the same) what we have just read would be the very final words recorded in the Old Testament

---

[1] The initial deportation of Judah commenced when King Nebuchadnezzar was Viceroy in the year 608/607 BC, which commenced the 70-year captivity of Judah, with the return to rebuild the wall of the City of Jerusalem given by the decree of the Persian King, Artaxerxes I Longimanus in the year 444 BC. The full 70-year captivity of Judah ended in 537 BC at the decree of Cyrus the Great.

[2] The term *canon*, from a Hebrew-Greek word meaning "cane" or "measuring rod," passed into Christian usage to mean "norm" or "rule of faith." It refers to the closed corpus of biblical literature regarded as divinely inspired. The Canon of Scripture is the list of all the books that belong to the Bible. The Church Fathers of the 4th century CE first employed it in reference to the definitive, authoritative nature of the body of sacred Scriptures.

Scriptures (aka, the Hebrew Scriptures). The Word of God is infallible (completely reliable, trustworthy and truthful) and by declaring its inerrancy, authority, infallibility and clarity we can only concur that it was not by chance that the Holy Spirit wanted these very words there, at the closing of the Jewish Bible.

With this choice, I believe that the Holy Spirit is bringing to our focus the last words of the Tanakh[3] for the unveiling of a specific and timely message to our generation. These very words are the reenactment of the Cyrus edict with which it inaugurated the movement of return of the Jewish people back to their own Land of promise after the Babylonian captivity. Cyrus's proclamation[4] ends with an imperative, to wit: *"Who is among you of all His people? May the LORD his God be with him, and let him **go up!**"*

Placed at the end of the book of 2 Chronicles the phrasal verb—**go up**—is loaded with a very significant meaning as God,

---

[3] The Hebrew Bible is often known as the TaNaKh, an acronym derived from the names of its three divisions: Torah (Instruction, or Law, also called the Pentateuch), Nevi'im (Prophets), and Ketuvim (Writings). The Torah contains five books: Genesis, Exodus, Leviticus, Numbers and Deuteronomy. The Nevi'im comprise eight books divided into the Former Prophets, containing the four historical works Joshua, Judges, Samuel, and Kings, and the Latter Prophets, the oracular discourses of Isaiah, Jeremiah, Ezekiel, and the Twelve (Minor—i.e., smaller) Prophets—Hosea, Joel, Amos, Obadiah, Jonah, Micah, Nahum, Habakkuk, Zephaniah, Haggai, Zechariah, and Malachi. The Twelve were all formerly written on a single scroll and thus reckoned as one book. The Ketuvim consist of religious poetry and wisdom literature—Psalms, Proverbs, and Job, a collection known as the Five Megillot (Five Scrolls; i.e., Song of Songs, Ruth, Lamentations, Ecclesiastes, and Esther, which have been grouped together according to the annual cycle of their public reading in the synagogue)—and the books of Daniel, Ezra, and Nehemiah, and Chronicles. The final redaction and canonization of the Torah book, therefore, most likely took place during the Babylonian Exile (6th–5th century BCE). *Encyclopedia Britannica biblical-literature/Old-Testament canon, texts-and-versions.*

[4] Many modern biblical researchers were skeptical about the wording of the declaration as described in the Book of 2 Chronicles and Ezra. Among other things, they claimed that it was improbable that a Persian king would have made a declaration in Hebrew or declared that he was acting as a messenger of the God of Israel. But archeological excavations conducted in the ancient city of Babylon in 1879, discovered a clay cylinder bearing a long inscription (it can be visited at the British Museum in London). The inscription included a plea made by King Cyrus to the Babylonians. *"I, Cyrus King of Babylonia... built for them a permanent Temple. I gathered all their inhabitants and restored their place of residence."* This archeological discovery strengthened the view that Cyrus was sympathetic and supportive of all the peoples under his rule and that the Declaration which appeared in the Hebrew Bible was an accurate reflection of history. https://mfa.gov.il/MFA/IsraelExperience/History/Pages/Israel-Post-issues-Cyrus-Declaration-stamp-16-Apr-2015.aspx

the author of the sacred Scriptures, wanted to use this particular word and insert it in its proper context to close out the Hebrew Bible, to leave a particular message to all readers of Holy Writ. The original Hebrew can help us in discovering the intrinsic import of the phrase *"let him **go up**,"* where in the original manuscript it is expressed by one word only—*yaal* (יַעַל)—which comes from a primitive root—*alah*—which literally means *ascend* (Strong's H#5927 עָלָה 'aw-law'—the verb became a technical term for 'making a pilgrimage') and it appears more than 300 times in the Bible with this meaning. It's verbal at the infinite form (לַעֲלוֹת - la'alot) is used accurately and figuratively to mean *to arise, cause to* or *make to ascend* or *come up, depart*. It designates the act of going up, of ascending towards a higher place and it is the word from which derives the expression **Aliyah**[5], namely, the *going up* or *ascend* to Eretz Israel, to the promised land of Israel. In fact, the origin of this term refers to the biblical description of the ascent of the Israelites to the Holy Land after the Exodus from Egypt as it is said that they went down to Egypt but then went up from there. At the end of the life of Jacob the Lord spoke to him saying:

> *"I am God, the God of your father," he said. "Do not be afraid to go down to Egypt, for I will make you into a great nation there. **I will go down to Egypt with you, and I will surely bring you back again**"* (Genesis 46:3-4).

In the weekly Torah portion[6] *Be'shallach* (lit. 'when he let go'—Exodus 13:17) I've found what perhaps is the first mentioning of this ascent when it says that *"the children of Israel **went up** (alu* in Hebrew—from *la'alot,* to go up, ascend) *in orderly ranks*

---

[5] עֲלִיָּה *aliyah,* ("ascent") is the immigration of the Jewish people from the diaspora (captivity) to the Land of Israel (*Eretz Israel* in Hebrew). Also defined as "the act of going up"—that is, towards Jerusalem —"making aliyah" by moving to the Land of Israel is one of the most basic tenets of Zionism. *Aliyah* is very significant for the people of Israel an important Jewish cultural concept and message that is set in the Bible from the very beginning and that is found everywhere in the Old Testament and stands as a fundamental component of Zionism. Someone who "makes aliyah" is called an *oleh* (pl. *olim*).

[6] It is a custom among Jewish communities worldwide for a **weekly Torah portion,** popularly referred to as a **Parashah** (lit. portion) to be read during the services on Saturdays, Mondays, and Thursdays. It formally means a section or portion of a biblical book in the Masoretic text of the Tanakh (Hebrew Bible). Each Torah portion consists of two to six chapters to be read during the week. There are 54 weekly portions or *parashot* in a year's cycle.

out of the land of Egypt" (Exodus 13:18). The act of descending and ascending needs to be seen in its general and all-inclusive meaning that has to do with the deliverance of the children of Israel. God so loved His ancient people that when he introduced His name to them through Moses (*"Say to the children of Israel: I am the LORD"*—Exodus 6:6)—not for the first time (ref. Genesis 15:7)—He wanted to make sure that He would fulfill the promise to the patriarchs in the exodus generation as the name יהוה (YHVH) would always be connected with the mercy and deliverance of God (although deliverance is a step by step process since it was not so easy to get Egypt out of Israel). In other words, "the guarantee of the fulfillment of the Divine promises lay in the nature of the Being Who had given the promises."[7] Not only is God set to perform His part in the covenant with them, but He definitely associates Himself to this peculiar people calling Himself to be their personal God, *"I will take you as My people, and I will be your God"* (Exodus 6:7).

The word **Aliyah** moreover denotes the **pilgrimage** which the children of Israel made three times a year in their ascension towards Jerusalem on occasion of the three major convocations; the fixed times of the biblical calendar they were required to attend (Passover, Pentecost, Tabernacles). According to the ***New International Dictionary of Old Testament Theology & Exegesis***, its root meaning of *ascent* (alah):

> ". . . is essentially literal, for travelers did indeed ascend when they made their way to the Holy City. In a most significant passage, the annual pilgrimages of the people to the central sanctuary are described as 'going up ... to appear before the LORD your God (Exodus 34:24).'"[8]

This three-times a year pilgrimage was called *aliyah le-reghel* (lit. ascent by foot), describing the holy pilgrimage that all Jewish pilgrims walked in their way to the temple in Jerusalem—*"Jerusalem, where the tribes go up"* (Psalms 122:3-4), because one

---

[7] Hertz, Rabbi Joseph; The Soncino Press, **Pentateuch & Haftorahs** (p. 232)
[8] **New International Dictionary of Old Testament Theology & Exegesis**, Vol. 3, p. 403 (Zondervan)

must always *"go up"* going to Jerusalem since it's elevated with respect to all others. Hence it follows that throughout the ages the Jews have made the effort to return to the land of Israel and live there or at least to take a journey to Eretz Israel, despite a multiplicity of obstacles.

God spoke clearly in Exodus 6:4 saying:

*"I have also established My covenant with them, to give them the land of Canaan, the land of their **pilgrimage**."*[9]

The ***Dictionary of Biblical Imagery*** defines the word ***pilgrimage*** as a:

". . . metaphor for the shape of the earthly life of anyone who is headed toward a heaven beyond this world. In all instances, the image implies a journey to a sacred place, and both facets are important–the pilgrim is always a traveler, but a fixed and glorious goal is always the final destination that motivates the journey."

Wherever they were, there was a Land waiting for them, and a journey. In modern history, from the late 19th century, there were mass migrations of Jews escaping from anti-Semitism in Eastern Europe and inspired by Zionist aspirations on the heels of the first Zionist Congress of 1897 promoted by Theodor Herzl. He is the one who promoted Jewish immigration to Palestine in an effort to form the Jewish State. Herzl is known to be the father of the modern Jewish State (as stated in the Declaration of the Establishment of the State of Israel—aka the Declaration of Independence[10]).

Fostered by a renewed interest in the formation of a national homeland for the Jewish people, the ensuing waves of ***aliyot*** (Hebrew plural form of Aliyah) continued throughout the 20th century, including Jewish refugees from Nazi occupied Europe before and after the Holocaust and those from Arab countries. After the birth of the State of Israel in May 1948, a policy of the in-

---

[9] The word ***pilgrimage*** appears 11 times in the Bible.
[10] https://www.knesset.gov.il/docs/eng/megilat_eng.htm

gathering of the Jewish exiles became a prime task of the new government when Jews from all over the diaspora were encouraged to make Aliyah. Subsequently, in 1950 a law of the Knesset gave legal right to all Jews to come and live in Israel and to gain Israeli citizenship. In its Section 1 it declares that "Every Jew has the right to come to this country as an *oleh* (immigrant)."[11]

Whether it occurred in time past or in the modern era, each case of Aliyah has been considered to be born from a point of view of someone being in exile. The term *exile* can be considered the state of a person who is banished.

> "While banishment is the moment in which a person becomes an exile, being an exile is the condition of life that follows. Exile encompasses a social role involving fringe status and a psychological state that includes as its salient features a sense of loss or deprivation and a longing to return to (or arrive at) a homeland" (**Dictionary of Biblical Imagery**).

With this helpful information we can already begin to define and delineate the message that the Hebrew Bible left with us, as being the *going up*, referring to the return to Israel by the Jewish people in exile through a call to leave their captivity, and to a moving on up to a better hope in Zion.

At this point it is essential to make it clear that my contribution surrounds the return of the Jews as it started from the going up to Jerusalem after the Babylonian captivity and in no way tries to encompass the whole migration of the "nation" of Israel at the time of the Exodus from Egypt. In this regard, about the return from Babylon the Bible speaks of two exiles. The first involved the Ten Northern Tribes—known as **Israel**—at the time when Assyria conquered and deported them in 721 BC. The second exile involved **Judah** (the Two Southern Tribes—Judah and Benjamin).

---

[11] https://knesset.gov.il/laws/special/eng/return.htm

My focus stretches from the time when Babylon was the conqueror and the waves of return that ensued,[12] in particular, with the closing words of 2 Chronicles. I am examining the first return, as confirmed by Nehemiah 7:5, to wit, *"And I found a register of the genealogy of those who had come up in the first return."*

Cyrus, God's Shepherd

It is in this context that in order to launch this vast exodus from Babylon and to signal the end of the deportation the Lord had in mind to use someone you wouldn't really expect:

"Now in the first year of Cyrus king of Persia, that the word of the LORD by the mouth of Jeremiah might be fulfilled, ***the LORD stirred up the spirit of Cyrus king of Persia***, *so that he made a proclamation throughout all his kingdom"* (2 Chronicles 36:22).

Cyrus, this first ruler of the first ancient superpower of the time received a mandate from the Creator of the universe to let the exiles of Israel go free, allowing them to go back to their land, thus showing that God was in control of their history. In ***History of the Jews***, Paul Goodman writes that:

"It was a decree of incalculably far reaching consequences, worthy to inspire that wonderful Psalms which sang of the resurrection of a people"[13] (Psalms 126).

Indeed, and as we will see, what this decree has meant for the Jews throughout the centuries brings with it the import of a worldwide call to move up.

The figure of Cyrus the king of Persia is central in the plan of God for the restoration of His people to their Land as He chose him as a particular instrument for the fulfillment of this prophetic moment in the history of the ancient people. In his figure, we have a gentile whose service to the children of Israel was prophesied no

---

12 For an overview, three were the return to Zion. The first under Cyrus, the second 90 years later when Artaxerxes I was on the Persian throne. Then, around 14 years later, Nehemiah returned with a few craftsmen.

13 Paul Goodman, ***History of the Jews*** – p. 36 (E.P. Dutton & Company, INC, New York, 1953)

less than a hundred and fifty years before he ascended the throne and Babylon was taken by him. None but God himself could have mentioned so long before the name of him who should deliver the Jews from bondage. Isaiah witnessed it when prophesied about Cyrus on behalf of the Lord:

> *"For Jacob My servant's sake, And Israel My elect, I have even called you by your name; I have named you, though you have not known Me. I am the LORD, and there is no other; There is no God besides Me. I will gird you, though you have not known Me"* (Isaiah 45:4-5).

Cyrus would do that which is God's pleasure should be done; for if God called him, and brought him forth, he would certainly make his way prosperous. But Cyrus was a foreign king that didn't know God nor was acquainted with His ways but that, nonetheless, served YHVH to perform all His pleasure. It is God Almighty Who declares of him:

> *"Who says of Cyrus **He is My shepherd**, and he shall perform all My pleasure, saying to Jerusalem, 'You shall be built', and to the temple, 'Your foundation shall be laid'"* (Isaiah 44:28).

The word *"My"* here implies that Cyrus was under the direction of God and that he was employed in His service for this peculiar purpose. It is for Jacob, the children of Israel, that God has called Cyrus by his name— distinguishing him from other rulers and giving him titles of honor such as *anointed* and *shepherd*. He was favored by the Lord God in being made the instrument to deliver His people. The design for which God would do this would be so that He might deliver Jacob and that the world might know YHVH was the true and only God. He is to be known as the One who had made the heavens and the earth and all things, and the One Who had raised up Cyrus for the purpose of delivering and comforting His people. As the Lord, the maker of heaven and earth overrules and directs the actions of kings and rulers, so He had solemnly set apart Cyrus to perform a strategic and divine service in His cause. He girded him for war and conquest on account of His people. For us today, the King of Persia stands figuratively as a representative of the Gentile peoples (the nations). In his role we can get a glimpse of that prophetic collaboration between Jews and Gentiles in the fulfillment of the prophetic Word. This divinely orchestrated co-operation is well expressed in Isaiah 14:1-2, where the prophet says:

> *"For the LORD will have mercy on Jacob, and will still choose Israel, and settle them in their own land. **The strangers** (viz. Gentiles) **will be joined with them, and they will cling to the House of Jacob. Then people will take them and bring them to their place**, and the house of Israel will possess them for servants and maids in the land of the LORD; they will take them captive whose captives they were, and rule over their oppressors."*

Aliyah – A Legacy Through Succession

Even today, as security for the return of the remnant of Israel, God wants to use us among the nations. At all times God uses people like Cyrus for the implementation of this purpose; yes, those who have understood the value of the message of Aliyah. Just consider, the echo of that edict still resonates as then and as in the past, all of us can take part at the restoration of Israel and feel involved in God's prophetic plan. To me, sharing God's portion in the re-establishment of national Israel is one of the most amazing and fascinating things a child of God can be called to do. Therefore, guaranteed by the presence of a Will (Testament) the message of Aliyah becomes the inheritance that the Hebrew Scriptures left us, thus becoming a legacy through succession.

It is all the more significant that the Hebrew Scriptures end with a message regarding the return of the Jewish people to Israel to a Land of Promise in view of their final salvation. This legacy, found in the Old Testament, has left us a message that still resounds today. The message is clear: the captivity of Israel has ended, and the time has come for her restoration, with a view climaxed in Israel's full salvation. In this light, the message of Aliyah becomes the warrant (the "guarantee") of the Hebrew Scriptures for all of us to embrace. Furthermore, we need to realize this is a common heritage—this mandate is not for a limited group of people or for a selected few. It cannot ever be said that "God hasn't called the Gentiles to support the Jewish people" if He is calling us today to consider it and looks to hand over to us this valuable heritage.

Cyrus' edict is later picked up by Ezra in chapter 1 of his text, where the same words are repeated.[14]

> *"Thus says Cyrus king of Persia: All the kingdoms of the earth the LORD God of heaven has given me. And He has commanded me to build Him a house at Jerusalem which is in Judah. Who is among you of all His people? May his God be with him, **and let him go up** to Jerusalem which is in Judah, and build the house of the LORD God of Israel (He is God), which is in Jerusalem"* (Ezra 1:2-3).

When we meet with repeated verses in the Bible we are in front of catch-lines. It was common in ancient times to place catch-lines at the end of a scroll to enable the reader to pass on to the correct second book after the reading of the first. Now, however, if the book of 2 Chronicles concludes with Cyrus' proclamation—taken up by Ezra—the book of Ezra then adds some details to the proclamation by following the Jews of Judah in their trail to their own Land where the narrative is centered on the promise of the return to Jerusalem as prophesied by Jeremiah—the very one that announced their exile (Jeremiah 25:11), but that after seventy years God would make them return to their own land (Jeremiah 29:10).

The act of assisting the Jewish people in their return to the promised land of Israel validates the Word of God in the eyes of the world. Ezra brings the message to a higher level of comprehension giving us a complete picture concerning the very words of Cyrus by adding the following statement:

---

[14] It is generally recognized among scholars that the two books of Chronicles (originally, one, uninterrupted book) and the Book of Ezra (which comprised the book of Nehemiah as well. Originally, Ezra and Nehemiah were considered one book entitled "Ezra.") are the work of a single author, who is often referred to as the Chronicler. The four (actually two) books together are sometimes called the Chronistic Work. https://www.baslibrary.org/bible-review/2/3/6

*"And let each survivor, in whatever place he sojourns, **be assisted by the men of his place** with silver and gold, with goods and with beasts, besides freewill offerings for the house of God that is in Jerusalem"* (Ezra 1:4 ESV).

The Hebrew word for "**assisted**" means *extolled, carried, gathered, transferred, dislocate.*

It comes from a primitive Hebrew root (Strong's H#5375 – נָשָׂא *nasà*) which means precisely to transport, *to transfer, to dislocate, to carry* and *to bring* and it implies a practical help in their journey home. This means that the local people helped the Jews in exile in their way back to Israel. Likewise, the prophetic Scriptures abound with references to a practical help coming from Gentiles towards the chosen people. For example, in the following passages:

"Thus says the LORD God: "Behold, I will lift up my hand to the nations, and raise my signal to the peoples; and they shall bring your sons in their arms, and your daughters shall be carried on their shoulders" (Isaiah 49:22).

"Who are these who fly like a cloud, And like doves to their roosts? Surely the coastlands shall wait for Me; And the ships of Tarshish will come first, To bring your sons from afar, Their silver and their gold with them, To the name of the LORD your God, And to the Holy One of Israel, Because He has glorified you" (Isaiah 60:8-9).

Please understand that as it was then, you and I can take part in the restoration of Israel and subjectively enter into God's prophetic plan. The existence of the modern State of Israel is the powerful testimony of the fulfillment of the Word of God, whereby the Jewish people in their return to the promised land, validates His Word in the eyes of the world. It means bearing witness to the nations that God is faithful, that He is real and sovereign. It is an act of courage and faith at the same time. Of courage, because it demonstrates that we have chosen to take sides with the truth, and of faith, because it demonstrates our trust in Him who said that one day *"All Israel"*[15] shall be saved. The practice of anticipating and embracing our prophetic destiny with Judah, looking at the time of our unity in Messiah (when *"ALL ISRAEL shall be delivered"*) gives tremendous credit to the prophetic role that Israel and the Church (both His "elect") will have, prior to its fulfillment, that peculiar assistance offered by the *"elect from among the nations"* to the Jewish people. This is but an anticipation of the glorious prophetic testimony we shall be summoned to give together on the world stage, during the final drama of history known as Daniel's Seventieth Week (Daniel 9:24-27).

Now, back at the time of Cyrus, the message of Aliyah had an immediate impact because we read that:

> ***"And all those who were around them*** *encouraged them with articles of silver and gold, with goods and livestock, and with precious things, besides all that was willingly offered"* (Ezra 1:6).

My dear friend Johannes Barthel, whose commitment to the cause of the Jewish people is outstanding and on whom I recognize that the Lord has bestowed a portion of anointing for coordinating the Aliyah of the Jewish people from the Gentile's side, explains in his book that this message promulgated by Cyrus was so clear that all their neighbors understood, believed, and obeyed it. Cyrus was not the only King whom God used in those times to enable the Jewish people to return home. In the Book of Ezra and Nehemiah we find reports of how God used the Persian Kings Darius and Artaxerxes IV Logimanus in the building of the Temple and the rebuilding of the city of Jerusalem.

Not only did they provide the authority to rebuild, but they generously gave large amounts of gold, silver, and other materials. In addition, they ensured that the Temple implements were returned. Ezra and Nehemiah had access to the treasures of these

---

[15] It is the author's persuasion that *"All Israel"* as stated in Romans 11 refers to the globality of the saved ones that form the Commonwealth of Israel (Ephesians 2), comprised of Jews (Judah) and Gentiles (aka those from among the "nations"—even so, those *"swallowed up among the Nations"*—Hosea 8:8-10).

Kings. Why was this? These Kings understood that in blessing Israel they would be blessed. What a better world it would be today if our governments had this knowledge.[16] My prayer is that the Holy Spirit may enlighten as many eyes as possible for people to see that our duty towards the Jewish people is a warrant or promise for all and our legacy for today. Cyrus's proclamation enabled and facilitated a mass return of the Jews, not only through a public announcement of the purposes of God for their return, but through a practical support for their *Aliyah* and the protection on their way home. In his proclamation, and subsequent practical help, we find a balanced approach to our duties towards the Jewish people today.

Will you be picking up this legacy yourself? Certain projects require cooperation and as then, you can participate at the restoration of Israel towards the fulfillment of Bible prophecy.

So, dear friend, the prophetic Scriptures have left us with a heritage and a mandate. What will you do with it?

≈ ≈ ≈ ≈ ≈ ≈

Prayer

Heavenly Father, stir up the spirit of those who are listening to the message that still resounds from the pages of Scriptures, that the time of favor for Zion has come, and that as in the days of Cyrus, great would be today the company of those who respond to the call of carrying the Jewish people home because they have understood that this is their legacy and their mandate for this day and hour for the time of the Final Redemption, in Jesus name I pray.

---

[16] Johannes Barthel, *Aliyah – The Miracle of the Jewish Return* (Ebenezer Emergency Fund International, 2018)

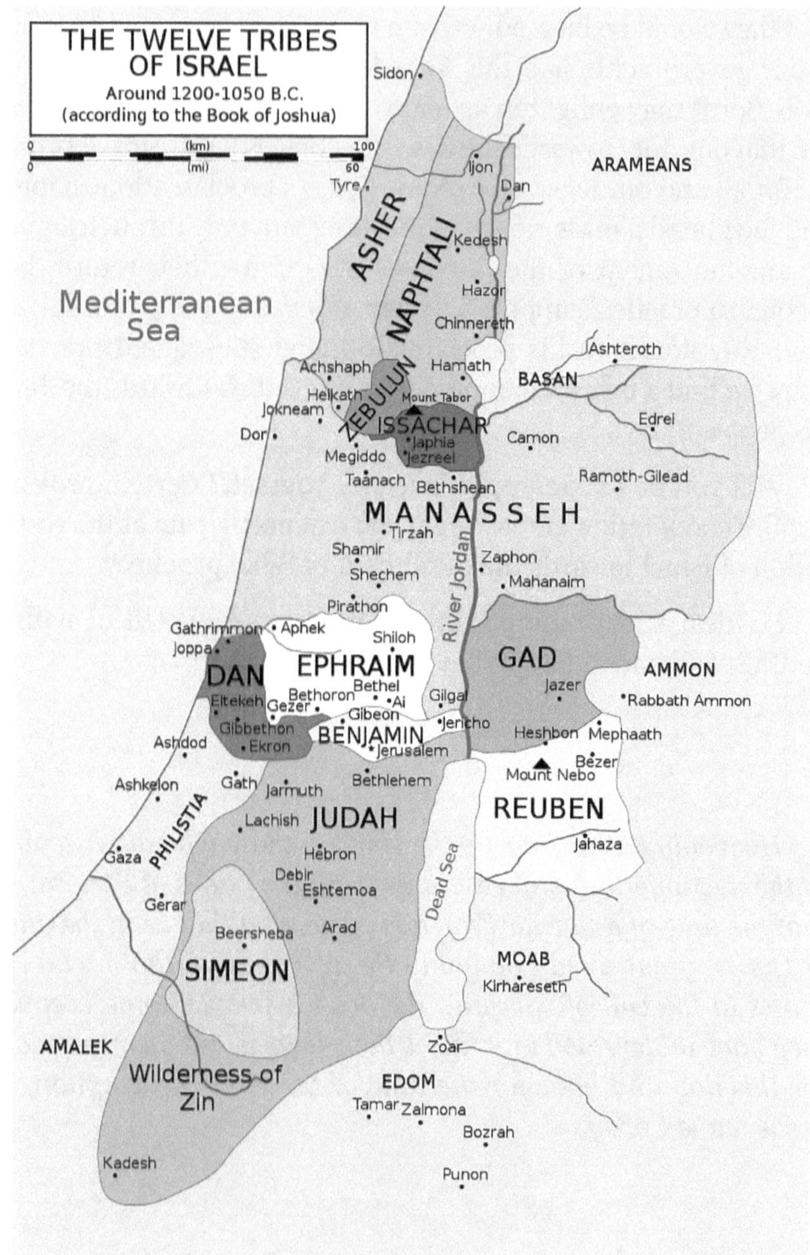

Figure 10 - The 12 Tribes of Israel - Book of Joshua

Chapter 2
On Their Shoulders We Stand

"I am God and there is none like Me, declaring the end from the beginning, and from ancient times things that are not yet done, saying 'My counsel shall stand, and I will do all My pleasure.'"

(Isaiah 46:9-10)

"It is high time for Christians to interpret unfulfilled prophecy by the light of prophecies already fulfilled. The curses on the Jews were brought to pass literally, so also will be the blessings. The scattering was literal, so also will be the gathering. The pulling down of Zion was literal, so also will be the building up. The rejection of Israel was literal, so also will be the restoration."

J.C. Ryle (1879)

"Surely it becomes a wise man, at a time like this, to return to the pages of prophecy and to inquire what is yet to come. At a time like this the declarations of God concerning His people Israel ought to be carefully weighted and examined. 'At the time of the end', says Daniel, 'the wise shall understand'" (Daniel 12:10).

J.C. Ryle (1858)

"What your attitude to Israel should be, is plainly shown in the Word of God."

Horatius Bonar (1855)

"Let us speak reverently of the Jew, if not for what he is, at least for what he was, and what he shall be, when the Redeemer shall come to Zion and turn away ungodliness from Jacob."

Horatius Bonar (1870)

"We shall at once profess our attachment to the premillennial school of interpretation, and the literal reading of those Scriptures that predict the return of the Jews to their own Land."

Charles Haddon Spurgeon (1866)

Gleanings from the Past

WITH THIS CHAPTER MY INTENTION IS TO PROVIDE MATERIAL[1] ABOUT THE END-TIME THEOLOGY OF A VAST GROUP OF RENOWN GODLY MEN of God of the past who believed, long before us, in the restoration of the Jews to their Land according to God´s Word. These godly men, long before the Zionist movement emerged at the end of the 19th Century, believed in the restoration of the Jews just because, by examining the Holy Scriptures with an unbiased eye, they saw that many of the Old Testament prophecies pointed to a glorious end-time regathering and spiritual awakening of the Jewish people and nation. They did their hermeneutical work well, and they rightly believed it. I firmly believe that this perspective on eschatology is lacking in many evangelical circles today in that the immediate tendency is to keep the Church totally disconnected with its complementary part, Israel, looking with apathy to any form of prophetical collaboration of the two.

For others, instead, the destiny of the Church and Israel seems to run parallel to one another—yet, never meeting. This means that a gulf of indifference separates numerous leaders, pastors, and teachers from the blessedness of seeing themselves in the Commonwealth of Israel (more on that in chapter 9). On the other hand, there are many whose aim is the repairing of the longstanding breach between Jews and Christians, the Fathers and the Children if you wish, allowing the Holy Spirit to shed light into the marvelous purpose of God for our mutual co-operation in the end-times. Indeed, could it be that this is precisely what Malachi 4:6 alludes to in reference to: *"And he* [Elijah] *will turn the hearts of the fathers to the children, and the hearts of the children to their fathers?"* Is this the restoration which shall occur within the

---

[1] Some of the information in this chapter is taken from an article I have published in the Educational Bulletin of Ebenezer Operation Exodus called **L'Hitamek** (*to go deeper* in Hebrew), 1st Edition, and can be retrieved at: https://indd.adobe.com/view/c6567f5c-1679-4678-ad95-704793dfaea9

"Household of God" prior to that *"great and dreadful day of the LORD"* (Malachi 4:5)?

Those who allowed the Scriptures to reveal this restorative plan can look further ahead by standing on the shoulders of those men of God who were enlightened years ago. Among those great servants of God, was John Charles Ryle (1816-1900). Ryle was a prolific writer, vigorous preacher, faithful pastor, and the first Anglican bishop of Liverpool. Charles Spurgeon considered him to be the best man in the Church of England. Ryle was educated at Eton and Oxford and considered entering Parliament but, upon his conversion in 1837, decided to go into the ministry instead. Throughout his ministry he remained one of the strongest defenders of the evangelical reformed faith within the Church of England.

In 1867 Rev. J. C. Ryle published a book containing seven highly significant sermons on eschatology entitled: ***Coming Events and Present Duties: Being Miscellaneous Sermons on Prophetical Subjects***[2] where he strongly defended the view that Israel would be restored to the land in fulfillment of God's promises in the Old Testament. Here I would like to insert some relevant extracts of one of those sermons entitled *"Scattered Israel to be gathered,"* where he carefully stated his understanding of the future of the Hebrew people, as well as the regathering of the Jews to the promised land. The substance of this address was originally preached as the Annual Sermon on behalf of the London Society for promoting Christianity among the Jews, at the Rectory Church, Mary-le-bone, in May 1858. Please note that Bishop Ryle's book from which this sermon was taken, was published in 1867. This was long before the formation of the State of Israel in 1948 and even before the Jewish Zionist movement began with Theodor Herzl in 1897. Ryle's interpretation of the Old Testament passages relating to the future of Israel was exactly correct: they would be regathered to *Eretz Israel*, the land given to

---

[2] London; Ipswich: William Hunt, 1879.

them as an "everlasting possession" (Genesis 17:8) that they may be positioned there before the return of their Messiah.

EXTRACTS FROM SERMON 5 "SCATTERED ISRAEL TO BE GATHERED"

By Rev. J. C. Ryle

"Hear the Word of Yahweh, O ye nations, and declare it in the isles afar off, and say, 'He who scattered Israel will gather him, and keep him as a shepherd does his flock'"

(Jeremiah 31:10)

Reader, the whole body of Gentile Christendom is specially addressed in this text. There is no evading this conclusion on any fair interpretation of Scripture. We ourselves are among the "nations" to whom Jeremiah speaks. It is a voice to all Christendom. And what does the voice say? It bids us proclaim far and wide the will of God concerning the Jewish nation. It bids us keep one another in memory of God's past and future dealings with Israel. *"He who scattered Israel will gather him."*

The other of these points is the future literal gathering of the Jewish nation and their restoration to their own land. I tell no man that these two truths are essential to salvation and that he cannot be saved except he sees them with my eyes. But I tell any man that these truths appear to me distinctly set down in holy Scripture, and that the denial of them is as astonishing and incomprehensible to my own mind as the denial of the divinity of Christ.

Now what says our text about the future prospects of the Jews? It says, *"He who scattered Israel will gather him."* That gathering is an event which plainly is yet to come. It could not apply in any sense to the ten tribes of Israel. They have never been gathered in any way. Their scattering has never come to an end. It cannot be applied to the return of the remnant of Judah and Benjamin from the Babylonian captivity. The language of the text makes such an application impossible. The text is addressed to the Gentiles, "the nations." The declaration they are commanded to make is *"to the isles of the sea."* In the days of the Babylonian captivity, the "nations" of the earth knew nothing of the Word of the Lord. They were sunk in darkness and had not even heard the Lord's name. If Jeremiah had told them to proclaim the return of the Jews from Babylon under such circumstances, it would have been useless and absurd. There is but one fair and legitimate interpretation of the promise of the text. The event it declares is yet future. The "gathering" spoken of is a gathering which is yet to come.

Reader, I place these texts before you without note or comment. They all point to a time which is yet future. They all predict the final gathering of the Jewish nation from the four quarters of the globe and their restoration to their own land.

Now is there anything ***contrary to this gathering in the New Testament***? I cannot find a single word. So far from this being the case, I find a chapter in the Epistle to the Romans where the subject is fully discussed. An inspired Apostle speaks there of Israel being once more "received" into God's favor, "grafted in," and "saved." (See Romans 11:15-32.)

Is there anything ***impossible*** in this gathering of Israel? Who talks of impossibilities? If an infidel, let him explain the present condition and past history of Israel, if he can.

For another thing, I charge every reader of this address never to forget the close connection which Scripture reveals between the time of Israel's gathering and the time of Christ's second advent to the world. In one Psalm it is expressly declared, *"When the Lord shall build up Zion, He shall appear in His glory"* (Psalms 102:16). Where is the true believer who does not long for that blessed day? Where is the true Christian who does not cry from the bottom of his heart, "Thy kingdom come"? Let all such work and give and pray, so that the Gospel may have free course in Israel. The time to favor Zion is tightly bound up with the restitution of all things. Blessed indeed, is that work of which the completion shall usher in the second coming of the Lord!

That of bishop Ryle is not an isolated case among the thousands of religious teachers of the past centuries who have not drawn erroneous conclusions as to the future fulfillment of the prophecies concerning the Jews. Many were the men of the Book and thoroughly versed in the Scriptures, able to bring forth treasures, *"things new and old"* (Matthew 13:52). They took by heart that Scripture must be interpreted in conformity to the Analogy of Faith, that key principle of interpretation taught by the Reformers which teaches that Scriptures should interpret Scriptures.

Beyond other times of history, there is this substantial Christian movement which predated Zionism and the subsequent great first wave of Aliyah of 1882-1903. This movement has left us with a spiritual legacy that to this day can boast of having countless spiritual children in every nation of the world. You will be amazed at what you are going to discover as my quest into those men of God of the past has led me to the outstanding research made by Dr. John Garr (PhD), to whom I am commended to give credit for the insurmountable learning contribution I have received from his writings in the compilation of this chapter.

I consider his work, *"God and Israel"*[3] to be one of the finest investigations on this subject. Dr. Garr really went deeper, offering insights into a vast period of time spanning the centuries in a way to present the sovereign hand of God in both the formation of the modern State of Israel and in the newly-discovered interest by Christians in praying for the peace of Jerusalem. In his outstanding research, after having demonstrated that for centuries the history of the Church exudes with individuals, movements, and entire denominations that lost sight of the purposes of God toward Israel and which haughtily displayed contempt for the Jews, both in Israel and in the diaspora. Dr. Garr points at that period of time when, centuries before the nation of Israel was resurrected from the ashes of the Holocaust, before the time of prophetic restoration of the Land, an increasing number of people came forward to support the restoration of Israel.

---

[3] John D. Garr, ***God and Israel: The Chosen People, the Holy Nation and the Promised Land*** (2016 Golden Key Press). His material can be purchased at https://www.hebraiccommunity.org

From the Restorationism Period to Zionism

As a matter of fact, early Christian hopes, and expectations regarding the rebirth of Israel were collectively deemed "Restorationism,"[4] because the focus was on the renewal of the ancient faith and practices of the Jews and the earliest formation of Christianity. So, many were the leaders in the Church that shared their expectation that the Jews themselves had long held for the restoration and renewal of their nation, in opposition to those who held contrary opinion, like those predisposed to Replacement Theology (aka *Supersessionism*). These men of valor believed the "spiritualization of prophecy" to be naught but a great error. These "biblical literalists" approached Scripture based on a historical-grammatical approach to every text (i.e. John Charles Ryle). For them, the issue of Israel was not simply a point of doctrine to be objectively dissected; no, they subjectively loved Abraham's descendants with a fervent love. They wrote, led, and taught that the Church should and would embrace the biblical mandate of provoking Israel to divine jealousy. Also, they had a passion for promoting and proclaiming a Pre-Millennial eschatology. Many of them were of Reformed origin, but, unlike many of Reformed persuasion, these men rejected Augustinian-Origen spiritualization and Catholic eschatology—tending toward a Post-Millennial world view. They took Scripture at face value and spoke openly about the logic and scriptural legitimacy of the futurity of the Millennial reign of Christ,[5] eschewing amillennial notions which formed the basis of a "Triumphal Christianity."

Several years ago, I came across a very interesting book entitled "*The Controversy of Zion and the Time of Jacob's*

---

[4] **Restorationism** denoted the Christian belief that Jews will be restored to their homeland in biblical Israel as a sign of God's impending millennial reign, usually just before, after or during a mass conversion of Jews (Stephen R. Haynes, ***Reluctant Witness: Jews and Christian Imagination*** - Louisville, KY, 1995). Haynes points out that Restorationist thought was a feature of all the various millenarian movements in the sixteenth through the eighteenth centuries and that Restorationism was also central to Puritan theology in Holland, Britain, and America during that time.

[5] Garr, John D., *Ibid.*

Trouble"[6] by Dalton Lifsey in which, on par with John Garr, the author presents a selection of extracts from the writings of these men of God of the past pertaining to one issue in particular, namely, how to read the prophecies of Israel's restoration. For example, Charles Haddon Spurgeon (who was a leading supporter of Restorationism and an avowed Calvinist) believed in a literal interpretation of the Scriptures when it came to the restoration of the Jewish people to their ancient homeland. Quoting from Dennis M. Swanson's[7] description of Charles Spurgeon's methods of studying prophecy, Lifsey includes the following extract from one of his sermons on Ezekiel 37 to show how Spurgeon understood correctly to be the 'dry bones,' to wit:

> "This passage, again, has been very frequently and I dare say very properly, used to describe the revival of a decayed Church. This vision may be looked upon as descriptive of a state of lukewarmness and spiritual lethargy in a Church when the question may be sorrowfully asked- 'Can these bones live?' … But while we admit this to be a very fitting accommodation of our text, yet we are quite convinced that it is not to this that the passage refers. No, he was talking of his own people, of his own race and of his own tribe. He surely ought to have known his own mind and led by the Holy Spirit, he gives us an explanation of the vision. Not - 'Thus says the LORD, My dying Church shall be restored,' but - 'I will bring My people out of their graves and bring them into the land of Israel.'"[8]

Spanning across the vast ocean of those of Reformed persuasion, another man that had a substantial impact on the Church of

---

[6] Lifsey, Dalton in ***The Controversy of Zion And The Time of Jacob's Trouble*** (2011 Dalton Lifsey)

[7] Dennis M. Swanson, *Charles H. Spurgeon and the Nation of Israel: A Non-Dispensational Perspective on a Literal National Restoration* www.spurgeon.org/misc/eschat2.htm#note50.

[8] Charles Spurgeon, Sermon #582, *The Restoration and Conversion of the Jews*, June 16, 1864 — Although Spurgeon specifically refers to the obfuscation of the Jews in the Ezekiel 37 vision of the Valley of Dry Bones, it must be noted that Commonwealth Theology, on the other hand, would include BOTH the Church (aka Ephraim from among the nations now His Elect) with Judah (the Jews) in this end-time revival . . . the newly-released text, ***Commonwealth Theology Essentials - 2020***, clearly defines the expansion of this end-time restoration and revival to include both Israel and Judah (Israel being that of Ephraim, Jezreel, Samaria scattered among the Nations).

his time in the 17th century was Robert Murray M'Cheyne,[9] who, like Spurgeon, approached the prophetic texts to observe their primary meaning unadulterated by spiritualization. On Isaiah 62:6-7 he comments:

"If any of you know the Hebrew of [it], you will see at once the true rendering of *'I have set watchmen over thy walls, O Jerusalem, which shall never hold their peace day nor night. You that are the Lord's remembrancers, keep not silence, and give Him no rest till He establish, and till He make Jerusalem a praise in the earth.'* Oh, my dear brethren, into whose hearts I trust God is pouring a scriptural love for Israel, what an honor is it for us, worms of the dust, to be made watchmen by God over the ruined walls of Jerusalem, and to be made the Lord's remembrancers, to call His own promises to His mind, that He would fulfill them, and make Jerusalem a blessing to the whole world!"[10]

Time elapsed until we encounter Iain Murray (The Puritan Hope), of whom Dr. Garr writes:

"By the mid-seventeenth century, Restorationism had become well entrenched in England, especially among the Puritans, who, though they viewed themselves as a re-embodied Israel, also believed that the Abrahamic covenant still applied to the patriarch's physical descendants. The strong interest that the Puritans maintained in the restoration of Israel in all likelihood resulted primarily from the fact that they placed much greater emphasis on the Hebrew Bible than other dissenters of their time did."

Among the activists of the period were also Thomas Newton, Bishop of Bristol (1704-1782) who supported the return of the Jews to Israel and their conversion in a book called "***A Dissertation On the Prophecies***," and Joseph Priestly (a prominent 18th Century English chemist, natural philosopher and Clergyman). Priestly spoke of the divine choice in choosing the Jews, that, at the end, will have been resettled in their own country.

---

[9] Robert Murray M'Cheyne (21 May 1813 – 25 March 1843) was a minister in the Church of Scotland from 1835 to 1843. M'Cheyne was a preacher, a pastor, a poet, and wrote many letters. He was also a man of deep piety and a man of prayer.

[10] Andrew A. Bonar, ***Memoir and Remains of Robert Murray M'Cheyne*** (Edinburgh: Banner of Truth, March 1, 1966)

Along the same line, a number of English intellectuals were attracted to the theme of the return of the Jews in their land and of their subsequent salvation, among whom was Sir Isaac Newton (1642-1727). Besides being famous for being a physicist, astronomer, and mathematician, Newton was a wonderful devoted Christian and a prolific author. He also contributed to untying the mystery of the Seventy Weeks of Daniel and many more things pertaining to divine measurements. Not everyone knows, however, he wrote a religious tract called ***Of the Day of Judgment and the World to Come***, in which he predicted the return of the Jews from their captivity and the establishment of a future Jewish kingdom. His thesis was based on the scriptural facts of the Abrahamic Covenant—believing that the Covenant is a permanent Covenant and unchanging and that cannot be revoked; and that the final restoration of Israel would most certainly take place. Of his period we also find the American writer Herman Melville who penned a poignant statement in his epic poem, ***Clarel: A Poem and Pilgrimage in the Holy Land***[11] in which he penned:

> "The Hebrew seers announce in time the return of Judah to her prime; Some Christians deemed it then at hand here was an object. Up an On. With Seed and tillage help renew-Help reinstate the Holy Land."

The ***"Up and On'"*** I affirm, is an amazing portrait of those ***Called to a Holy Pilgrimage***.

Above all, the passion that these people had for Israel is well reflected in a classic hymn composed by Charles Wesley published in 1762, entitled *"Almighty God of Love,"* which enshrines the vision that God would regather the Jewish people to a restored Israel. Here is the hymn in its original version[12]:

1 ALMIGHTY God of love,
Set up the attracting sign,
And summon whom thou dost approve
For messengers divine;
From favored Abraham's seed

---

[11] It is a poetic fiction about an American young man named Clarel, on pilgrimage through the Holy Land with a cluster of companions who question each other as they pass through Biblical sites.

[12] https://www.wesley-fellowship.org.uk/Zionist_Hymn.html

The new apostles choose,
In isles and continents to spread
The dead-reviving news.

2 Them, snatched out of the flame,
Through every nation send,
The true Messiah to proclaim,
The universal friend;
That all the God unknown
May learn of Jews to adore,
And see thy glory in thy Son,
Till time shall be no more.

3 O that the chosen band
Might now their brethren bring,
And, gathered out of every land,
Present to Zion's King!
Of all the ancient race
Not one be left behind,
But each, impelled by secret grace,
His way to Canaan find.

4 We know it must be done,
For God hath spoke the word:
All Israel shall the Saviour own,
To their first state restored;
Rebuilt by his command,
Jerusalem shall rise;
Her temple on Moriah stand
Again, and touch the skies.

5 Send then thy servants forth,
To call the Hebrews home;
From East, and West, and South, and North,
Let all the wanderers come;
Where'er in lands unknown
The fugitives remain,
Bid every creature help them on,
Thy holy mount to gain.

6 An offering to their God,
There let them all be seen,
Sprinkled with water and with blood,

> In soul and body clean;
> With Israel's myriads sealed,
> Let all the nations meet,
> And show the mystery fulfilled,
> Thy family complete!

I am fully persuaded that if today we can look with confidence at the sure fulfillment of the promises and prophecies of God pertaining to the final salvation of the Jewish people it's because these visionaries of the past had fought their fight of faith and even died without seeing the realization of what they believed—but only seen them from afar. That is why we are called to stand on their shoulders.

The research of John Garr on this period of history is extraordinary; suffice it to say that he brought to light that emphasis put on the restoration of Israel at the time of the *Restorationism* movement, when Napoleon Bonaparte invaded Palestine in 1799. Even so, the French *Restorationists* petitioned him to approve the restoration of the Jewish homeland. In response, Napoleon issued a *"Proclamation to the Jewish Nation,"*—a most dramatic appeal to European Jewry in which he encouraged them to begin working on restoring their ancient nation:

> "Hasten. Now is the moment that may not return for thousands of years, to claim the restoration of your rights among the population of the universe that had been shamefully withheld from you for thousands of years, your political existence as a nation among the nations, and the unlimited natural right to worship Yehovah in accordance with your faith, publicly and in likelihood forever."[13]

A New Understanding

Another aspect of the *Restorationism* of the Puritan era was that it encouraged and favored the importance of returning to the

---

[13] Napoleon Bonaparte, quoted in Lawrence J. Epstein, *A Treasury of Jewish Inspirational Stories* (Northvale, NJ: Jason Aronson, 1993), p. 180

Hebrew texts of the Bible and recovering the Hebraic foundations of the Christian faith as fundamental to the Reformation, with the consequence people began to understand the power and perdurability of God's promises to Abraham and his descendants. As a matter of fact, the religious impulse to restore Israel (aka, the Jewish people) began in the political arena in the Twentieth Century and succeeded with the establishment of the Jewish State in 1948. American writer Paul C. Merkley had an important role in ascertaining that not only did England have an important role in the formation of the Zionist political entity, but that the cause of "Restoration" of the Jews to Zion first became a viable political force in the United States with the publication in 1891 of the "***Blackstone Memorial***."

Moreover the model for collaboration between Christian Restorationists and official Jewish Zionists was formalized by Theodor Herzl himself at the time when many significant friendships between Christian Zionists and official Jewish Zionists served to win the public mind and the cooperation of the politicians for actions that would lead to the creation of the State of Israel in 1948. Merkley searched Presidential archives, Jewish historical libraries, and official Zionist records in both the United States and Israel for evidence of dealings between official Zionists and active Christian Restorationists. Much of this record appears in print for the first time in the book ***The Politics of Christian Zionism 1891-1948*** in which he writes that "Political Jewish Zionism was inspired and directly influenced by its contemporary, Christian Zionism."[14]

Over time, Christians began to understand the *mystery* of the Gentiles' inclusion into the Commonwealth of Israel (Ephesians 2:12) and their being engrafted into the one Olive Tree of Salvation (Romans 11:16-24; Jeremiah 11:16-17) that by the late Nineteenth Century the Restorationist movement had taken on the title of Christian Zionism. Later on, a significant portion of evangelical Christianity continued the tradition of Restorationism by

---

[14] Paul C. Merkley, *The Politics of Christian Zionism 1891-1948* (New York: Routledge, 1998)

maintaining their support for the Jewish people and the establishment of a Jewish national homeland in the Holy Land. Anita Shapira is right when saying that Christian Zionists of the 1840s passed the notion (biblically based arguments) on to Jewish circles.[15] Dr. Garr adds:

> ". . . this fact rests on the 500-year-long continuing quest by Restorationists and Christian Zionists to pray for, support, and work to effect the restoration of the land of Israel to the sovereignty of the Jewish people. While Christian Restorationists had had significant influence on the birth of Zionism, Zionism would have a much more powerful impact on the church because the restoration of Israel would force the church to come face to face with the fallacy of its supersessionist triumphalism vis-à-vis the Jews. Perhaps the greatest light that Restored Israel has brought and will bring to Christianity is the restoration of the inherent Jewish roots of the Christian faith that will enable Christianity to recognize its supreme debt to Judaism and to the Jewish People."[16]

But perhaps there's another example I should like to mention here that stands representative of the many people who lived in the years preceding Israel's declaration of independence and that saw the birth of the State of Israel as a result of a fervent intercession. Rees Howells (1879-1950), the founder of the Bible College of Wales in Swansea was neither a Zionist (in terms of publicly advocating the rights of the Jews to their land), nor a follower of Restorationism, he was simply known as the "great intercessor." Once the Holy Spirit took possession of him in 1906, Rees Howells was led deeply into a ministry of intercession for all sorts of needs including healing and conversions with the scope of challenging the results of spiritual death at home and abroad on the mission field. By prayer and by faith alone he could see revivals and the start of many works for the kingdom of God during his lifetime, as well as countless answers to prayer.

---

[15] Anita Shapira, **Israel: A History** (London, UK 2014)
[16] John D. Garr, p. 236

The Lord, as well, put in his heart a burden for the Jewish people. He saw the need for them to go back to their homeland as was promised to them by God. He also bought an estate in Swansea (Wales) to be served as a refuge for Jewish children in 1938. He and his college, through years of intercession for the Jews, saw the fulfillment of their prayers in the actual return of the Jews and the establishment of the modern State of Israel. Norman P. Grubb wrote a biography[17] on Rees Howells in which he succinctly describes the role of intercession in the restoration of Israel, by saying:

> "It reminds us that no great event in history, even though prophesied beforehand in Scriptures, comes to pass unless God finds His human channels of faith and obedience. Prophecies must be believed into manifestation, as well as foretold."

These were the years of WWII, and despite all the other problems they had to face at the Bible College of Wales, Howells and his people had always the time to pray for the Jews. In another instance, in October and November 1947 there were days at the College given to prayer on behalf of the Jews to return to their ancient homeland. Mr. Howells said:

> "We pleaded that because of His covenant with Abraham four-thousands years ago, God would take His people back to their Land, and Palestine should again become a Jewish State."[18]

And so, it was, on May 14, 1948, the Jewish people declared their independence. He and many others could see the birth of the State of Israel as the result of their efficacy in prayer. It is really true that *"The effective and fervent prayer of a righteous man avails much"* (James 5:16).

Upon Israel's Declaration of Independence, the following day, the newly born State of Israel was attacked by the combined armies of Syria, Lebanon, Jordan, Egypt, and Iraq (Saudi Arabia sent hundreds of troops serving under the Egyptian flag), giving way to the interminable cycle of wars of independence, the Arab-

---

[17] Norman P. Grubb, **Rees Howells Intercessor**, (the Lutterworth Press, 1952)
[18] Ibid.

Israeli wars. Egypt invaded the land from the south, Syria, and Lebanon from the north; Jordan and Iraq came from the east and the Mediterranean Sea to their west—the Jewish people had their backs to the sea. Israel's total Jewish population was a mere 650,000. The total population surrounding Israel was from 100 to 150 million. The land the Arabs occupied was nigh two hundred times larger that Israel, besides, their armies were better equipped than the Jewish forces. But God had not preserved a remnant and brought them back to the land so that they could be driven into the sea! Not only did the Jews survive but they thrived by gaining more land. With Israel now established as a sovereign nation, Jews from around the world began to come back to their Land of promise. Within a couple of years, the population doubled in Eretz Israel. The new immigrants came mainly from the neighboring Arab countries, then from Europe.

New waves of returnees of the Jewish people began in accordance to the many biblical references that saw in Eretz Israel the final consummation of the destiny of the world's Jewish diaspora. This phenomenon of the return to the land came officially to be called Aliyah. It is not an overstatement to say that Aliyah, the return of the Jewish people to their ancient homeland, was the greatest miracle of the Twentieth Century.

≈ ≈ ≈ ≈ ≈ ≈

Prayer

Thank You, Lord, for the examples of those who have gone before us in fighting the fight of faith. It is so amazing to see how these people were visionaries. Lord, today we are experiencing the fulfillment of what they believed; yet, they were not allowed to see its fulfillment. Help us to take from where they left off while standing on their shoulders, to look further ahead. Enable us to bring their beliefs to the proper level of comprehension for us today. Give us days of alignment with Your purposes on earth for the restoration of the Jewish people to their homeland in anticipation of the arrival of their and our Jewish Messiah!

Chapter 3
Called Back to the Land

Thus says the Lord GOD: "I will gather you from the peoples, assemble you from the countries where you have been scattered, and I will give you the land of Israel."
(Ezekiel 11:17)

The Lord builds up Jerusalem; He gathers together the outcasts of Israel.
(Psalms 147:2)

THE TIMES WE ARE LIVING IN REQUIRE THAT WE MOVE ON UP TO A GREATER LEVEL OF COMPREHENSION REGARDING THE PURPOSES OF GOD about the gathering of the House of Jacob to their promised land of Israel and to what end it leads and the spiritual ramifications associated with it. Undeniably, we need to realize behind King Cyrus' calling to serve the Jewish people in their return from Babylonian exile, there was a greater determination wrought by the Lord concerning all peoples who would come to know that He is the God Who oversees, controls, and supersedes all events.

This concept of the sovereignty of God is clearly expressed in His very words in Isaiah, *"That they may know from the rising of the sun to its setting that there is none besides Me"* (Isaiah 45:6). This is the wonderful deliverance of the Jews proclaimed to all the world, that the Lord is God, and there is none else. What does this mean aside for us to know that all flesh is to possess this knowledge? In this passage the Lord is referring to the entire inhabited earth which must know there is no other *god* besides Him, the Creator of heaven and earth. So, in what sense did the release of the Jewish people from Babylon and their making Aliyah cause all flesh to know that the Lord is the true and only God? Bible expositor Edward J. Young makes this perfectly clear:

"The return of the exiles from Babylon did not accomplish this end per se, nevertheless this was the end for which Cyrus was raised up. He was set apart that the Jews might return to Judah that their Messiah could be born in Bethlehem and that when redemption had been accomplished and its message proclaimed there might be a universal acknowledgment that the God of Israel is the true God."[1]

So, here we are faced with an expansion of our understanding of the intents of the Lord which contains both the gathering and redemption of the Jews, with salvation afforded the whole world.

God's Faithfulness to His Covenant

The promise of the covenant between God and Moses depended on Israel's obedience to the divine command.

"Now it shall come to pass, if you diligently obey the voice of the LORD your God, to observe careful all His commandments which I command you today, that the LORD your God will set you high above all nations of the earth" (Deuteronomy 28:1).

God warned, by every possible means, of the serious consequences to which their disobedience would lead. He sent prophets to every generation, warning them of exile. Firstly, the Ten Tribes of the North (Israel-Ephraim) rebelled, falling to the Assyrians in 721-722 BC (their capital, Samaria). One century afterwards, Judah and their capital, Jerusalem, received the same prophetic warnings, but they, as well, did not listen to the prophets. Eventually, Nebuchadnezzar began the process of deportation by stages, which led to the Fall of Jerusalem in 586 BC. Notwithstanding, our Heavenly Father, still faithful to His promises, made the Persians and the Medians to arise in order to defeat the Neo-Babylonian Empire and set Judah free from their 70-year Captivity cir. 537 BC. While only a remnant came back to Judah, the Jews[2] decided to become fiercely attached to this land to fulfill the purpose of God's covenant. After Jesus' death and resurrection,

---

[1] Young, Edward J. ***The Book of Isaiah – Vol. III*** (Eerdmans Publishing Co., 1972)

[2] The term *Yehudi* (יְהוּדִי) occurs 74 times in the Masoretic text of the Hebrew Bible. The plural, *Yehudim* (יְהוּדִים) first appears in 2 Kings 16:6 where it refers to a defeat for the Yehudi army or nation, and in 2 Chronicles 32:18, where it refers to the language of the Yehudit (יְהוּדִית). Jeremiah 34:9 has the earliest singular usage of the word *Yehudi*. In Esther 2:5-6, the name "Yehudi" (יְהוּדִי) has a generic aspect, in this case referring to a man from the tribe of Benjamin. (Source - Retrieved: Wikipedia – 07.29.2020).

God gave Israel another approximately 40 additional years to accept the most generous of all His gifts. Notwithstanding, the leaders of the people followed the wayward path of their fathers; therefore, He handed them over to the Roman Tenth Legion under Titus who destroyed Jerusalem and the Temple in 70 AD, and the Jews were dispersed among the nations (Luke 21:20-24). But never forget, as Paul teaches us, that through their rejection, we, non-Jews from the nations, secured entry into the Kingdom of God—although we were ". . . *aliens from the Commonwealth of Israel and strangers from the covenants of promise, having no hope and without God in the world*" (Ephesians 2:12). Yet Paul reaffirms His covenantal mercies to Judah-Israel in Romans 11:1-2:

> "*I say then, has God cast away His people? Certainly not! For I also am an Israelite, of the seed of Abraham, of the tribe of Benjamin. God has not cast away His people whom He foreknew.*"

We never could show enough gratitude towards Israel, through which we got the Bible and much more: the knowledge of the true God and of our Savior Jesus-Christ. And we could never forget: "*salvation is from the Jews*" (John 4:22b) . . . for "*The scepter will not depart from Judah, nor the staff from between his feet, until Shiloh comes and the allegiance of the nations is his*" (Genesis 49:10—Berean Study Bible Version).

The Diaspora

At the entry *Diaspora* the Encyclopedia Britannica says:

> "**Diaspora**, (Greek: "*Dispersion*") Hebrew *Galut* (Exile), the dispersion of Jews among the Gentiles after the Babylonian exile or the aggregate of Jews or Jewish communities scattered 'in exile' outside Palestine or present-day Israel. Although the term refers to the physical dispersal of Jews throughout the world, it also carries religious, philosophical, political, and eschatological connotations, inasmuch as the Jews perceive a special relationship between the land of Israel and themselves. Interpretations of this relationship range

from the messianic hope of traditional Judaism for the eventual 'ingathering of the exiles' to the view of Reform Judaism that the dispersal of the Jews was providentially arranged by God to foster pure monotheism throughout the world."

While the term *diaspora* is generally accepted to refer to the Jewish communities outside of Israel, others prefer to talk about **dispersion** as it renders much better the idea of the scattering from the biblical point of view ("*James . . . to the twelve tribes in the dispersion*" (James 1:1 ESV).

Regardless, it always points at the condition of those who are found living outside the land of Israel. It is interesting to note that the Septuagint (LXX), indicates the diaspora is derived from two Hebraic root forms from the word *galah*—these are *golah* and *galuth*. *Galah* is a verb whose initial sense is to be naked, as well as to make naked, which includes a semantic field which is as much a denudation as that which uncovers or of revelation understood as fact showing things which were initially concealed. It is only by extension of this primary meaning that *galah* may also signify the fact of depopulating a land, dispossessing its inhabitants, that is, to leave a land, voluntarily or involuntarily. So, *golah* and *galuth* cannot be understood without reference to the land. Both have an abstract collective sense of exile.[3]

In any event, the existence of this worldwide diaspora is a modern testimony of an ancient disobedience committed collectively by the children of Israel (viz., Judah cir. 70 AD). Once more, the most terrible of the prophecies would be fulfilled: "*You, however, I will scatter among the nations*" (Leviticus 26:33a NASB). To be chased away from the land and isolated from God's presence was for them the most terrible of all judgments. To be deprived of the covering of His presence, of the joy of the celebrations of the great feasts in Jerusalem.

During the centuries Abraham's progeny were scattered throughout the whole earth—here we realize that the tribes of

---

[3] Stéphane Dufoix, *The Dispersion* (Brill's Specials in Modern History, 2016)

Ephraim (known as Jezreel, Samaria, and, of course, as Israel—i.e. the Ten Tribes of Northern Israel), and the Jewish (Judah-Israel) communities which exist today disbursed to almost all the nations. Wherever Judah went, anti-Semitism followed them. Pogroms and massacres decimated them. They were chased away from many nations. We can hold up the example of the attempt at the extermination of the Jewish people by Haman, minister under Darius II, Artaxerxes the Great, king of Persia (521-485 BC—book of Esther); the Inquisition and the expulsion of the Jews from Spain in 1492; the pogroms since the 17th century in Poland; the gulags in Russia during the 19th Century; the Holocaust during World War II, where Jews were terrorized, persecuted, and six million assassinated.

But the Jewish diaspora is one of the greatest *miracles* of our God! Any other people, spread out in small groups in the middle of other nations, would assimilate themselves and disappear within two generations, or three at the maximum. Nevertheless, sixty generations after the scattering of the people of Israel we can easily recognize Jewish communities in numerous countries. Throughout Israel's history, despite the people's sin and rebelliousness, God never abandoned His chosen. As Dr. Marvin Wilson has written in his outstanding work:

> "From Bible times to the present day, some have sought to dismiss the notion of Israel's election, but the Bible is clear: the preservation of the people of Israel from generation to generation has reflected God's faithfulness, grace, and ultimate purposes in history. But God did not abandon them, for His reputation and honor among the nations was at stake. Thus, He kept His word, despite Israel's unbelief and failure, He remained faithful to those covenant promises He made to His own people."[4]

---

[4] Marvin R. Wilson, ***Our Father Abraham – Jewish roots of the Christian Faith*** (Eerdmans Publishing Company, 1989)

Full of compassion, the Lord perseveres and gives until today the possibility of repentance, forgiveness, and return. This is Israel's hope today. The present restoration of Israel is the greatest proof of His compassion.

Figure 11 - Rebirth of the State of Israel

Standing in the Gap

Before taking up the call to go back to the Land, I should like to clarify one point which has to do with our participation, as His elect among the Gentiles, in the fulfillment of the biblical prophecies pertaining to Israel in the end times. While the Jewish people are divinely called to the Land, these *"elect from among the nations"* are called to make the difference in the return of the Jews to Eretz Israel. With this I would just go on record as expressing my support for the many ministries which have been raised up by God to take a stand for the cause of the Jewish people of Israel. These are those who were inspired by the Hebrew prophets who spoke of a future restoration of Israel and the role of the Nations (aka Gentiles) in Judah-Israel's fulfillment.

These elect from among the nations took to the letter the many passages that speak in favor of Zion, the likes of Isaiah 62:1 which proclaims: *"For Zion's sake I will not keep silent, And for Jerusalem's sake I will not keep quiet"* (NASB). They knew that God's promise to the Jewish people still stands; and that while some individuals and nations have been cursed for their indifference and hostility towards Israel, others have been blessed greatly for having blessed the nation of Israel. They counted the cost for standing with Zion and defended its right to the Land according to the Covenant God made with Abraham. Yes, it holds that the modern restoration of Israel is not a political anomaly, but the evidence of God's on-going faithfulness to His people through His Covenant made with the patriarch Abraham. They comforted, and still comfort, the descendants of Jacob because they have felt the bowels of God's compassion expressed in many passages of the Scriptures, like the following:

> *"'Comfort, yes, comfort My people!' Says your God. 'Speak comfort to Jerusalem, and cry out to her, that her warfare is ended, that her iniquity is pardoned; for she has received from the LORD's hand double for her sins"* (Isaiah 40:1-2).

As reviewed in the previous chapter, all Christian efforts in aligning with the restoration of Israel went hand-in-hand with the first phases of Aliyah and with greater thrust at the birth of the

State of Israel in 1948 and beyond. The tragic, sad, and true story in between is enclosed within the words of an acquaintance of yours truly, Nigel Woodley:

"As the first signs of the restoration of Zion began to dawn in 1882, when the first wave of Jewish immigrants began to head home to Zion in what is referred to as the first Aliyah, so the devil, in opposition to such a threat, decided to put a stop to this restoration. The threat that Satan was concerned about was the fact that the restoration of the people of Israel would herald the coming of Messiah and usher in the Messianic Age .... The Satanic plot would end such Zionist ambition, so through Hitler and the Shoah, he tried to abort the birth of the State of Israel. In His sovereignty, the Lord had to allow the Holocaust, the outcome of which was a homeland for the Jewish people."[5]

Others, like Dr. Tom Horn, have written much in connection with this regathering:

"God began His chosen nation's restoration to Palestine nearly a century before the Nazi beast began its genocidal work. Migration, though a trickle at first, began about 1838. The revival of national Jewish life in that land started in earnest in 1878. Then came the event that distinguished it as perhaps the most important signal that Apocalypse is near. Jerusalem was reclaimed for the Jews in precisely the manner the prophet Isaiah had foretold more than 2,700 years earlier: *"As birds flying, so will the Lord of hosts defend Jerusalem; defending also he will deliver it; and passing over he will preserve it"* (Isaiah 31:5). The prophetic fulfillment of the Isaiah's prophecy occurred when General Allenby, in 1917 took Jerusalem for the Jews out of the hands of the Turks. He then ordered airplanes to fly over Jerusalem and took the Turks by surprise that they had to surrender the city and so, Isaiah's prophecy was thus fulfilled: 'As birds flying,' God delivered Jerusalem, the city was defended while aircraft passed over. As a result,

---

[5] Woodley, Nigel. *Holocaust Exposed. The Biblical Enigma* (Solid Trust Ministries, New Zealand, 2009)

the Balfour Declaration was signed on November 2, 1919, recognizing Palestine as the rightful homeland for the Jew. The regathering began to take new dimensions.'"6

Defending Jewish Rights to the Land

The legal rights of the Jews to their land have always been the motivator for all Christian support to the cause of Zion, undergirded by the biblical declarations of the Hebrew prophets pointing to a future national home for the Jews in *Eretz* Israel.

It is then widely assumed that the State of Israel was born as a result of UN Resolution 181 in 1947. Then, on May 14, 1948, on the day in which the British Mandate over Palestine expired, the Jewish people's council gathered together at the Tel Aviv Museum, declaring the establishment of the State of Israel. In the words of the Declaration of Independence (*Megilat Ha'Atzmaut*) we can feel the emotion and the sanctity of this milestone event in prophetic history:

> "Eretz-Israel (the Land of Israel) was the birthplace of the Jewish people. Here their spiritual, religious, and political identity was shaped. After being forcibly exiled from their land, the people kept faith with it throughout their Dispersion and never ceased to pray and hope for their return to it and for the restoration in it of their political freedom. Impelled by this historic and traditional attachment, Jews strove in every successive generation to re-establish themselves in their ancient homeland. In recent decades they returned in their masses . . .. The State of Israel will be open for Jewish Immigration and for the Ingathering of the Exiles."7

The truth is that the legal rights of the Jewish people and Israel as a nation find their foundations solidly embedded in International Law well before the very existence of the United Nations, dating back to international legal instruments agreed upon by the

---

6 Thomas R. Horn, *The Rabbis, Donald Trump, and the top secret plan to build the Third Temple* (Defender Publishing, 2019)

7https://mfa.gov.il/mfa/foreignpolicy/peace/guide/pages/declaration%20of%20establishment%20of%20state%20of%20israel.aspx

principal allied powers of World War I meeting in San Remo (Italy) in April 1920 as a follow-up to the meeting in Paris in 1919 of the victorious allies after WWI. It was at this place and time, in San Remo, that the historical claim of the Jewish delegation to a "national home" became essentially legal in character in the form of the San Remo Resolution of 1920 by the adoption of the Mandate for Palestine by the League of Nations. The Mandate's relevant provisions remain valid and legally binding to this day.[8] The Conference commenced on 18 April 1920 at the Villa Devachan in the Italian Riviera town of San Remo. As Hugh Kitson confirms:

> "The Hebrew scriptures record that the Almighty God, whom Christians and Jews worship, gave the title deed to the land of Israel to the descendants Abraham, Isaac and Jacob as an everlasting possession some 4,000 years ago. What God did at San Remo was to enshrine that title deed into International Law in the modern era. The San Remo Resolution, which raised the Balfour Declaration to the status of an international treaty, could be likened to the 'Cyrus Decree' for the modern era. So, why is this latter-day Cyrus Decree so crucial in the purposes of God? I would suggest that it is to prepare the Jewish people (who have been largely scattered across the face of the earth for two millennia), the Land of Israel and the city of Jerusalem, for the second coming of Messiah. His mission this time? To rule and reign over the whole earth from His throne – the throne of David – in Jerusalem."[9]

Let me also quote from one of the most influential politicians of the Twentieth Century:

> "When it is asked what is meant by the development of the Jewish National Home in Palestine, it may be answered that it is not the imposition of a Jewish nationality upon the inhabitants of Palestine as a whole, but the further development of the existing Jewish community, with the assistance of Jews in other parts of the world, in order that it may become a center in which the Jewish people as a whole may take, on grounds

---

[8] Dr. Cynthia D. Wallace, ***Foundations of the International Legal Rights of the Jewish People and the State of Israel*** (Creation House, A Charisma Media Company, 2012).
[9] Hug Kitson (retrieved at https://prophecytoday.uk/general/item/1789-archive-san-remo-100.html)

of religion and race, an interest and a pride. But in order that this community should have the best prospect of free development and provide a full opportunity for the Jewish people to display its capacities, it is essential that it should know that it is in Palestine as of right and not of sufferance."[10]

Exactly so, the Jewish people are back in their promised land based upon legal binding rights established by International Law. Not only was the Jewish State formed because of a legal recognized right to apply sovereignty—as we read in the Mandate for Palestine accorded to Great Britain in August 1922, where the League of Nations recognized "The historical connection of the Jewish people with Palestine and the grounds for reconstituting their national home in that country"—but the Jewish people's right to settle in all of Judea and Samaria need to be considered an extension of their rights to the land. Today these areas are at the core of the whole conflict in the Middle East, as well as being at the center of worldwide political debate. According to International Law, the Jews are the indigenous people of this land, also known as first peoples, aboriginal peoples or native peoples of the land referred to as Judea and Samaria, and therefore fulfill the criteria required by International Law. The Jews are the ethnic group who were the original settlers of Judea and Samaria some 3,500 years ago, when the land was bestowed upon the Jews by the Almighty.

Leaders of this world, who chose to make revisionist history, purposefully misleadingly the community of nations by referring to Judea and Samaria as the "West Bank" of the Jordan River (which includes Israel) or the "Occupied Palestinian Territories"[11] do so with historical subterfuge. At the moment of this writing the Judea and Samaria Area is administered by the Israeli Defense Forces Central Command, and with military law applied.

---

[10] Winston Churchill – British Secretary of State for the Colonies -June 1922.
[11] Extracts from: https://www.israelhayom.com/opinions/applying-sovereignty-in-judea-and-samaria-does-not-violate-international-law/

Applying sovereignty to Judea and Samaria is therefore legal. Caroline Glick, in her best-selling book, ***The Israeli Solution***[12] has given an enormous contribution in solving the longstanding dilemma regarding the conundrum of a Two State Solution vs. a One State Solution. She explains that when Jordan, Egypt, Syria, Lebanon, and Iraq invaded Israel after their Declaration of Independence, the following:

> "Under international law, this war was an illegal war of aggression. All Jews who had been living in the areas that the Jordanians conquered were expelled from their homes. Under international law Israel has the strongest claim to sovereignty over the areas, and from a national historical perspective, Judea, and Samaria, as well as Jerusalem, are the cradle of Jewish civilization. Following the destruction of Jerusalem in 70 CE, during the Jews' nearly two thousand years of homeless exile, it was for their return to Jerusalem, Hebron, Beit El, Susia, Elon Morech, and Beitar that they prayed. The end of the war found Jordan illegally occupying Judea and Samaria. Israel's legal claim to sovereign rights over Judea and Samaria is clearly stronger than that of the Palestinians. In truth, the Jewish people's rights to sovereignty over Judea and Samaria, as with their rights to the rest of the Land of Israel, are overwhelming"; for example, Shiloh, which is in the heart of Samaria, "was the Jewish people's first capital in the Land of Israel. The Two State formula is based on the proposition that the root cause of the Palestinian conflict is Israel's unwillingness to surrender sufficient lands to the Palestinians, rather than the Palestinians' rejection of Israel's right to exist and their continued commitment to its destruction."

That is why many believe that the Israeli Solution—the One State Solution, where under Israel civil and legal sovereignty all parties involved can claim their human rights and privileges—might be the only possible peaceful solution.

---

[12] Caroline B. Glick, ***The Israeli Solution*** (Crown Forum, New York, 2014)

Repairing the Breach and Reversing History

Indeed, what the enemy meant for evil, God turned into good. By revealing to countless people the love that God has for Israel, *"Because the LORD has loved Israel forever"* (I Kings 10:9), the Holy Spirit made the impossible possible, and thus, from the day Israel was born more than 70 years went by and Israel began to experience the collective effort of many, who, from the ranks of Christianity and enlightened by the unalterable Word of God, started to visit Israel and pray, help, and declare the Word of the Lord in light of Israel's restoration. Then the entire environs of Jerusalem were returned to its people in 1967 as mentioned earlier. This was an extraordinary and prophetic event that saw the beginning of even a greater movement of believers flocking to Israel with the aim of repairing the breach that for so many centuries had kept the Church and Israel separated by a gulf of ignorance and when, by pretending to be spiritual, turned the cross into the sword.[13]

English Bible teacher Ken Hepworth has fairly written why most Christians are unaware of how Jews have been treated by the established Church throughout the ages.[14] No doubt, Christian help to the Jewish people has made the difference in so many areas during these past seventy-plus years from the birth of the State of Israel to the present. It's been a very long period of time in which the majority of pro-Israel ministries have focused mainly on the restoration of the Land and of its people, directing all their efforts at helping the Jews arise out of the ashes of the Holocaust to their present liberation.

Over the years, we discovered Israel's role in Bible Prophecy; we learned to read the signs of the times as we understood that Israel was the clock signaling the season of the return of Messiah. We remembered that God keeps covenant with the Jewish people because of the covenant he made with their forefathers. And, we commenced in repairing the longstanding breach between Israel

---

[13] Bolender, Merrill. *When the Cross Became A Sword* (Merril Bolender 2011)
[14] Hepworth, Ken. *Their Blood Still Cry Out*, Zaccamedia 2013

and the Church whereupon many ministries were birthed to stand in the gap and favor the reconciliation through acts of reparation.

Somehow, we have been acting as the "Ruth Church." The book of Ruth tells us while Orpah decided to leave Naomi and returned to her Gentile people, Ruth—the Moabite—decided to throw her lot in with Naomi, to serve and protect her. Her reward was great, even in becoming the great-grand-mother of David. Alas! A Gentile in the bloodline of Yeshua, the Messiah. She declared:

> *"For wherever you go, I will go; And wherever you lodge, I will lodge; Your people shall be my people, And your God, my God"* (Ruth 1:16).

Ruth represents that part of the Church (aka His "Ekklesia") that is willing to go out of its way to bless the Jewish people and to help them fulfill their divine call to return to their land and to their God; thus, healing this more than two-thousand year rift. It demonstrates that to show gratitude for the things that the Jews have done for us in terms of our spiritual legacy, we can be and act like Ruth deciding to throw in our lot with Naomi, to serve and protect her.

About this, it should be noted that:

> ". . . those who believe in the God of Israel know that supporting Israel in biblically-consistent ways has its rewards, even though it is a value in and of itself, for those who help Israel are helping to fulfill God's purposes in this world. Those in the Gentile world who don't yet understand this would be wise to read chapter 12 in the book of Genesis, in which the Lord made his eternal promise to the first Patriarch of Israel."[15]

But not only this, we learned to pray for Israel and for the Jewish people through a much better understanding of the role of prophetic intercession. Perhaps no one has taught countless numbers of people how to pray and intercede for the Jewish people as Rees Howells (aka the great intercessor – see chapter two), the founder

---

[15] David Rubin, ***God, Israel & Shiloh Returning to the Land*** (Shiloh Israel Press, 2011)

of the Bible College of Wales in Swansea. Here I quote some entries from his diary on September 1938. Referring to the Jewish plight under two gruesome characters of the time he wrote:

> "I have a great burden for these people, and I want God to lay their burden on me. The devil, through Hitler and Mussolini, is being used to send them back to their own land; it is the fulfillment of prophecy; it is another sign that this is the closing of the age. I am longing to help God's people to return to their land ... I want God to touch me deeper still with the feelings of what these are suffering ... God moved Cyrus, the one who had held them back in captivity, to supply the money to take them back! He will do this again, if someone will believe Him. I firmly believe the times of the Gentiles are drawing to a close, and the Jews must be back in their own land when the Master returns.....I shall buy the new estate, probably next week, and I am willing to risk my all in order to help the Jews."[16]

In 2017 I had the privilege of spending a weeklong Prayer Advance initiative held at the Bible College of Wales in Swansea. I will never forget the time spent in the halls and rooms of the place in which Rees Howells and his company of intercessors changed the pages of history by their dedicated efforts in intercessory prayer. The air was filled with what the old Pentecostals would call "holy hush" just because a man decided to stand in the breach and pray.

Allow me to digress on the personal, given that I've just mentioned Rees Howells prayer over a situation that saw some of the most dreadful characters who so much affected the fate of the Jewish people in the Twentieth Century. One of them is Benito Mussolini, known as the Dux of Fascism. It is he who in 1938 pronounced the ominous words, "Hebraism is a irreconcilable enemy of Fascism," thus heralding and implementing the racial laws against the Jews of Italy.

---

[16] Norman Grubb, **Rees Howells, The Intercessor** (The Lutterworth Press, 1952)

Not everybody knows that Benito Mussolini was born in a small village called Predappio—the smallest village with the biggest fascist-inspired buildings—in the region of Emilia-Romagna, just a few kilometers from the town where I live. The seeds of antisemitism were present in the Fascist regime since its inception, though antisemitism was not yet official policy. By 1943, the Fascists began confiscating Jewish property in Italy and rounding up Jews for deportation, and abruptly many of those who had not protested against anti-Jewish laws rushed to save Jews. Of the 45,000 Jews counted in Mussolini's census of 1938, about 8,000 died in Nazi camps.

About 7,000 managed to flee. About 30,000 lived in hiding before being liberated by Allied troops. But even fewer people know that the "Dux of Fascism" was buried in the local cemetery family crypt. Because of this, Predappio hosts parades of nostalgic post-fascists dressed in black shirts, singing songs, and raising their arms for the "Salute to the *Duce*" in ceremonies commemorating Mussolini's March on Rome on 28 October 1922 which marked the beginning of fascist rule. From my house I can see in the distance Mussolini's tower of his summer residence which rises tall on a hill. Sometimes I ponder the fact of my vicinity with these memorials of a terrible past of Italian history; I see myself as the product of the reversal of the curse once placed over the Jewish people because of fascism. Right from here, a few kilometers away from a place so much connected with racial laws, anti-Semitism, and a terrible alliance with Nazi Germany, began, now, I work for the rebuilding of the breach and the restoration of the State of Israel, where I am involved in decision-making for the benefit of the Aliyah of the Jewish diaspora throughout the world.

Truly I can say that there is nothing impossible with God for nothing can stand in the way of His purposes on earth. In His plan, He works contrary to all expectations when it comes to choosing one of the *nothings of this world* to confound the works of the spirit of Antichrist by placing this brother right in a symbolic place to show to the world that He is the one who watches over His people Israel by turning the curse into a blessing for them!

These and many other things have happened since 1948. Thus, more than seventy years were needed to fix foundational concepts such as the physical restoration of Israel and its people to the Land; these godly efforts have been at the forefront of Jewish emancipation and restoration.

Still, the ingathering of the exiles unto salvation, namely their spiritual restoration was not a priority during these initial years. But today, what is taking place before our eyes through the return of the Jewish people to Eretz Israel from the four corners of the world, transcends the post-exilic regathering as it precludes the final spiritual restoration of Israel and the final harvest of the elect from the Nations. Here we have the balance between the physical and spiritual restoration coming together as the Land, the People and the Nation of Israel are progressively being restored, gathered, and spiritually delivered (saved). So, we have understood that debt Christianity owes to the Jewish people, which is fourfold, as taught by Dr. Richard Booker,[17] ours is a written debt. If it wasn't for the Jews, we wouldn't have the Bible today. Virtually, all the writers of the Book were Jews, who risked and gave their lives to preserve the Bible for us, the revelation of God to mankind for the salvation of the world. "Every time a sermon or teaching is presented from the Bible, it is a message from God to us written by a Jew."

In sum, it is a moral debt. By moral debt we mean the unique standard of behavior set by God by means of the Ten Commandments through which man can enjoy a good and blessed life without destroying himself. The fabric of all western moral law stands on the ten "words" of God, the basis of the Jewish Law (Torah) that comes from the Jews. It is also a spiritual debt. Everything we have in the Gospel is a spiritual debt we owe to the Jewish people. The religious system given by God was only a

---

[17] Notes on teaching by Richard Booker – ***Christian Debt to Jews, Israel and the Nations in Prophecy*** (The Institute for Hebraic Christian Studies)

shadow of the good things to come, pointing to the mediator of the New Covenant by means of death. The blessings of the Messiah have come to us through the Jewish people. Yes, the New Covenant found in Jeremiah:

> *"Behold, the days are coming, says the LORD, when I will make a NEW COVENANT* (my emphasis) *with the house of Israel* (Northern 10 Tribes) *and with the House of Judah* (Southern 2 Tribes)—*not according to the covenant that I made with their fathers in the day that I took them by the hand to lead them out of the land of Egypt, My covenant which they broke, though I was a husband to them, says the LORD. But this is the covenant that I will make with the house of Israel after those days, says the LORD: I will put My law in their minds, and write it on their hearts; and I will be their God, and they shall be My people. No more shall every man teach his neighbor, and every man his brother, saying, 'Know the LORD,' for they all shall know Me, from the least of them to the greatest of them, says the LORD. For I will forgive their iniquity, and their sin I will remember no more"* (Jeremiah 31:31-34).

This is the "amazement!" The so-called "lost tribes of Israel"—who were "swallowed up of the Nations" throughout the four corners of the globe (Hosea 8:7-10; Isaiah 11:10-13) have been found! Our connection to the Jewish people is through Jesus (Yeshua) the Messiah. In other words, all that comes out through Jesus to us (who are grafted in and have become part of the Commonwealth of Israel) in terms of redemption and salvation as "Ephraim-Israel" have been included into the singularity of the Commonwealth of Israel via the SAME New Covenant—this is an insurmountable spiritual debt we owe to the Jewish people. The "Scepter"—the Royal-Line—*"shall not depart from Judah"* (Genesis 49:10):

> *"And in that day there shall be a Root of Jesse, Who shall stand as a banner to the people; for the Gentiles shall seek Him, and His resting place shall be glorious"* . . . *"It shall come to pass in that day that the LORD shall set His hand again the second time to recover the remnant of His people who are left, from Assyria and Egypt, from Pathros and Cush, from*

Elam and Shinar, from Hamath and the island of the sea . . . He will set up a banner for the nations, and will assemble the outcasts of Israel, and gather together the dispersed of Judah from the four corners of the earth . . . also the envy of Ephraim shall depart, and the adversaries of Judah shall be cut off; Ephraim shall not envy Judah, and Judah shall not harass Ephraim" (Isaiah 11:10-13).

So all-inclusive is the Salvation, this all-encompassing Deliverance—for not only has the "Savior of Israel" incorporated His dispersed into this promised New Covenant, He has wrought a most glorious reconciliation between both the House of Judah and the House of Ephraim. The breach of Jeroboam has been healed by the Root of Jesse—for:

"David My servant shall be king over them, and they shall all have one shepherd; they shall also walk in My judgments and observe My statutes, and do them . . . and My servant David shall be their prince forever. Moreover I will make a COVENANT OF PEACE with them, and it shall be an EVERLASTING COVENANT with them; I will establish them and multiply them, and I will set My sanctuary in their midst forevermore . . . My tabernacle also shall be with them; indeed I will be their God, and they shall be My people. The nations also will know that I, the LORD, sanctify Israel, when My sanctuary is in their midst forevermore" (Ezekiel 37:24-28).

The *"elect from among the Nations"* do NOT subsume the Jewish people (Judah) – no, no, no—they (the *"elect from among the Nations"*) are incorporated into the Commonwealth of Israel via the New Covenant through the Redeemer of Israel—and it is He Who has inaugurated His COVENANT OF PEACE between them (Judah and Ephraim). This is truly the Tabernacle of David—the United Kingdom of David!

Even so, it is a civil debt as well—for clearly it is written:

"For if the Gentiles have been partakers of their [viz. Jewish/Jerusalem] *spiritual things, their duty is also to minister to them in material things"* (Romans 15:27).

Western civil and penal jurisprudence owes much debt to the civil laws that God gave the Jewish people as a rule of conduct in all areas of life, such as, family laws and individuals laws—let alone the aforesaid "spiritual things" given to us by the Jewish people. When these principles are rightly implemented, they become an invaluable heritage of Judeo (and Christian) core values for life. Indeed, we Christians support Israel because God's gifts and calling to Israel are *"irrevocable"* (Romans 11:29; Numbers 23:19). So, as far as practical help, the principle applied is: because the Gentiles have been blessed with spiritual blessings from the Jews, they have an obligation to help them in the material way of life, *for it is time to show favor to Zion, the appointed time has come.* This is the financial debt of gratitude we have.

Moreover, we can counter biased news with these unalterable scriptural viewpoints. We can assure our Jewish friends that we are standing with them and with Israel in these days when hatred towards the Jews is again raising its ugly head. Then we can pray for the fulfillment of the Lord's plan crying out for Zion's sake until God fulfills all that He has said He would do. This is NOT presumptuous behavior on our part—it is simply the plain Word of God, our compass, our obligation before God and man!

Paul wrote to the Romans remembering our greatest example, Messiah, who . . .

> *". . . has become a servant to the circumcision for the truth of God to confirm the promises made to the fathers and that the Gentiles might glorify God for His mercy as it is written: 'For this reason I will confess to you among the Gentiles and sing to Your name.' And again He says: 'Rejoice O Gentiles with His people"* (Romans 15:8-10).

The Messiah is our example, Who became a servant to the Jewish people to show God's truthfulness and to show God's mercy. This is the basis of our trust; and though one might question this, because not all Jews have followed Yeshua, God will make good His promises to the patriarchs and He will do this through His servant of the Jewish people, Yeshua, the Messiah. And God's mercy is demonstrated by causing the Gentiles to glorify God. So, because the Gentiles have shared with the Jews in these spiritual matters, they have an obligation to help the Jews in material matters out of gratitude, and not for the Jews who believe only, but for all, especially those that are regathered to the Land—even in unbelief.[18] For the Almighty has included us all in *"disobedience"* that *"He might have mercy on us all"* (Romans 11:32) – and more so:

> *"I say then, have they stumbled that they should fall? Certainly not! But through their fall, to provoke them to jealousy, salvation has come to the Gentiles. Now if their fall is riches for the world, and their failure riches for the Gentiles, how much more their fullness!"* (Romans 11:11-12)

. . . it is "their fullness" which awaits the Final Redemption—to God be all the glory!

Aliyah, God's Sign to the Nations

Now, going back to Cyrus' proclamation, as mentioned in the opening of Chapter One, the book of Ezra picks up from 2 Chronicles to give the same message: *"Who is among you of all His people? May his God be with him and **let him go up** to Jerusalem"* (Ezra 1:3). The background of it is Jeremiah's prophecy that the Jews would go into captivity for 70 years (Jeremiah 25:11-12; 29:10). The full 70-year captivity ended in 537/536 BC at the very decree of Cyrus who allowed the first wave of Aliyah to Jerusalem in pursuant of the mandate from God to favor the rebuilding of the temple in Jerusalem (cf. Isaiah 44:28).[19] Their captivity commenced in the year 607/608 BCE under Nebuchadnezzar who was then Viceroy to the King of Babylon.

---

18 David. H. Stern, ***Jewish New Testament Commentary***, p. 437

19 Cyrus was king over the entire region that had once been Assyria and Babylon. Assyria had deported the northern kingdom beginning in 745 BC – and in 722 BC the capital of Northern Israel (Samaria) fell to the Assyrians—their final deportations occurred at King Sennacherib's demise in 711-712 BC (2 Chronicles 32:20-23); thus, some 33 years of deportations of the Northern Ten Tribes. Babylon had taken the Southern Tribes (Judah and Benjamin) commencing cir. 607/608 BC and then on the 9th of Av in 586 BC Jerusalem and her Temple were destroyed by then King Nebuchadnezzar (the 70-year captivity was then calculated from 607-537 BC). Therefore, when the Medo-Persian Empire came to power, Cyrus' proclamation of freedom went to all original 12 tribes, but only Judah and Benjamin could adequately respond and return to rebuild God's temple—nigh 200+years (745-537 BC) had elapsed between the initial Assyrian deportations of the 10 tribes of the northern kingdom until the Decree of Cyrus the Great of Persia;

As we know, the return from Babylon ensued in waves wherein Zerubbabel (whose name means *offspring of Babylon*), with the blessing of Cyrus, led the first band of captives back to Jerusalem. Zerubbabel was in charge of the first return (Ezra 2:2; Haggai 2:23). Cyrus made him governor of Judah and for some twenty years was strongly associated with prophets, priests, and kings, until the new temple was dedicated (some 49 years later—Ref. Zechariah 4). On God's instructions, Haggai promised Zerubbabel a special blessing:

> *"I will take you, Zerubbabel My servant, the son of Shealtiel, says the LORD, and will make you a signet ring; for I have chosen you"* (Haggai 2:23).

God was pleased with him in bringing the first captives home, less than 50,000[20] Jews. This was just the beginning of a new era in which God would truly begin to fulfill the promises of the prophets concerning a glorious future occasioned by their return and restoration. It is interesting to note that with Cyrus and Zerubbabel there was both a proclamation (the edict) and practical help (assistance in the return). This is exactly what we have seen for the last decades with the Lord raising up Christian ministries which combine a Cyrus/Zerubbabel anointing together in one.[21] Nowadays, several international Christian ministries devoted to helping the Jewish people in their homecoming to the land of Israel according to the biblical prophecies concerning their return offer a wide range of services to the *olim*[22] in need of help. Everything from providing humanitarian aid and services to Holocaust survivors and poor families in the former Soviet Union in

---

thus, the Northern Ten Tribes had been fractured and dispersed by Assyria and Babylon; most likely, many may have been unsure of their real heritage.

[20] Precisely, 42,360 were the people who returned, plus 7,337 servants, and 200 singing women for a total of 49,897.

[21] Ministries like Ebenezer Emergency Fund Operation Exodus have a *Cyrus anointing*. The ministry of Ebenezer Emergency Fund International, for example, began thirty years ago with an offering of just two USD. Since then, by the faithful giving of Christians around the world, it has helped thousands of Jews making Aliyah in fulfillment of the prophetic Scriptures. For more info please visit: https://operation-exodus.org.

[22] *Olim* is a Hebrew word that means new immigrants. The singular form is *oleh* (m) and *olah* (f).

need of financial support, to anyplace in the world where the diasporic Jewish people in need of assistance are found—there the Christian expression of love can make the difference to thousands of people in their God-given desire to move to Israel.

The Lord has inspired countless Christians to pray, help and practically assist the Jewish people. For example, shipping costs of household goods are provided to families that are moving to Israel as well as flight tickets, or the covering of costs for passports and any other documents proving their Jewish identity that potential *olim* need from the archives to prove they have the right to make Aliyah. In their endeavor, Christians reach these Jewish families who are in stark poverty and by assisting them in returning to the land of Israel they rescue them from anti-Semitism returning them to a better hope.

At times, projects of bringing home some of the most ancient tribes—like those from the Bnei Manasseh of India and the Ethiopians Falash Mura—are sponsored. Volunteers from many nations just give their practical help by picking up the *olim* at their home with all of their luggage and transporting them to the airport for their flight home. Others, instead, are committed to pray for protection during their journey home, while some are given to prayer and intercession on behalf of those that are still unwilling to leave the ease and comfort of their countries because they don't have the urgency to do so at this time. Despite the multi-colored variety of these services, education is a common denominator in all these ministries. They provide the right information and teaching to the churches about God's plan and Covenant for His people throughout the ages. Their particular function as "return ministries" is what the Lord had in mind in view of the promises regarding the return of the Jews to their homeland. In this way they carry a special anointing containing both the proclamation of the purposes of God for the return of the Jewish people and practical help in their Aliyah from the four corners of the world. This has been their task for decades now, to be the mouthpiece of the Lord for their return home to their promised land, precisely what is written in Jeremiah.

"Hear the word of the LORD, O nations, And declare it in the isles afar off, and say, 'He who scattered Israel will gather him, And keep him as a shepherd does his flock'" (Jeremiah 31:10).

Not only so, but also to be instruments in the hand of the Lord, helping in their return!

"For the LORD will have mercy on Jacob, and will still choose Israel, and settle them in their land. The strangers will be joined with them, and they will cling to the House of Jacob" (Isaiah 14:1).

"Behold, I will lift My hand in an oath to the nations, and set up My standard for the peoples; They shall bring your sons in their arms, and your daughters shall be carried on their shoulders" (Isaiah 49:22).

These passages clearly demonstrate that any Christian involved in the restauration of Israel is working with God in a prophetic preparation for the return of Messiah. This is much greater than everything else put together. To suggest that "God doesn't need your help" to do this "Second Exodus" is, in a word, preposterous—if I can be so blunt. Why? Yes, the Lord's hand is not so short that He cannot save to the uttermost; however, God is not seeking robots to accomplish His feats of grandeur—He desires human cooperation in His plan and purpose for the ages. We are not deists—we are of the Faith of Abraham who believed God and it was imputed to him for righteousness! God Almighty told Eve in the Garden that her Seed would crush Satan's head (i.e., the Serpent's head—Genesis 3:15)—and through the Messiah, the Seed of the Woman (Galatians 3:15-25; Romans 16:20) He is doing just that!

One of the most incredible stories I've heard in relation to the involvement of the Assembly of the Living God (aka "the Ekklesia" or "Church") as expressed in the Prophetic Scriptures (Romans 16:26) just examined, goes back to the testimony of Steve Lightle, who during a six-day fast in 1974 in Germany, had a powerful vision. Gustav Sheller, founder of Operation Exodus, condensed Steve Lightle's powerful testimony in his book:

"The power of God came in the room. It was so strong I couldn't get off the floor . . .. On the last day I got up and sat in a large, overstuffed chair. I saw a giant screen with a multitude of Jewish faces. There were so many of them. There were hundreds of thousands of Jewish people. They were on the screen and I began to see them as they began to come together and to mill around. And I could see their faces just as I can see you across the table. And then I saw the nation they were within, and it was the Soviet Union. I could see the borders of that land. I'm sitting there watching this. This is something new. Nothing like this has ever happened to me before. They came together to one place and there then appeared a highway that God Himself went and built. Nobody could get on that highway except whom the Lord permitted, and these were Jewish people. They got on this specially built highway and they began to walk and they began to come forth. And at the same time God raised up men with ministries as great or greater than that of Moses, who went to the authorities in the Soviet Union and proclaimed to them, 'Thus saith the LORD God of Israel, 'Let My people go!' And the authorities refused and wouldn't. Their hearts became hardened and they would not let the people go. And prophecies began to come, and plagues and judgment began to come against the Soviet Union until they were brought to their knees, that whole nation. And they just coughed up all these people on that highway. God built it and those Jews, hundreds of thousands of them, began to walk out."[23]

Ebenezer Emergency Fund International Operation Exodus was born following the footsteps of men of God like Gustav Sheller and Steve Lightle. I had the privilege of getting to know Steve Lightle[24] personally and listening to him teaching and preaching many times in the course of my years of involvement on the International Board of Ebenezer International. Gentile believers in Yeshua worldwide have continued to respond to the challenge to help carry the Jewish people home through prayer and financial

---

[23] Gustav Sheller, **Operation Exodus**, 1998

[24] The incredible life changing stories of Steve Lightle can be found in his two books, **Exodus II, Let My People Go** and **Operation Exodus II**.

support through the ministry of those pioneers who had the burden of the Lord to see these prophecies concerning the Exodus of the Jewish people.

Yes, we have received "blessings and cursing"—accolades, blessings and adoration from both Jews and Christians regarding our labor of love . . . contrariwise, we have been grossly misunderstood by friends and foes alike from both Houses, if you would. Notwithstanding, our charge, we affirm, is aligned with the Word of God, and in keeping with the present legacy of God's people—both Jews and Christians whose resolute support demonstrated in this manner can both endure criticism and enjoy praise . . . we know how to abound and to be abased for we can do *"all things through Messiah who strengthens me"* (Philippians 4:13).

In the course of my ministry I've had the opportunity and the joy of participating in the distribution of food parcel programs (life changing was the one my wife and I did in Ukraine) and thus sharing promises from the Hebrew prophets with Jewish families and giving the message of the return. I have also helped several *olim* making Aliyah, whether it was by driving a van to carry them in their transit from their homes to the airport, or holding their suitcases, I have always witnessed and affirmed the validity of the Prophetic Scriptures in my journey. I remember the day that my wife and I were carrying two Jewish children on our arms while coming out of an El Al plane at Ben Gurion Airport in Tel Aviv on occasion of a special Aliyah flight from Italy (cf. Isaiah 49:22: *"They shall bring your sons in their arms, and your daughters shall be carried on their shoulders"*). Looking back at the pictures that were taken we realized that we were part of the fulfillment of Bible prophecy, and a countless number of people have done and are doing things like these and many others in accordance with the prophetic Scriptures. One of the most incredible Bible verses is found in Jeremiah 32:41:

> *"Yes, I will rejoice over them to do them good, and I will assuredly plant them in this land, with all My heart and with all My soul."*

If you do a Bible word search on this verse you would find that this is the only place in the Bible where the Lord says that He is going to do something with all of His heart and all of His soul. It's so unique what the Lord does for the House of Jacob in returning them to their land that He has chosen to reserve a special place in the Scriptures where He sets the records straight by having all know that He has reserved all His attention to the welfare of His people as He gathers them to the Land. *"And I will assuredly plant them in this land."* There is a specific word in Hebrew to describe the work of an immigrant absorption, it is *Klitah*.[25] The word itself means *reception* or *naturalization* and comes from the verb *kalat* (to absorb). Because of this primary root, it is connected to another word, *miklat*, which stands for shelter. From here it comes also to mean a place of refuge, as in the cities of refuge found in the Bible (*irim miklaot*) to which perpetrators of accidental homicide could flee and receive asylum from vengeful relatives of the victims. Therefore, whenever a Jew makes Aliyah to Israel, at his arrival at Ben Gurion airport in Tel Aviv, he or her receives a *sal klitah* (an absorption basket or financial grant) provided by the Ministry of Aliyah and Integration. It shows that God doesn't only gather His people to the Land of promise but has raised a governmental institution that caters for the welfare of new immigrants and the National Institutions like the Jewish Agency for Israel[26] and Keren Hayesod[27] and many other volunteering associations that serve the scope of Aliyah and integration.

---

[25] Klitah was an important part of the lexicon of old-fashioned Zionism. New immigrants were received in *mercazei klitah* (absorption centers) that were a little more welcoming than army barracks. People would enquire, "How's your klitah going?" which was a way of asking, "Have you learned Hebrew, do you have a job, have you met the love of your life and how are you dealing with the crazy bureaucracy?" all in one question.

[26] One of the Israel's three National Institutions, the Jewish Agency for Israel is best known as the primary organization fostering immigration (Aliyah) and absorption of Jews and their families from the Jewish diaspora into Israel. Since 1948 the Jewish Agency for Israel has brought over 3 million immigrants to Israel and offers them transitional housing in "absorption centers" throughout the country.

[27] Keren HaYesod—United Israel Appeal—is an official fundraising organization for Israel and works in coordination with the State of Israel and the Jewish Agency to further the national priorities of the State of Israel.

Thus, through the Aliyah of His people and their settlement in the land of Israel, God is sending a clear sign to the nations that He is the One that has entered history as the One Who is having mercy on Zion, *"For the time to favor her, Yes, the set time, has come....So the nations shall fear the name of the LORD...For the LORD shall build up Zion......When the LORD shall build up Zion, he shall appear in his glory"* (Psalms 102). In other words, the return of Israel to the land witnesses for God and the display of His faithfulness in rebuilding Zion would bring the nations to recognize His sovereignty over His people as the rebuilding of Zion must precede and prepare for the Lord's return in glory.

This is precisely what we see taking place today. The Lord is restoring and rebuilding the nation of Israel. The rights of Israel to the Land confront head on a blatant lie: the Jewish people are foreign colonialists in their own ancestral homeland. Any talk in the process of annexation makes clear that the Jewish people have a valid, legal, historic, and moral claim to Judea and Samaria which supports Israel's sovereignty over the many Jewish communities there as they are an integral part of the historic Jewish homeland. After all, they are called Jews because they are the people of Judea. That is why all Christian support for Israel takes these factors into consideration. These important areas are also an integral part of our Christian identity and heritage. Believers know that under Israeli sovereignty, our common heritage can be protected. In a region where Christians are on the run and live in fear because of persecution, Christians in Israel can thrive and are free to profess their identity.

The gathering of the House of Jacob to their homeland as prophesied by the Hebrew prophets of old, needs to be viewed in stages, as set in a prophetic sequence of the events, of which *Aliyah (ascent to the Land),* with its other side of the coin, *Klitah (absorption and integration),* stands as the first phase of the plan of God.

This is indeed a "Land call" for the restoration of the nation of Israel in fulfillment of the covenant made by God to Abraham regarding the Land. Certainly, the regathering of the exiles to their ancient homeland is a testimony that there is a God in heaven whose name is the Lord God of Israel. David in fact once said:

"And who is like Your people Israel Your very own people forever; and You, O LORD have become their God . . .. So let it be established, that Your name may be magnified saying, 'The LORD of hosts, the God of Israel, is Israel's God'" (1 Chronicles 17:21, 23).

However, the gathering of the House of Jacob to their land is embedded with a spiritual finale that stands as the last milestone of the prophetic sequence. I would say one glaring observation—you might call it the "elephant in the room." That is this: There is a kind of metaphysical, Gnostic-style denial, by many who profess (sad to say) belief in Yeshua, as Messiah, of the "materiality" or "physicality" of today's Israel. This denial commenced almost simultaneously with the rise of historic Christianity wherein the millenarian aspects of the Prophetic Scriptures were denied the Jews; in particular, by many of the early "Church Fathers" who grossly allegorized the Scripture (aka, "Replacement Theology")—like Marcion and Origen—claiming that only the elect from the Nations were the True or Exclusive Israel of God (i.e., ALL Israel). They had and still many have the conviction that all the promises of God now accrue only to themselves—today's Jews are collectively rejected by the Almighty because of their "unbelief" and alleged disregard as His "covenant people."

They defame we who adhere to a "literal hermeneutic" of the Prophetic Scriptures. I do not have the time to theologically debate this "Rejection Theology" in this tome; however, suffice it to say, their rejection of the Jew befits their rejection of the literal Word of God and is utterly contrary to the statements of Paul found in Ephesians 2:

"For He Himself is our peace, who has made both one, and has broken down the middle wall of separation, having abolished in His flesh the enmity, that is, the law of commandments contained in ordinances [lit. "dogma"], so as to create in Himself ONE NEW MAN from the two [from Jew and Gentile], thus making peace, and that He might reconcile them both to God in one body through the cross, thereby putting to death the enmity. And He came and preached peace to you who were afar off and to those who were near. For through

Him we both have access by one Spirit to the Father" (Ephesians 2:14-18).

Yes, this is our "inhouse food fight" – yes, we are "one in Messiah" – yet, many of us who affirm Messiah's salvation, act as if this "middle wall of separation" engendering hate and animosity between the two was never abolished by the work of the cross! Only in His mercy can He open our eyes to the reality of what the Cross of Messiah has wrought for us all. How dare we claim inheritance in the Commonwealth of Israel—all the while denying membership of the Jews in their own Commonwealth! What contorted interpretation of Scripture have we here to deny the House of Judah full rights to their own Commonwealth? Sadly, this tortured theology afflicted wide swaths of the European Church during Europe's most horrid rise of Fascism and Hitler's reign of terror. Despite of the "material universe"—when God said, *"and it was good"*—makes a mockery of His Word: *"For the earth is the Lord's and the fullness thereof"* (Psalms 24:1-3). Indeed, if the "material" is by definition "evil"—then why should there be a *"new heaven and NEW EARTH"* (Ref. 2 Peter 3:13; Isaiah 65:17; 66:22)? Indeed, the "this worldly" Jews is contrasted by our "Replacement" brethren who claim their own status as "other worldly" being superior to the "Jewish orientation!" Enter Messiah, our Yeshua:

> *"Nathanael answered and said to Him, 'Rabbi, You are the Son of God! You are the King of Israel!' Jesus answered and said to him, 'Because I said to you, 'I saw you under the fig tree,' do you believe? You will see greater things than these.' And He said to him, 'Most assuredly, I say to you, hereafter you shall see heaven open, and the angels of God ascending and descending upon the Son of Man"* (John 1:49-51).

This is the same "Jacob's Ladder" which Jacob viewed bridging HEAVEN and EARTH—uniting the two and smashing to smithereens the dimensional divide while placing on the EARTH (as did Jacob/Israel) a pile of stones, calling it *Bethel*, even *El-Bethel—"God, the House of God."* Apparently, the Son of God (heaven) has every intention of coming to the earth (Son of Man)

. . . deprecating the Almighty's quest to inhabit both heaven and earth is NOT in accordance with His plan and purpose of the ages.

BOTH the Jew and the believer in Yeshua await the Deliverer (Messiah) who shall come OUT OF ZION and so ALL ISRAEL shall be delivered! (Romans 11:26-27) . . . Yes, the *"Heavenly Mt. Zion"* to which believers in Yeshua have come and are presently engaged (Hebrews 12:22) shall and is uniting with earth's Zion; for He is not only the Son of God (heavenly) He is the King of Israel (earthly)—that is precisely why He is entitled *"the heavenly MAN"* (1 Corinthians 15:48).

But first, let us examine the next loop in the order of things. . .

≈ ≈ ≈ ≈ ≈ ≈

Prayer

Father, we acknowledge that you have chosen to hallow your great Name through the Aliyah of your people to the promised land of Israel. May this sign be raised as a banner throughout the nations so that the world may see your faithfulness to your promises and come to know you as their Savior and Lord—the Son of God—and Son of Man, the King of Israel!

Figure 12 – Ebenezer Emergency Fund Int'l Operation Exodus

Chapter 4
Called to Relationship

After seventy years are completed at Babylon, I will visit you and perform My good word toward you, and cause you to return to this place. For I know the thoughts that I think toward you, says the Lord, thoughts of peace and not of evil, to give you a future and a hope. Then you will call upon Me and go and pray to Me, and I will listen to you. And you will seek Me and find Me, when you search for Me with all your heart.

(Jeremiah 29:10-13)

The Beginning of Redemption

THE SAGES OF ISRAEL HAVE ALWAYS SEEN THE IN-GATHERING OF THE EXILES AS *ATCHALTA De'GEU-LAH*[1], THE BEGINNING OF REDEMPTION, HENCE, a pivotal point in time since it is the initial stage of the salvation and redemption process. From this perspective Aliyah is considered a greater *Mitzvah* (lit. commandment, in a sense of a moral deed in keeping with the Law). Aliyah is a *mitzvah* in the sense of a preparatory act because it enables one to perform not only the *mitzvot* (commandments) connected to the land but all of the *mitzvot*. For example, only in Israel can one observe Shabbat and all of the Jewish holidays with ease because the entire country is on Jewish time and calendar. Israel is conducive to Torah study both in terms of vast opportunities and in terms of enabling the Bible to come to life, and why not, living in Israel allows one to learn and master Hebrew and thereby connect to one's heritage. It is therefore believed that one should make *Aliyah* because living in Israel is a *mitzvah* in and of itself as well as a preparatory act which enables one to observe all of the *mitzvot* and to live a full Jewish life by living in a Jewish State.

In a public lecture delivered in Jerusalem in 2019 Jewish scholar and international speaker Rabbi Mendel Kessin told us:

---

[1] **Atchalta De'Geulah** lit. *"the beginning of the redemption"* is the period of time in which occurs a new stage of revival in the process of the redemption and the coming of Messiah. (Wikipedia).

"The issue is that it is time to remove the influence of people who have nothing to do with furthering God's Torah. The Jewish people must be prepared and must be elevated in order to begin the process of redemption."[2]

In essence, renowned Rabbi Kessin is maintaining that in order for Messiah to come, the Jewish people must return to Torah which elevates them in preparation for the arrival of Messiah in view of the full redemption. This is basically the thought of the sages of Israel who would see that the act of ingathering of the exiles in the land of Israel will bring about the coming of Messiah, as the hand of God is demonstrating in the events of the creation of the State of Israel. In this light, the gathering of the exiles (in Hebrew - *Kibbutz Galuyot*) is embodied by the idea of going up (Aliyah) since the Holy Land is considered to be spiritually higher than any other land. According to The Oxford Dictionary of the Jewish Religion the word *exile* refers to the condition, not the persons. For almost as long as the Jewish nation has existed, it has been persecuted and forced to wander from land to land: starting with slavery in Egypt, to the destruction of both temples in Jerusalem, to the Crusades, the Inquisition, the pogroms, the Holocaust, and finally, modern-day anti-Semitism.

These times of national displacement are known in Hebrew as *galut,* exile. The term *galut* expresses the Jewish conception of the condition and feelings of a nation uprooted from its homeland and subject to alien rule. The beginning of all *galut*, the root from which it grew and branched off, was when Jacob and his children left Canaan (as Israel was then called) because of famine and traveled to Egypt for food. Expressed in the Torah and later developed by the former prophets, the concept of the gathering of the Exiles (*Kibbutz Galuyot*) became entrenched in the weekday Jewish liturgy. The tenth blessing of the 18th benediction reads:

---

[2]https://www.breakingisraelnews.com/137468/rabbi-predicted-trump-presidency-shocking-new-prediction-israels-election-messiah/?fbclid=IwAR2F_lsaH7YuHM9DchcYIPRGR7bpxgT2H73Cma1FBVlMZZ2Q9MzvKANM8Yk

"Sound the great shofar to herald our freedom, raise high the banner to gather our exiles. Gather us together from the four corners of the earth."

This tells me that a Jew could not be complete as a Jew without the connection to his land. Let us look at some other prayers:

"Have pity on us, O Lord, in the land of our captivity, and do not pour Your wrath upon us—for we are Your people, the members of Your covenant" (from the Tachanun Prayer); "Blow the great shofar for our Liberty, and miraculously ingather our exiles, and gather us together from the four corners of the earth. Blessed are you O Lord, who ingathers the dispersed of His people Israel" (from the thrice daily Amidah prayer).

This benediction in the Amidah is a central part of Jewish liturgy. It is the earliest benediction wherein an appeal is made concerning subjects related to Jewish nationality and restoring the existence of the Hebrew nation as an independent nation.

All these prayers express the idea that God will return the scattered Jewish people to their ancestral homeland and improve their lives when they repent for their sins.

Assuming now, as it has been for the first stage of the prophetic sequence whose protagonists are the Jewish people in their calling to go up, make Aliyah—to the Land of Israel— we can now view the book of Ezra to help us in understanding that their ascent is progressive and that their second phase entails a moving on up to a greater degree of relationship with their God, the Holy One of Israel. Therefore, I believe that according to God's greater design there is more to it than just a mere and physical return to the land, albeit always in view as the initial stage.

That is why we need to realize that the land concept itself was never meant to be a salvific issue in God's eyes in terms of obtaining a spiritual ticket to heaven to be received with the Israeli passport. No, because salvation is always accompanied by confession of sin, repentance, and subsequent restoration. In light of this, the gathering of the Jews serves a double purpose in the sight of God. The first is to be the means whereby God—

once the restoration of the Land of Israel sets the stage for the return of Messiah—creates the second instrument unto the salvation of His people. In the middle between these dynamics, there is what many Hebrew prophets looked at, namely a return to the God of Israel by means of *teshuvah*[3] (return) nurtured by the Torah—i.e., the interim preparation for Messiah arrival and subsequent salvation.

We can expand this further by looking at Ezekiel 36 where we cannot help but recognize that the gathering of the Jewish people is of God and that it is contingent upon the Lord repeatedly expressing His will in wanting to save them. A careful reading will highlight this pattern before our eyes.

> *"I scattered them among the nations, and they were dispersed throughout the countries; I judged them according to their ways and their deeds. When they came to the nations, wherever they went, they profaned My holy name—when they said of them, 'These are the people of the Lord, and yet they have gone out of His land.' But I had concern for My holy name, which the house of Israel had profaned among the nations wherever they went. "Therefore say to the house of Israel, 'Thus says the LORD God: "I do not do this for your*

---

[3]Teshuvah, from the Hebrew תשובה, literally, "return," pronounced "tshuvah" or "teshuvah," is the forsaking of sin and turning to God. It is one of the principal tenets of Judaism. Judaism recognizes that everybody sins on occasion, but that people can stop or minimize those occasions in the future by repenting for past transgressions. Thus, the primary purpose of repentance in Judaism is ethical self-transformation.

Maimonides said, "Even if a man has sinned his whole life, and repents on the day of his death, all his sins are forgiven him" (Maimonides, Yad, Teshuvah 2:1). One should repent immediately. A parable is told in the Talmud (*Shabbat* 153a) that Rabbi Eliezer taught his disciples, "Repent one day before your death." The disciples politely questioned whether one can know the day of one's death, so Rabbi Eliezer answered, "All the more reason, therefore, to repent today, lest one die tomorrow." (quoted in Telushkin, 155)

Reish Lakish said: "What is the meaning of that which is written: 'This is the law [*torah*] of the burnt offering, of the meal offering, and of the sin offering, and of the guilt offering, and of the consecration offering, and of the sacrifice of peace offerings' (Leviticus 7:27)? This teaches that anyone who engages in Torah study is considered as though he sacrificed a burnt offering, a meal offering, a sin offering, and a guilt offering" (Menahot 110a).

sake, O house of Israel, but for My holy name's sake, which you have profaned among the nations wherever you went. And **I will** sanctify My great name, which has been profaned among the nations, which you have profaned in their midst; and the nations shall know that I am the Lord," says the LORD God, "when I am hallowed in you before their eyes. For **I will** take you from among the nations, gather you out of all countries, and bring you into your own land. Then **I will** sprinkle clean water on you, and you shall be clean; **I will** cleanse you from all your filthiness and from all your idols. **I will** give you a new heart and put a new spirit within you; **I will** take the heart of stone out of your flesh and give you a heart of flesh. **I will** put My Spirit within you and cause you to walk in My statutes, and you will keep My judgments and do them. Then you shall dwell in the land that I gave to your fathers; you shall be My people, and I will be your God. **I will** deliver you from all your uncleannesses. **I will** call for the grain and multiply it, and bring no famine upon you. And **I will** multiply the fruit of your trees and the increase of your fields, so that you need never again bear the reproach of famine among the nations. Then you will remember your evil ways and your deeds that were not good; and you will loathe yourselves in your own sight, for your iniquities and your abominations. Not for your sake do I do this,' says the LORD God, 'let it be known to you. Be ashamed and confounded for your own ways, O house of Israel!' 'Thus says the Lord God: 'On the day that **I** (will) cleanse you from all your iniquities, **I will** also enable you to dwell in the cities, and the ruins shall be rebuilt. The desolate land shall be tilled instead of lying desolate in the sight of all who pass by. So they will say, 'This land that was desolate has become like the garden of Eden; and the wasted, desolate, and ruined cities are now fortified and inhabited.' Then the nations which are left all around you shall know that I, the Lord, have rebuilt the ruined places and planted what was desolate. I, the LORD, have spoken it, and **I will** do it.' 'Thus says the LORD God: '**I will** also let the house of Israel inquire of Me to do this for them: **I will** increase their men like a flock. Like a flock offered as holy sacrifices, like the flock at Jerusalem on its feast days, so shall the ruined cities be filled with flocks of men. Then they shall know that I am the LORD.'" (Ezekiel 36:19-38).

Fifteen times the Lord repeatedly says '*I will*' to demonstrate His full intention and determination of saving His people. As righteousness is of God actualized, so it is redemption. Nevertheless, salvation is certainly not a mechanical thing for anyone moving to the land of Israel, nor is it given with the status of Israeli citizenship. So, Jacob has been regathered first, not because they have repented, but for God's great name and purpose that they could be a distinct people again, not for their own sake, but as an example to the world of the Lord's own ability to save.

Not Land Only

As stated earlier, the importance of Torah for the Jewish people in making *teshuvah* (returning to God) is such that if we look at the "Land Call" concept we see that it was never given as a stand-alone promise but that it is always connected with the doing of the Torah. Let us look at Psalm 105:11, 44-45:

> ***"To you I will give the land of Canaan as the allotment of your inheritance*** *. . . He gave them the lands of the Gentiles and they inherited the labor of the nations,* ***that they might observe His statues and keep His laws***."

In other words, the very possession of the Land was for the purpose of serving the Lord God of Israel by doing His commandments as it is clearly shown in Moses' famous speech in Deuteronomy, ***"And you will again obey the voice of the Lord and do all His commandments which I command you today"*** (Deuteronomy 30:8).

Similarly, the very Ten Commandments themselves were given to be put into practice in the Land of promise as the fourth commandment shows, *"Honor your father and your mother, that your days may be long upon the land which the LORD your God is giving you"* (Exodus 20:12). Afterall, the very first commandment reads: *"I am the LORD your God,* ***who brought you out*** *of the land of Egypt, out of the house of bondage. You shall have no other gods before Me"* (Exodus 20:2-3). This is even stricter because it is an appeal to all the Jewish people of the world irrespective of the fact that they have made Aliyah or not. Another example is found in Deuteronomy 30:19-20 where it says:

". . . therefore choose life, that both you and your descendants may live; that you may love the LORD your God, that you may obey His voice, and that you may cling to Him, for He is your life and the length of your days; and that you may dwell in the land which the LORD swore to your fathers, to Abraham, Isaac, and Jacob, to give them."

From the testimony of the Scriptures it looks to me that there is a pattern throughout the Old Testament of a 'Land for Torah' principle. Here is another passage:

"You shall therefore keep His statutes and His commandments which I command you today, that it may go well with you and with your children after you, and that you may prolong your days in the land which the LORD your God is giving you for all time" (Deuteronomy 4:40).

Furthermore, there is another aspect which surrounds the 'Land for Torah' principle that has to do with a relationship with God stemming from obedience to Him as if to say that the focus and the finality of the command is about a God-children relationship, not land *per se*. What I'm saying is that the people of Israel were never meant to possess the Land if not to fulfill God's purposes of having a testimony on earth of a people set apart for Him, a peculiar and special nation distinct from the nations, known for following the Lord in the Land of Promise. After all, Cyrus' decree was issued with a purpose which is even beyond the 'Land call' principle.

At the time of king Darius, the enemies of the Jews began to hinder their work and sent a letter to Darius urging him to stop the work of building the house of God at Jerusalem. Darius, however, after learning of the original decree of Cyrus, reconfirmed it and the work continued without further hindrance and the temple was finished in the 6th year of the reign of Darius. In a letter sent by Tattenai we read the report by the elders of the Jews explaining that *"In the first year of Cyrus king of Babylon, king Cyrus issued a decree* **to build this house of God**" (Ezra 5:13), furthermore a scroll was found and in it a record was written thusly:

> **"Cyrus issued a decree concerning the house of God at Jerusalem: 'Let the house be rebuilt, the place where they offered sacrifices; and let the foundations of it be firmly laid'"** (Ezra 6:3).

Whereupon Darius issued a decree concerning the building of the house of God granting assistance in whatever they needed to accomplish this God-given task:

> *"And whatever they need let it be given them day by day without fail,* **that they may offer sacrifices of sweet aroma to the God of heaven"** (Ezra 6:9-10).

So, here we have the restoration to the Land and restoration to the service of God going on at the same time. There cannot be one to the exclusion of the other.

Even more, incorporated in the original Decree of Cyrus there is a specific mentioning about the foundations of the temple to be firmly laid. In other words, it was the gathered Jews' responsibility to act out the command of the Lord for the building of solid foundations so as to ensure the stability of the Temple and the continuity of sacrifices of sweet aroma to the God of heaven. Land, obedience, and relationship are concepts interwoven together in the New Covenant in Yeshua (announced by Ezekiel and Jeremiah) where God cleanses His people following their regathering to the Land. **The theological proposition behind the New Covenant itself is that returning to the Land is in view of their turning to God.** It presupposes a later and subsequent return to Him Who has been merciful in bringing them home. Therefore, in this second phase of the going up, people are placed at the center as they are marching upward to a new level of relationship with the very God of the Land.

Theirs is really a call to a higher and Holy Pilgrimage. In other words, the promise that God would become their God and that they would be a people for Himself starts right at the moment they enter into a covenant relationship with Him to do all His commandments, in the Land of Promise. In a sense, the thesis that returning to the Land is sufficient for salvation is very weak in itself. It does not pass the test of Scripture. There has got to be something in between. That is why YHVH had to cry out to a people that was in compromise:

> **"Remember the Torah of Moses my servant, which I commanded him in Horeb for all Israel, with the statutes and judgments.** *Behold, I will send you Elijah the prophet before the coming of the great and dreadful day of the LORD"* (Malachi 4:4).

The word *remember* comes from the Hebrew *zichru* (זִכְרוּ Strong H#2142) the imperative form of the verb *zakar* which means *to mention, to recall, to think about, to acknowledge, to make known*. Its basic meaning indicates a process of mentioning or recalling either silently, verbally, or by means of a memorial sign or symbol. So, the end-time scenario depicted by Malachi reveals that prior to the coming of Elijah the prophet, the Jewish people should have taken heed to this final warning lest they miss the blessing of receiving the One Who was to come. In fact, the last sentence of Malachi recites *"Lest I come and strike the earth with a curse"* (Malachi 4:6). In the gospel of Luke, we read that an angel speaks to Zechariah in the temple saying that his son, John, would go in the spirit and power of Elijah (Luke 1:17) and in Matthew's Gospel it is said that *"Jesus answered and said to them, 'Indeed, **Elijah is coming first and will restore all things"** (Matthew 17:11). In simple terms, before the *". . . coming of the great and dreadful day of the LORD,"* just as John the Baptist moved in the anointing and power of Elijah to prepare the way of the Lord, there is to be another release of this type of ministry before the second coming of Jesus.

Some commentators have suggested that the Elijah that is to come can also represent a prototype of the end-time awakening that is to come, when a prophetic mantle will fall on the end-time Church enabling her to be a prophetic witness against the powers of darkness (Ref. Revelation 11:6). Once again, the pattern presented by the Scriptures is that anytime a revival breaks out it is accompanied by a *teshuvah* to the Lord by means of His word that brings forth repentance. In fact, the promise still stands as the Elijah who is to come will *"Turn the hearts of the fathers to the children, and the hearts of the children to their fathers"* (Malachi 4:6). This means that a spiritual restoration of lost biblical truth will precede the return of the Lord. For the Jewish people it starts with remembering and recalling the Torah of Moses. There needs to be a time in the sequence of the events that a national return to God's word occurs prior to the second coming of Messiah ben David. But if Elijah—who is to come—stands for the last outpouring of the Holy Spirit, a return to Torah is precursory to the national revival. There is a connection between Torah and revival. Malachi 3:1 says: **"And the LORD whom you seek will suddenly come."**

In other words, the Lord will come back only after a great revival characterized by intense prayer for seeking Him. Again, *"Behold, I will send you Elijah the prophet before the coming of the great and dreadful day of the LORD"* (Malachi 4:5). Malachi is saying that before the second coming of the Lord, the entire world will experience a period of prophetic witness, here symbolized by Elijah, that will catch the attention of the nations in a time of revival of a great magnitude. The interesting thing is that according to Malachi, the spiritual end-time revival is preceded by a revival of Moses. **"Return to me"** (Malachi 3:7) (TORAH), **"And I will turn to you"** (Malachi 3:7) (REVIVAL). Isn't it amazing? The precondition to revival is the willingness to go back to Torah.

I might also add that the phrases in Malachi 4:6 wherein *"And he will turn the hearts of the fathers to the children, and the hearts of the children to their fathers,"* is an intensely familial interchange dealing with fathers and children; in other words, dealing with the Household of God, the family of God which appears that all "estrangement" and "broken relationships" shall be overwhelmed by this end of days revival and restoration. Could this not be, as well, the anointing ministry of the end-time prophet(s) of BOTH houses of Israel UNITED in mission and purpose? Could this be the restoration, that Covenant of Peace "between them both" (i.e., between the Household of Judah—the Jewish people; and the Household of Ephraim—those elect from the Nations)?

The sense of profound depth of this statement leads me to affirm such a restorative ministry of the prophet shall occur BEFORE that great and terrible day of the Lord. Likewise, He Who judges righteously cannot do so—for all judgment has been committed to the Son—until He "gets His House in order!" Therefore, He will surely *"purify the sons of Levi that they may offer unto the Lord a sacrifice in righteousness"*—for *"judgment must begin at the House of God first"*—wherefore shall the ungodly abide? Yes, He will restore us—for among His *"brethren according to the flesh"* – *"blindness in part has befallen them"* – but among those elect from among the Nations, *"we see through a glass dimly"*[4]— eventually, we both shall know our Joseph as He unveils Himself to us in the midst of the end-time famine which shall affect the whole earth! This revelation of His "relationship" with us both— both His brethren after the flesh and the Egyptians which He has saved—shall unite us on that day . . . but He—Joseph—must make His move and reveal Himself for neither one of us knows Him in fullness until we see Him AS HE IS!

In one of his sermons, *The Perpetuity of the Law*, Charles Spurgeon once said:

> "You have deprived the gospel of its ablest auxiliary when you have set aside the law. You have taken away from it the schoolmaster that is to bring men to Christ. No, it must stand, and stand in all its terrors, to drive men away from self-righteousness and constrain them to fly to Christ. **They will never accept grace till they tremble before a just and holy law; therefore, the law** serves a most necessary and blessed purpose, and it must not be removed from its place."[5]

---

4 Misc. Ref. Malachi 3:3; 1 Peter 4:17; Romans 9:3; Romans 11:25; 1 Corinthians 13:12
5https://www.spurgeon.org/resource-library/sermons/the-perpetuity-of-the-law-of-god#flipbook/

In the next chapter we will pick up the book of Ezra to determine the importance and role that God has assigned to the Torah in the leading up to the final phase of His plan for His people.

≈ ≈ ≈ ≈ ≈ ≈

Prayer

Father, we marvel at Your plan. At the beginning of the redemption, You have brought the children of Israel back to the Land choosing to have a witness on earth through them and the Torah has an important role in it. But you are a God of relationship and we pray that through the reading of your Word their eyes may be opened to see the wonderful reality of Messiah and our eyes as well. O Lord God . . . may Your prophetic witness grip our hearts in these end of days . . . "turn the hearts of the fathers to the children, and the hearts of the children to their fathers"— spare us the curse, and grant us your blessing!

Chapter 5

Called to Moses

For until this day the same veil remains unlifted
in the reading of the Old Testament,
because the veil is taken away in Christ.
even to this day, when Moses is read,
a veil lies on their heart.
Nevertheless, when one turns to the Lord,
the veil is taken away.

(2 Corinthians 3:14-16)

Torah and Teshuvah

THE PURPOSE OF THIS CHAPTER IS TO LOOK AT THE ROLE THAT THE TORAH HAS IN ACCOMPLISHING THE WORK OF *TESHUVAH* IN THE JEWISH PEOPLE, of turning their hearts to the God of Israel. In this respect I believe with my Jewish brethren that the Torah is for all time and ages since the day Moses received it at Sinai. Even Jesus confirmed it when he said: *"Don't think that I came to destroy the Law or the prophets. I didn't come to destroy but to fulfill"* (Matthew 5:17).

However, the Scriptures show a pattern describing a set time in the sequence of events that Torah has been most effective in turning the hearts of the people to the Lord their God, meanwhile, at other times, Torah has been completely neglected, unkempt, even forgotten. I affirm with the apostle Paul who has said that *"Even to this day, when Moses* [The Torah] *is read, a veil lies on their heart. Nevertheless, **when one turns to the Lord, the veil is taken away***" (2 Corinthians 3:15-16). Again, it is precisely the relationship between turning to the Lord and the unveiling of Yeshua unto salvation through Torah, which will be the main object of this chapter.

Now, after about an eighty-year gap, from the first return promoted by Cyrus' decree (cir. 537 BC) unto another decree made by Artaxerxes Logimanus (465-425 BC his reign) in approximately 458 BC[1] (or 444-445 BC) . . . a second wave of Aliyah occurred with Ezra as its leader (79 to 93 years after the first decree under Cyrus the Great). This decree authorized Ezra[2] to be its leader to return with a more sizeable group of Jews from Babylon. Here are the terms and conditions of the new decree, which, by the way, was incorporated into Aramaic:

> *"Artaxerxes, king of kings, To Ezra the priest, a scribe of the Law of the God of heaven: Perfect peace, and so forth.* ***I issue a decree that all those of the people of Israel and the priests and Levites in my realm, who volunteer to go up to Jerusalem, may go with you.*** *And whereas you are being sent by the king and his seven counselors to inquire concerning Judah and Jerusalem, with regard to the Law of your God which is in your hand; and whereas you are to carry the silver and gold which the king and his counselors have freely offered to the God of Israel, whose dwelling is in Jerusalem"* (Ezra 7:12-15).

> *"And whatever seems good to you and your brethren to do with the rest of the silver and the gold, do it according to the will of your God"* (Ezra 7:18).

Compared to the first wave of returnees, for in this new stage we are talking about a smaller remnant going up to the land—approximately two-thousand men, plus families. It comes in a period when the walls, the altar, and the temple were already built, but the moral situation of the people was a great concern to Ezra. It wasn't, at this time, very exciting living in Jerusalem because people had to struggle to make a living. They were poor and building the temple was slow work. It needed two prophets (Haggai and Zechariah) to urge them to keep going. But first, there must be someone to get the truth instilled in them wherein God must

---

[1] Known as Artaxerxes I Longimanus, he temporarily halted the rebuilding program at Jerusalem that Cyrus, his predecessor, had encouraged but later allowed it to continue. In the seventh year of his reign, he authorized the mission of Ezra to head a large number of Israelites back from the Captivity to Jerusalem. This is the decree to rebuild the Temple and the City of Jerusalem. Other scholars would date Artaxerxes decree in 444/445 BC but all within the span of his reign from 465-425 BC.

[2] The first mention of Ezra is in connection with a royal decree granting him permission to lead a band of exiles back to Jerusalem. This Edict was issued by king Artaxerxes.

come first in their life as people. It was so important that they went back to Jerusalem as God's people. Once again, the temple would be the very center of their return and their hopes, but tragically they had returned to their land but not to their Lord. Upon his arrival Ezra learned of intermarriages between the children of Israel and pagans in the region. He wept and prayed for the nation. His honest confession led to a national repentance and revival. Confession opened the door to a spiritual restoration.

Ezra was a direct descendant of Aaron and was, therefore, qualified to occupy the priestly office. Furthermore, he was a scholar and had authority to render interpretations of it, as well as making legal copies. He was a man who was shaped by God for such a time as this. His name—Ezra—literally means *help*. It shows us that his mission was to help God in advancing His plans, but in a rather different way than Zerubbabel in the first return. In fact, he was remembered most for being the man of the Scriptures, one who not only studied it, but lived it and taught it.[3] He was a man of great moral strength, learning, humility, self-denial, zeal, prayer, and faithfulness to God and His people, a fascinating character.

Indeed, this constituted a second phase in the timeline in the life of those who chose to go up to the Land. Ezra said, *"So I was encouraged, as the hand of the Lord my God was upon me; and I gathered leading men of Israel to go up with me"* (Ezra 7:28).

In the book, ***History of the Jews***, Paul Goodman offers a concise but complete review of Ezra's mission:

> "The rebuilding of the Temple in Jerusalem would have availed little had it not been for the appearing of Ezra, who, with the moral earnestness and zeal gave an entirely new tendency to Jewish history. The Jews became first and foremost a religious community, in which the study of the Sacred Writings and the observance of their institutions were to be the

---

[3] Tradition says that Ezra was the president of the great synagogue which settled the question of the Jewish Canon of Scriptures and began building synagogues in Jewish communities. From that time on, the order of service in the synagogue would follow Ezra's directions, even today.

great purpose of Jewish life. This regenerator of Judaism, of whom it was afterwards said that he restored the Torah which had been forgotten, came from Babylon bringing with him a decree of King Artaxerxes Longimanus which gave full authority for the carrying out of the object he had in view. Of epoch-making importance was his establishment of the Torah of Moses as the basis of Jewish life and thought, a measure which more than anything else ensured the continuance and vitality of Judaism."[4]

Ezra goes up to the Land with a purpose as this second wave of Aliyah was part of a program of religious education. In other words, Ezra arrives with education in view, which had to be the teaching of the Law of the Lord. This was a turn in the lives of many for he brought clarity as to what were the reasons behind their return. Ezra set the way for this second stage of the pilgrimage, a going up to spiritual maturity. *"For Ezra had prepared his heart to seek the Law of the LORD, and to do it, and to teach statutes and ordinances in Israel"* (Ezra 7:10). This is the reason behind Ezra summoning volunteers to go up with him and teach Torah. *"And you, Ezra, according to your God-given wisdom, set magistrates and judges who may judge all the people who are in the region beyond the River,* **all such as know the laws of your God; and teach those who do not know them**" (Ezra 7:25).

This is, in every sense of the word, a moving on **up**, a progress towards spiritual maturity. What amazes me is that it involved only a remnant. The numbers itself spoke of the trend because if in the first return under Zerubbabel 42,360 people came back, here we have a considerably smaller group. It shows that those in the first wave did it just because they saw an opportunity to move to the Land in a framework of a "Land call" only. With Ezra, however, yes there is Aliyah but it's about an ascent with a mission where the exiles are positioned in a favorable situation in which they would be willing to accept their God-given call to live up to

---

[4] Paul Goodman, ***History of the Jews***, pp. 37-38 (E.P. Dutton & Company, INC. New York, 1953)

the standards of the Torah. That's why Ezra speaks into the spiritual situation of the people. As it was then, Ezra's spiritual principles and dealings with the people serve as a frame of reference and comparison with the spiritual situation of today's modern Israel. Essentially, what Ezra did was to highlight the breaking of the law in the Land of promise as something which could provoke God's anger. For example, a life lived in the Land of promise without fearing God yields its spiritual fruits. One of the saddest features of the book of Ezra is that when the people got back, they quickly returned to their sinful practices. It had cost them their land; they had been away from home for seventy years and yet upon their return they started ignoring the commandments of God. In Ezra 9:1-2 it shows us Aliyah without Torah produces intermarriages; in fact, the most common sin was marrying outside the people of God, a practice forbidden to Israel:

"When these things were done, the leaders came to me, saying, 'The people of Israel and the priests and the Levites have not separated themselves from the peoples of the lands, with respect to the abominations of the Canaanites, the Hittites, the Perizzites, the Jebusites, the Ammonites, the Moabites, the Egyptians, and the Amorites. For they have taken some of their daughters as wives for themselves and their sons, so that the holy seed is mixed with the peoples of those lands. Indeed, the hand of the leaders and rulers has been foremost in this trespass.'"

A reformation therefore was then needed:

"And now for a little while grace has been shown from the LORD our God, to leave us a remnant to escape, and to give us a peg in His holy place, that our God may enlighten our eyes and give us a measure of revival in our bondage" (Ezra 9:8).

In other words, for a little while, grace to return to the Land has been shown from the Lord to leave for them a remnant in Jerusalem, but now it was time for a heartfelt return to God. *"And now, O our God, what shall we say after this? For we have forsaken Your commandments"* (Ezra 9:10). How quickly people tend to forget! For this very reason, this verse is the key to unlock the book of Ezra helping us to understand that the second wave of return marks a further step in the line of events towards a more genuine return to their God. Here we are in a defining moment in the lives of the regathered Jews at the time when the issue of sin needs to be dealt with, in the Land of promise.

> *"O LORD God of Israel, You are righteous,* ***for we are left as a remnant,*** *as it is this day.* ***Here we are before You, in our guilt, though no one can stand before You because of this!"*** (Ezra 9:15).

Sin causes separation from God, and consequently, the people could not claim a right standing before Him. This time Ezra well knew that he was sorely afflicted for them and grieved and fasted on their behalf. Motyer explains:

> "There has been no moral reform or even recognition of the need of it. To come home to Canaan is not to come back to God."[5]

> *"Then Ezra rose up from before the house of God, and went into the chamber of Jehohanan the son of Eliashib; and when he came there, he ate no bread and drank no wa-ter,* ***for he mourned because of the guilt of those from the captivity"*** (Ezra 10:6).

No wonder that under him and Nehemiah a genuine and national revival occurred. It was a revival of a Torah rediscovered which brought repentance and alignment with God's moral standards. Thereafter, in that heartbreaking prayer made by Nehemiah we read that the whole issue of the children of Israel—brought back to their Land—was that they might go back to God's Torah. We read this in Nehemiah 9:28-29, to wit,

> *"Yet when they returned and cried out to You, You heard from heaven; And many times You delivered them according to Your mercies, And testified against them,* ***THAT YOU MIGHT BRING THEM BACK TO YOUR LAW."***

---

[5] Alec Motyer, p. 382

This is the essence of the second phase of the plan of God for the Jews. The House of Jacob is brought back to the land with a purpose, that they might be reoriented to a relationship with God by means of the Torah of Moses. It's definitely an Aliyah to Torah, if I may say, a further ascension towards their pilgrimage to the final destination.

What I want to further underline is that the Lord always calls for an inward change of heart. If we look at the context of Isaiah 1, for example, the prophet is addressing and rebuking the nation for their vain show of religious observances:

"When you spread out your hands, I will hide My eyes from you; even though you make many prayers, I will not hear you" (Isaiah 1:15).

It is astonishing to see how liturgical prayers and mechanical recitations can be of no effect. God will ignore that because prayer repeated over and over can become a motive of weariness to the Lord. What God desires of His people is that they would offer prayers with *kavanah* (the intention of the heart) as the sages of Israel would say. The sages say that prayer without *kavanah* is like a body without soul. In its simplest meaning, it refers to concentrating the mind in the performance of a religious act, ensuring that it does not devolve into rote, mechanical action. It is being profoundly aware of the One to whom you are speaking as you direct your heart toward heaven. Therefore, prayer and turning to God are knitted together, they go hand-in-hand as it relates to the heart. We see that throughout the Hebrew Scriptures there is this constant plea with His people for inward change:

"Wash! Purify yourselves! Remove your sinful deeds from my sight. Learn to do good, seek justice, relieve the oppressed; bring justice to the fatherless, plead the widow's cause' and 'Come now, let us reason together, says the LORD: though your sins are like scarlet, they shall be white as snow; though they are red like crimson, they shall become like wool" (Isaiah 1:16-18).

As messianic brother Pearson comments:

"This is the cleansing of the heart's intentions, the source of what move personal actions and renders decisions. Notice that the verb translated 'reason together' is related to the word for *reproof.* All sound 'reasoning' must begin with the foundational truth that people must turn away from their evil inclinations by returning to God in repentance (teshuvah). Ultimately God is always calling for our heartfelt teshuvah, and no matter how 'scarlet red' our sins might be, this word reveals that the gates of repentance are always open for those who sincerely desire to draw near Him for healing."[6]

In Torah portion *Ki Tisa* (lit. 'when you elevate' – Exodus 30:11) we are before a nation that is being elevated for the holy service of cleansing the Land of promise. The lesson is that God cares more about who we are than what we do. This is what God is looking for in His people. Through the Torah the Lord calls His children to move on up to a higher position of service to Him. As I have heard Rabbi Dr. Justin D. Elwell teaching on Torah saying:

". . . true holiness is expressed through the daily experience of the statutes and ordinances of God in the community of the redeemed (man's obedience), with the sure mercies that flow from a God, that never runs out of blessings (God's faithfulness). Being blessed does not make you holy; what makes you holy is how you live out your faith and life, if lived with even a hint of ethical consideration is immersed in responsibility, and should it be a life of faith, responsibility is a defining factor of that life."[7]

The Function of Torah to the Jewish people

Before looking at the Hebrew meaning of the word *Torah* it is important to understand that if certain branches of Judaism have given to the term a narrow definition within a legalistic framework, that does not confine Torah's meaning within a limited concept only. Ariel and D'vorah Berkowitz explain that the Hebrew word for *Torah* תּוֹרָה (Strong's H#8451):

---

[6]https://www.hebrew4christians.com/Scripture/Parashah/Summaries/Devarim/Haftarah/haftarah.html
[7] Rabbi Dr. Justin D. Elwell, *Torah 3 – Leviticus*

"... is derived from a root that was used in the realm of archery (y-r-h). The root word means *to shoot an arrow in order to hit a mark.* The word *Torah* is a word that means *direction, teaching, instruction,* or *doctrine.* It is instruction designed by God to hit the mark concerning who He is and what His righteousness is. In order to underscore the rendering of Torah as instruction it is helpful to note that there are at least two other related Hebrew words derived from the same root as 'Torah.' The first one is the word for *teacher,* the second one is *parent.* A parent is not a lawgiver, rather, a parent is a disciple-maker, and instructor of children. This indicates to us that one of the primary roles for a parent is to teach and instruct the child."[8]

As they elucidated, the Hebrew root of the word is linked to the idea of casting out something in the right direction or on a right course. It carries the meaning of directing, guiding, or instructing on a right course of action. Thus, Torah means teaching for a true course in life, as Clifford Denton explains.[9] Generally speaking, if we see Torah only in terms of law, whether Jews or Christians, we have not firmly set the Torah foundations of the Scriptures. Even more to that, the sages say that the whole Word of God can be considered Torah when understood as the good instruction of God to His children. Now we understand that Torah was never meant to bring salvation or to gain justification before God (it is written that *"Israel shall be **saved** by the LORD"* - Isaiah 45:17), but it only acts as a protector.

*"So then, the law was our **guardian** until Christ came"* (Galatians 3:24 ESV).

*"Accordingly, the Torah functioned as a **custodian** until the Messiah came"* (Galatians 3:24 CJB).

In his Jewish New Testament Commentary, Dr. David Stern has a personal rendering of this verse, that is, *"The Torah functioned as a harsh disciplinarian until the Messiah came."* When Paul talks in Galatians about the Torah functioning as *guardian* or *custodian* to the Jews, he is drawing upon a very familiar illustration from the ancient Greco-Roman world by using the Greek

---

[8] Ariel & D'vorah Berkowitz, ***Torah Rediscovered*** (Fifth Edition 2012)
[9] Clifford Denton, ***The Covenant People of God*** (Tishrei International, 2011)

word *pedagogo,* where families often hired someone to serve as a protector for the children when they sent them to their teachers. The protector was not the teacher, he was the one who was employed to make sure that the child would safely reach his or her teacher.

Likewise, we can ask, "How does God choose to preserve the Jewish people?" One way he does, is through the Torah. The Torah can function as a *pedagogue* as the Greek word for *guardian* or *custodian* should be translated. The pedagogue's duty was to conduct the boy to and from school and to superintend his conduct, but he was not the teacher. Hence, he was something like the boy's guard to help ensure the student safety on the way to his teacher. Seen in this light this verse emphasizes protection rather than imprisonment.

So, the Torah was intended to preserve the mental, moral, and social safety of all of the environment into which an individual was born and raised. In other words, the remnant of Israel is protected by Torah's boundaries until the date sent by the Father when the Spirit of God would lead them to their true teacher, their Messiah. Let me reiterate this concept: Torah is designed to put the hedges around God's people to protect them, functioning as a protective barrier. The Torah provides the boundaries that we can clearly see eliminating many gray areas in the lives of His people. For example, it defines honesty and integrity in clear words and yet clear illustrations. Moreover, it concisely defines such terms as sin, righteousness, holiness, and purity. It provides the whereabouts of where, when, and how to run this race.

Torah tells the truth, the difference between holy and unholy, clean and unclean, life and death, it is both a protection and a written revelation of the legal binding agreement between God and His own people. Israel, on the other hand, is bound to keep covenant as both parties involved (God and His people) are subject to certain legal conditions. Now we are beginning to see that the Torah serves a bigger scope. With this background let's go back to Paul's statement:

*"Even to this day, when Moses [The Torah] is read, a veil lies on their heart. Nevertheless, **when one turns to the Lord, the veil is taken away**"* (2 Corinthians 3:14-16).

Each stage of the plan of God brings with it a higher level of maturity. There is a need to have a natural progression from the carnal to the spiritual, a moving on up, a maturing, an ascending to a better level. Here the apostle Paul talks about a veil being on the Jewish people equal to the veil Moses had when he came down from Mt. Sinai. It is as if Paul is saying, "Listen, there was a veil placed on the minds of all of Israel, even back then, so that they couldn't fully understand Moses." We saw that in the times of Jesus and we see it today as well. The interesting thing is that as it was then, so it is now, the Torah comes alive in the life of a Jewish person when they discover Messiah and then the veil is lifted from Moses (so to speak) and Yeshua is found everywhere and everything comes alive. The Complete Jewish Bible adds an important element when it says: *"**But, says the Torah**, whenever someone turns to Adonai, the veil is taken away"* (2 Corinthians 3:16). It is a reference to Deuteronomy 34:34: *"But when he went in before Adonai for Him to speak, **he would take the veil off until he came out**."* It is the Torah itself that explains the process of what is inferred by the apostle Paul.

*"Unlike Moses, who put a veil over his face so that the children of Israel could not look steadily at the end of what was passing away. **But their minds were blinded**. For until this day the same veil remains unlifted in the reading of the Old Testament"* (2 Corinthians 3:13-14).

Paul interprets Moses' veil as covering the transitory glory and reads Deuteronomy 34 as a rabbinic style parable or proverb (*mashal*). The veil represents lack of enlightenment, but when Moses stood in the presence of God, he removed the veil. Paul represents the verb as passive—*"is removed"*—which supports his point, that truly turning to the Lord removes the veil. The veil is taken away in Christ, the true Teacher and schoolmaster after the protector (the Torah) has kept God's people within certain boundaries so that at the time of their *teshuvah* (return to God by means of the Torah) they may see Him face-to-face. It is interesting to note that the first Jewish disciples Jesus called to follow Him didn't have their eyes closed. When Philip found Nathanael, he said to him, *"We have found Him of whom Moses in the law, and also the prophets wrote—Jesus of Nazareth, the son of Joseph"* (John 1:45). His mind wasn't veiled as he saw the promised Messiah of whom the Torah was speaking about. That is why Jesus said, *"If you had believed Moses you would believe me, for he wrote about me. But if you believe not his writings, how shall you believe my words?"* (John 5:46). He was dealing with the rejection of the spirit of the Torah in favor of the traditions of men. It's a revelation of a spiritual principle to learn from today:

> ". . . disconnect the truths given to humanity through Moses, and you lose sight of the real Jesus."[10]

And this brings us back to the word *blinded* used by Paul in 2 Corinthians. There in the Greek it means not only to make blind but is a NT metaphor meaning *to blunt, to darken the mind.*

One of the chief ways the enemy works against us is that he uses mind games. Man was created a tripartite being—spirit, soul and body. The spiritual man fellowships with God, but the soul is the part of our being that can be affected by the powers of darkness whose main object is to try to derail us from God's track, alongside with darkening the minds so that people do not have the revelation of God.

The Function of the Torah for You

The Torah avails something only if it is put into practice through holiness and purity of life. For example, I should like to mention the concept of fidelity, that is, *an exclusive devotion to the one you share covenant with.* Yes, the life of faith stands on a covenant relationship. Likewise, the Torah speaks in terms of fidelity as a covenant relationship which is based upon the faithful-

---

[10] Dr. Michael Lake, ***The Sheeriyth Imperative***, Defender Publishing, 2016

ness of the parties joined together. It follows that it is in the practice of fidelity that our response to the commandments is exercised. Moreover, the study of the Torah reforms us on the inside so that our life can reflect the required holiness. What is holiness if not that which is set-apart from what is common, habitual, or profane? Rightly said the apostle Paul when he wrote "*For this is the will of God, your sanctification*" (1 Thessalonians 4:3). Holiness is an encompassing term that covers every area of the Christian life, but is best appreciated when it reflects the love we manifest to our neighbour according to the golden rule: "*Therefore, whatever you want men to do to you, do also to them, for this is the Law and the Prophets*" (Matthew 7:12). This latter statement of Jesus reveals and exposes what we deem to be not so important in our daily walk towards the path of righteousness.

The fact that God loves everyone is sometimes forgotten and missed, isn't it? After all, God cannot ask too much from us! But it is not so, for the Lord tests our abilities by putting us in situations that we need to exercise love even to the most difficult persons. This is not an easy thing to do, but when the ethics of the Torah reforms us from the inside, the things that we were not able to do, like love our neighbour as ourselves, now we can do with the help of the Holy Spirit. Holiness implies that we undergo a process of reformation so that our deeds might become rooted in *hesed* (Hebrew for *mercy*). From this change, we begin to interact and engage with people in a more appropriate manner.

Finally, to walk in purity is the standard we all must attend to. Being pure means dealings with the personal parts of our lives. What is holiness, after all, if not being morally pure? To walk worthy of our calling means to make a daily decision of living set-apart for the service of the Lord without being mixed with impure things. To me this is the heart of the Torah and the part that people do not wish to belabor. It comes at a stage of our walk with Him wherein giving all of ourselves to Him is imperative. Studying the Word is one way the Lord purifies the soul. My prayer is that all of us may reach the required degree of maturity that we may walk mindful of the purity and holiness of the calling of God in true biblical faith.

A Revival of Moses is Needed

I believe that a collective return to Moses will happen through a new interest in the Torah apart from the traditions of men. The author, S. Douglas Woodward, made an extended research in his book **Rebooting the Bible** in which he found out that one Rabbi, 2,000 years ago, led the campaign to corrupt our Old Testament (*the Masoretic Text* that all Protestant Bibles follow). And he succeeded—at least in a narrow sense. He is known as the father of Rabbinic Judaism. When the Temple was destroyed in 70 AD, at the end of the Jewish wars, Judaism split into two different religions, *Apostolic Christianity* and *Rabbinic Judaism*. Both were new. Christianity was led by Peter and Paul. *Rabbinic Judaism* was led, ultimately, by Rabbi Akiba ben Josef (50-135 AD).

Not only was Akiba responsible for creating a Judaism that was no longer dependent upon a Temple and its sacrificial worship, he sought to obscure Messianic passages in the Old Testament including the timing when Messiah was believed to arrive. What is important is that Akiba was indeed the principal figure responsible for establishing the Oral Law[11] (*"the law of commandments contained in ordinances"* [lit. *"dogma"*] – Ephesians 2:15) as superior to the Written Law (i.e., the Bible,) not Moses as rabbis today suggest. Akiba and his disciples were not interested in Moses' thoughts. *In fact, Moses must sit "eight rows back"* behind other listeners. Consequently, in Rabbinic Judaism Moses is inferior to Akiba. The Talmud states that "When Rabbi Akiba died, the glory of Torah ceased" (Sotah 49a).

Additionally, it was the intent of Rabbi Akiba ben Josef and the Jamnia Academy to muddle the biblical testimony that God Himself would come in the flesh as our Redeemer, thus blocking

------

[11] Although we do not view the Oral Torah as the inspired Word of God, there can be tremendous value in reading and studying rabbinic literature.

the Jews from turning to Yeshua by altering the Messianic passages Christian evangelists used to preach the Gospel. It followed that the new Judaism would respect the thoughts ("dogma") of the rabbis which became the authority on the matter pertaining to the Torah so that one of the main expressions today about views and interpretations on the Law is, "What they said, goes!" In the course of time Rabbinic Judaism would build its new religion by creating a new text (viz., Hebrew Bible).

Step one in this process was the creation of the **Mishnah** (the oral Torah was eventually written down by Rabbi Yehuda haNasi [aka Judah I] around the year 200 CE).

Step two was the **Gemara**, a commentary on the Mishnah. Together they constitute the **Talmud**, although in some instances, the Gemara and Talmud are spoken of as synonymous, and then a "new version" of the Hebrew text itself prepared at Jamnia's academy (cir. 1000 CE). This new Hebrew version, from which Aquila's New Greek Bible was translated, would one day become known as the **Masoretic** Text. However, what they did not calculate, which one day would spoil their strategy, was the discovery of **The Dead Sea Scrolls** hidden away by the Essenes which would survive despite Akiba's textual purges.

Aliyah, Jews, & Israel vs. Demonic Powers

Not only is there a spiritual need for a revival of Moses if all Israel wants to experience a genuine return to Torah in *teshuvah* (heartfelt return to God) and praying with *kavanah* (with heart's intention), but there are other things that constantly try to derail the people of Israel from their set path to their final redemption. Since the creation of the world, Abraham's lineage has been violently contrasted by Satan and his minions knowing that from them would come the One who would crush his head according to the Genesis 3 prophecy after the serpent seduced Eve into sin. We read God's answer to the serpent in verse 14-15 of Genesis 3:

"So the LORD God said to the serpent: 'Because you have done this, you are cursed more than all cattle, And more

than every beast of the field; On your belly you shall go, And you shall eat dust all the days of your life. And I will put enmity between you and the woman, and between your seed and her Seed; He shall bruise [lit. crush] your head, and you shall bruise His heel.'"

From that moment on, it has been a merciless and relentless fierce battle in order for Satan to discover who would be that Seed, born of the woman, who would defeat him at the end. At the Cross, Yeshua defeated Satan, the Serpent, and loosed principalities and powers making a public spectacle of them, triumphing over them in it (Colossians 2:15).

However, since the days of the Garden of Eden, Satan has been targeting the direct genetical lineage of Abraham's physical descendants; in particular, those of the House of Jacob: the Jews. From that day on, a ruthless hunt was in force to try to eradicate from the face of the earth the **earthly seed** who one day would give birth to the One of the tribe of Judah Who would declare the Serpent's demise (*"And once more, Isaiah says: 'The root of Jesse will appear, One who will arise to rule over the Gentiles* [aka "the nations"]; *in Him the Gentiles will put their hope'"* (Romans 15:12; Isaiah 11:1, 10).

That is why we need to realize that there are two destinies for Israel. There are two competing kingdoms from the very beginning. God has a destiny, and *"So the great dragon was cast out, that serpent of old, called the Devil and Satan, who deceives the whole world"* (Revelation 12:9) has his destiny as well. We know that Israel brought in our Messiah—the *"Root of Jesse, the Lion of the Tribe of Judah"* (Genesis 49:8; Revelation 5:5-6); contrariwise, the enemy (*"according to the working of Satan, with all power, signs, and lying wonders, and with all unrighteous deception"*—2 Thessalonians 2:9) has his own "unrighteous deception" for Israel to counterbalance what God wants to do (he wants Israel to produce the *son of perdition*—2 Thessalonians 2:3). Notwithstanding, God's Deliverance for Judah from the hand of the enemy *"will consume [the enemy] with the breath of His mouth and destroy* [him] *with the brightness of His coming*" (2 Thessalonians 2:8).

This dual deception is going on over in Israel right now due to the intense spiritual dynamics surrounding this, the nexus of earth's contestation between the *"children of light vs. the children of darkness."* Even so, the enemy is working hard to divert God's plan of salvation on behalf of the Jewish people using all methodologies at his disposal to derail and avert as much as he can in a vain attempt to delay his final demise. We should therefore not be surprised if in Israel and around the world the seducer has crept in with lies concerning Messiah, like inspiring those who promote the kabbalistic[12] concept that wants to bring to pass messianic prophecy towards Israel but without Messiah—denying *"The Deliverer will come out of Zion and He will turn away ungodliness from Jacob . . . For this is My covenant with them, when I take away their sins"* (Romans 11:26-27; Psalms 14:7; Isaiah 59:20-21; 27:9; Hebrews 8:12). One of the many examples of this distraction is the most crucial passage of the Tanakh, Isaiah 53, on which the Talmud asserts that the suffering servant who was cut off for the sins of the people is not a man but Israel itself—the "suffering servant's" personification, rejection, despising, and even the "bearing of our sins" is transferred to the suffering of the Jewish people, when only the Redeemer of Israel is worthy of such a prophetic entitlement and fulfillment!

Knowing where this spiritual conflict comes from, we now understand why the gathering of the exiles of the House of Jacob is so contested, at all levels. The devil has been trying to obscure this essential prophecy knowing that the fewer people who know it,

---

12 From **Kabbalah** (Hebrew: קַבָּלָה, literally "reception, tradition" or "correspondence") is an esoteric method, discipline, and school of thought in Jewish mysticism. A traditional Kabbalist in Judaism is called a *Mequbbāl* (מְקוּבָּל). The definition of Kabbalah varies according to the tradition and aims of those following it, from its religious origin as an integral part of Judaism, to its later adaptations in Western esotericism (Christian Kabbalah and Hermetic Qabalah). Jewish Kabbalah is a set of esoteric teachings meant to explain the relationship between God, the unchanging, eternal, and mysterious Eis Sof ("The Infinite"), and the mortal and finite universe (God's creation). It forms the foundation of mystical religious interpretations within Judaism.

the better. He has blinded scores of pastors and leaders to the restoration of Israel by allowing a legion of religious spirits swirling around this subject trying to impede the knowledge of truth, placing a gulf of ignorance to serve as a great divide.

To make matters worse, there is another cruel reality of this "duality of deception" that simply remains unchecked. Deuteronomy 32:8-9 seems to answer this quandary. It describes how God's dispersal of the nations at Babel resulted in His disinheriting those nations as His people.

> *When the Most High gave to the nations their inheritance, when **he divided mankind**, he fixed the borders of the peoples according to the number of the sons of God. **But the LORD's portion is His people, Jacob his allotted heritage**.* (ESV)

On this particular subject, Dr. Michael Heiser's groundbreaking work, *The Unseen Realm*, explains:

"In the distant past God disinherited the nations of earth as his family, choosing instead to create a new family from Abraham. The disinherited nations were put under the authority of lesser Elohim, divine sons of God. When they became corrupt, they were sentenced to mortality"[13] (Psalms 82:6-8).

From the context it appears that at the Tower of Babel God divorced humanity over the nations delimiting them to seventy of the principalities. The number seventy is derived from the so-called *Table of Nations* (seventy) in the Genesis 10 account. All humanity was turned over to seventy principalities and fallen immortals, that aligned themselves with Nimrod, and began to take control (power, politic, culture) and to mold the culture or civilization around them. In other words, the souls of men began to be highly influenced by these principalities and powers in their way of thinking. The only exception was for the nation of Israel because of the covenant God made with Abram to whom it is as if

---

[13] Michael S. Heiser, ***The Unseen Realm***, 2015 Lexham Press

He were saying, "I am going to bring you out of this Babylonian system and will make you into a nation." Therefore, eventually Israel became that special possession of God, although we know that through history these powers tried to come back under the guise of other gods through the promotion of idolatry. Likewise, in the moment we get saved we are no longer under these "dark lords" and their kingdom of darkness. Thus, the nations were estranged from the One True God, having succumbed to the first "kingdom" mentioned in the Scripture: *"Cush begot Nimrod . . . the beginning of his **kingdom** was Babel* (i.e., Babylon—Genesis 10:8-10); thus, the Kingdom of God vs. the Kingdom of Darkness—Babylon the Great vs. the Holy City, Jerusalem.

Now, many Jews were temporarily broken off from the Olive Tree of Salvation—from the common Root that is the source of Life (Romans 11:13-24), allowing us from among the nations— "elect" from among the nations—to be grafted into the same One and only Olive Tree (Jeremiah 11:16). At the time of their breaking off, these principalities tried to gain control over the minds of those that live in unbelief causing people to become misdirected, disoriented.

However, the "breaking off" of the *natural* branches vs. the grafting in of the *wild* branches must be understood in the context of Jeremiah 11:16 ("*The LORD called your name, Green Olive Tree*")—there is but ONE OLIVE TREE. Dividing God's people has been at the heart of Satan's strategy from the days of the United Kingdom of David and prior thereto with the selling of Joseph into slavery.

The expression "Tabernacle of David" as found in Amos 9:11 speaks of a day wherein it says:

"On that day I will raise up the tabernacle of David, which has fallen down, and repair its damages; I will raise up its ruins, and rebuilt it as in the days of old; that they may possess the remnant of Edom [LXX "Mankind" as per Obadiah 19 – even "Esau" or "Adam"], *and all the Gentiles who are called by My name,' Says the LORD who does this thing"* (Amos 9:11-12).

In chapter 9 I will extend the exposition into the intricacies of Israel's "Breach of Jeroboam" when the Ten Northern Tribes broke off from Judah (and Benjamin and the Levites—2 Chronicles 10; 1 Kings 11-12) thereby putting in ruins the Tabernacle of David known as the United Kingdom of David. Amos bespeaks of the judgment on Judah and the separate judgment on Israel (Amos 2:4-16); clearly, there are two houses. So righteously angered was the Holy One of Israel with the adultery of the Northern Ten Tribes that He gave them a ***"certificate of divorce"*** (Jeremiah 3:8) but, although Judah was more treacherous than Israel-Ephraim (aka, Jezreel, Samaria) He did not divorce her (Jeremiah 3:6-12).

Remarkably, Jeremiah, says of the Northern Ten Tribes and later of both Houses:

"'Return, backsliding Israel,' says the LORD; 'I will not cause My anger to fall on you. For I am merciful,' says the LORD; 'I will not remain angry forever. Only acknowledge your iniquity, that you have transgressed against the LORD your God, and have scattered your charms to alien deities under every green tree, and you have not obeyed My voice,' says the Lord. 'Return, O backsliding children,' says the LORD; for I am married to you. I will take you, one from a city and two from a family, and I will bring you to Zion. And I will give you shepherds according to My heart, who will feed you with knowledge and understanding. Then it shall come to pass, when you are multiplied and increased in the land in those days,' says the LORD, 'that they will say no more, 'The ark of the covenant of the LORD.' It shall not come to mind, nor shall they remember it, nor shall they visit it, nor shall it be made anymore. At that time Jerusalem shall be called THE THRONE OF THE LORD, and all the nations (i.e., the "Gentiles") shall be gathered to it, to the name of the LORD, to Jerusalem. No more shall they follow the dictates of their evil hearts. In those days the house of Judah shall walk with the house of Israel, and they shall come together out of the land of the north to the land that I have given as an inheritance to your father" (Jeremiah 3:12-18).

The Law of Moses clearly says that if a certificate of divorce is given while the husband is still alive, the woman, so divorced, cannot marry another—otherwise, she commits adultery. She can only remarry if her first husband dies (See: Deuteronomy 24:1-4)—otherwise, she commits adultery; however, if the first husband dies, she can remarry HIM! That is precisely what happened to the Northern Ten Tribes. First, He gives them a certificate of divorce; then He says, "*I am married to you!*" How can that be?[14]

Furthermore, this is all the more complicated when clearly the Ten Northern Tribes (aka Ephraim) was taken by the millions into Assyrian captivity over the course of some 33 years (745-712 BC) to the extent it is said of these ancient Israelites:

"Aliens would swallow it up. Israel is swallowed up; now they are among the Gentiles like a vessel in which is no pleasure. For they have gone up to Assyria, like a wild donkey alone by itself; Ephraim has hired lovers. Yes, though they have hired among the nations, NOW I WILL GATHER THEM; and they shall sorrow a little, because of the burden [lit. "oracle" or "proclamation"] *of the king of princes"* (Hosea. 8:7-10).

So, when did all this go down? When did YHWH (Jehovah) remarry her? When did He "*gather them*" from this place and that place throughout the world where they had been scattered, swallowed up of the Nations/Gentiles? And how could He ever remarry her who clearly played the harlot? Even if she married another while her first husband was alive, she could not remarry unless and until her first husband died!

Compounding her (Ephraim's) detestable situation, Hosea's accounting of her "state of affairs"—speaking clearly concerning Ephraim-Israel—the Almighty uses Hosea himself as His Own relationship with Ephraim and says to Hosea:

"When the LORD began to speak by Hosea, the LORD said to Hosea: 'Go, take yourself a wife of harlotry and the children

---

14 For an extended research on this topic see **Dr. Douglas Hamp** groundbreaking work **God's Divorce and Remarriage** in *One in Messiah: Perspectives on Commonwealth Theology* (Commonwealth of Israel Foundation 2019)

of harlotry, for the land has committed great harlotry by departing from the LORD' . . . So he went and took Gomer the daughter of Diblaim, and she conceived and bore him a son, Then the LORD said to him: 'Call his name Jezreel, for in a little while I will avenge the bloodshed of Jezreel on the house of Jehu, and bring an end to the kingdom of the house of Israel . . . it shall come to pass in that day that I will break the bow of Israel in the Valley of Jezreel" (Hosea 1:2-5).

But it gets much worse for this Israel—the so-called Ten Lost Tribes!

"And she conceived again and bore a daughter. Then God said to him: 'Call her name Lo-Ruhamah [Lit. "no mercy"], *for I will no longer have mercy on the house of Israel, but I will utterly take them away. Yet I will have mercy on the house of Judah, will save them by the LORD their God, and will not save them by bow, nor by sword or battle, by horses or horsemen.' Now when she had weaned Lo-Ruhamah, she conceived and bore a son. Then God said: 'Call his name Lo-Ammi'* [lit. "not My people"] *'for you are not My people, and I will not be your God"* (Hosea 1:6-9).

Just how bad can it get: Divorced, no mercy, swallowed up of the Nations, scattered to the four corners of the earth, and no longer His people! Then a "cosmic change of heart"—so it appears—and we hear this:

"'Yet the number of the children of Israel shall be as the sand of the sea [SAY WHAT?], *WHICH CANNOT BE MEASURED OR NUMBERED. And it shall come to pass in the place where it was said to them, 'You are not My people,' There it shall be said to them, 'You are the sons of the living God.' Then the children of Judah and the children of Israel shall be gathered together, and appoint for themselves one head; and they shall come up out of the land, for great will be the day of Jezreel! Say to your brethren, 'My people,' And to your sisters, 'Mercy is shown'"'* (Hosea 1:10-11 and 2:1).

The Almighty is either very "conflicted" or He has an amazing, awesome, glorious plan in healing this ancient Breach of Jeroboam in both remarrying Israel's Ten Northern Tribes and regathering them, multiplying them abundantly, and then reuniting them with the House of Judah and calling the lot of them "MY PEOPLE!" So, when does all of this happen?

Well, it has happened and is happening since Messiah, the Redeemer of Israel, came the first time. First of all, as found in Romans 7, we have this remarkable analysis of "the problem" of marriage, divorce, and remarriage—in accordance with the very Law of Moses, no less:

*"Or do you not know, brethren (for I [Paul] speak to those who know the law), that the law has dominion over a man as long as he lives? For the woman who has a husband is bound by the law to her husband as long as he lives. But if the husband dies, she is released from the law of her husband. So then if, while her husband lives, she marries another man, she will be called an adulteress [that's precisely what happened in Hosea's accounting of Ephraim-Israel]; but **if her husband dies**, she is free from that law, so that she is no adulteress, though she has married another man. Therefore, my brethren, you also have become dead to the law through the body of Christ, that you may be married to another—to Him who was raised from the dead, that we should bear fruit to God"* (Romans 7:1-4).

Do you see it? Messiah, the Christ, even YHWH, said He was married to these Ten Adulterous Tribes—and gave them a "certificate of divorce." How could He ever remarry her? That is the great mystery! The only way she could marry again (the "law" or "covenant" of remarriage) would be for her first husband to die—HE DID. Now, we can be married to another, even to Him Who was raised from the dead. Her first husband died but was resurrected—she is now about to remarry and NOT commit adultery!

But it gets much better—regarding these Gentiles, Paul declares from Hosea:

". . . and that He might make known the riches of His glory on the vessels of mercy, which He had prepared beforehand for glory, even us whom He called, not of the Jews only, but also of the Gentiles? [Note the question mark in the original Greek!] 'I will call them My people, who were not My people, and her beloved, who was not beloved. And it shall come to pass in the place where it was said to them, 'You are not My

*people,' There they shall be called sons of the living God.'
Isaiah also cries out concerning Israel: 'Though the number
of the children of Israel be as the sand of the sea, the remnant
will be saved. For He will finish the work and cut it short in
righteousness, because the LORD will make a short work
upon the earth"* (Romans 9:23-28).

Now, do you see it? Ephraim-Israel has been restored to the
"Root that bore her!" She remarried the One to Whom she was
originally betrothed—talk about mercy—HOW GREAT IS HIS
MERCY! And, more so, she is being reunited with the House of
Judah. Yes, disbursed and swallowed up of the Nations—she now
comes forth in "twos and threes" out from among the nations to
be regathered with Judah. This is a heavenly reality even now for:

*"But you have come to Mount Zion and to the city of the living
God, the heavenly Jerusalem, to an innumerable company of
angels, to the general assembly and ekklesia of the firstborn
who are registered in heaven, to God the Judge of all, to the
spirits of just men made perfect, to Jesus the Mediator of the
New Covenant, and to the blood of sprinkling that speaks better things than that of Abel"* (Hebrews 12:22-24).

Yes, the heavenly Zion is being united with the earthly Zion—
to God be the glory! Now, we rejoice with James' declaration—
who quoted from the same passage found in Amos 9:11-12:

*"Men and brethren, listen to me: Simon has declared how
God at the first visited the Gentiles to take out of them a people for His name. And with this the words of the prophets
agree, just as it is written: 'After this I will return and will
rebuild the tabernacle of David* [i.e., "the United Kingdom of
David"], *which has fallen down; I will rebuild its ruins, and I
will set it up; so that the rest of mankind* [LXX "Edom" or
"Esau"] *may seek the LORD, even all the Gentiles who are
called by My name, says the LORD who does all these things'"*
(Acts 15:13-17).

Amazing Grace! The "Lost Ten Tribes" have been found!
God's plan and purpose for BOTH HOUSES—the House of Israel
and the House of Judah—will not be thwarted. For after Romans
9-16 where Paul deals with the "oneness of God's people" (where

these profound passages we have witnessed are found in conjunction with the prophetic Scriptures)—after we have heard *"that He might have mercy on all"* (Romans 11:32)—then we read how through Messiah's "multiplication" that old Serpent, the Devil, even Satan, would have his head crushed: *"And the God of peace will CRUSH SATAN under your feet shortly"* (Romans 16:20). Not a word about Satan is heard throughout the entire book of Romans until the very end, after God's people are brought together in ONE—then, and then only, is the head of the Serpent crushed!

> *"He has made of the Two* [the Jew and the Gentile] *ONE NEW MAN, so making peace"* (Ephesians 2:15).

Alas! Yet, there is abundant evidence of the aforesaid disorientation rampant in Israel today seemingly thwarting the purposes of the Almighty (let alone the disquieting divisions within Christendom—that is another book). In his latest book, Dr. Michael Lake speaks about *Principality Wars*, a concept that sums up well all spiritual warfare stating:

> "... principalities, powers and rulers not only blind humanity to the gospel, but they also continue the war against the Creator by constructing cultures that are opposed to the Almighty."[15]

It is absolutely true that our warfare is against those dark forces that are in supremacy in the culture around us—the same applies to today's Israel. At the same time, the eyes of the Lord are all-year-long on His land and He considers the Land as His portion having attached His name to Jerusalem. *"But the LORD's portion is His people, Jacob His allotted heritage"* (Deuteronomy 32:9). There is a constant conflict going on over the Land of Israel for who is to be in control. That is why Israel is the center of all spiritual conflict in the world—even terrestrial consternation. Despite all that, we know in the end Israel will turn to the Lord to be saved as it is written:

---

[15] Dr. Michael Lake, *The Kingdom Priesthood*, p. 149 (Biblical Life Publishing, 2020)

*"Afterward the children of Israel shall return and seek their LORD their God and David their king. **They shall fear the LORD and His goodness in the latter days**"* (Hosea 3:5).

These will be the days in which they will behold the One who died and was raised for them. Of this national wondering moment, the prophet Isaiah had to say:

*"Hark! You watchmen raise their voices, together they shout for joy; **for eye to eye they see the return of the LORD to Zion**"* (Isaiah 52:12 ESV).

The phrase *eye to eye* indicates that the Jews will look upon the Lord directly in the eye. In that coming day, the veil will be taken away and they will no longer see through a mirror "in riddles," but rather *panim el panim*, "face to face" (1 Corinthians 13:12).

What was begun as a revival of religion in the days of Ezra was due to the fact that the faith of their fathers had become bound up in the Torah—Judaism had become primarily a religion of the Book. The people had returned to the land as God predicted because He had not forsaken the Covenant incapsulated in the Torah. He brought and is bringing them back to their Promised land in the hope that they will be ready to resume their obligation to Him. A thorough transformation awaited them, as we will consider in the next chapter.

≈ ≈ ≈ ≈ ≈ ≈

Prayer

How manifold are your thoughts oh Lord! You have kept your people, the Jews, within the boundaries of Torah that acted as a hedge of protection all around them while it served as a tutor to bring them to the true Teacher that is in heaven, Yeshua the Messiah. Send a revival of Moses among your people Lord and renew their interests for their Tanakh and that by the reading of it, the scales may fall off their eyes so as to contemplate the One who died and is coming back for them. This is a spiritual battle of immense proportion. Please open the eyes of the Church that it may realize that much of the solution to this conflict is predicated upon her taking side with you for her benefit, Israel's redemption and Satan's demise, in Jesus name!

Figure 13 - Luke 1:31 - He Will Reign Over the House of Jacob

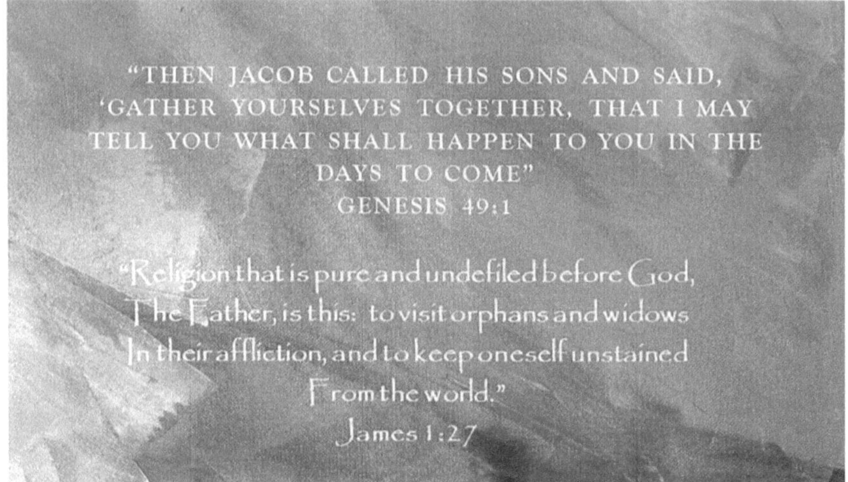

Figure 14 - Genesis 49:1 & James 1:27

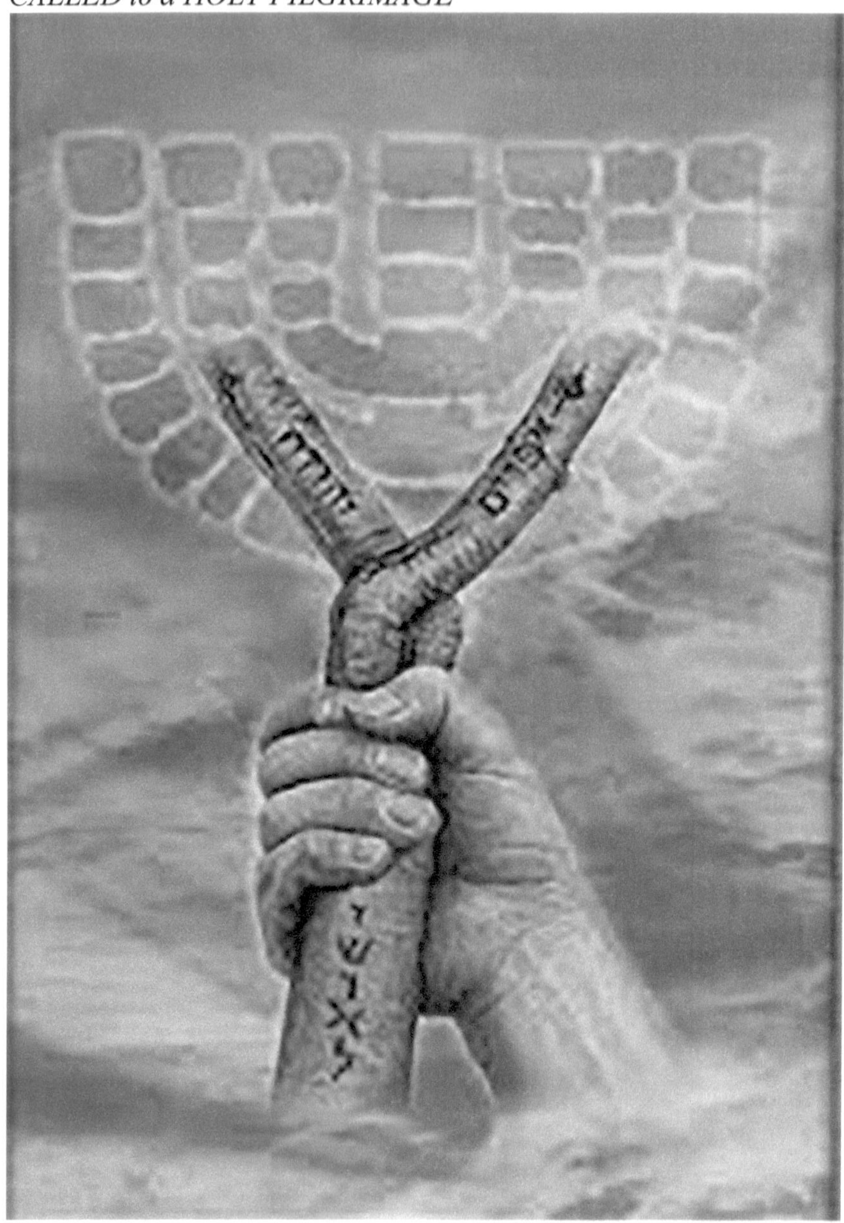

Figure 15 - One Stick in the Hand of the Lord

Chapter 6

Called to Transformation

Behold, I am with you and will keep you wherever you go, and will bring you back to this land; for I will not leave you until I have done what I have spoken to you.

(Genesis 28:15)

IN THE GENESIS ACCOUNT GOD PROMISED JACOB TO BRING HIM BACK TO HIS LAND AFTER DEALING WITH HIM ACCORDING TO HIS PROMISES. LITTLE did Jacob know of what would happen in the way of his pilgrimage that would grant him to become the person God intended him to be. Similarly, the God of Israel has been calling the House of Jacob to the promised land since then, yet in the final stage of their pilgrimage, a corporate and glorious transformation awaits them. In chapter 4 we saw that Ezekiel 36 speaks in favor of a turning of the heart after Jacob is regathered in the Land, but elsewhere we read that the turning to the Lord can happen in the nations as well. I also see much evidence in the Scriptures suggesting that the return to the Land of Israel is predicated upon the people seeking God while living in the diaspora – He has never prevented His people to turn to Him anywhere they live. Consider the following passages:

> *"Now it shall come to pass, when all these things come upon you, the blessing and the curse which I have set before you,* **and you call them to mind among all the nations where the LORD your God drives you, and you return to the LORD your God** *and obey His voice, according to all that I command you today, you and your children, with all your heart and with all our soul, that* **the LORD your God will bring you back from captivity, and have compassion on you, and gather you again from all the nations where the LORD your God has scattered you.** *If any of you are driven out to the* **farthest parts under heaven, from there the LORD your God will gather you, and from there He will bring you.** *Then the LORD your God will bring you to the land which your fathers possessed, and you shall possess it. He*

will prosper you and multiply you more than your fathers. And the Lord your God will circumcise your heart and the heart of your descendants, to love the LORD your God with all your heart and with all your soul, that you may live" (Deuteronomy 30:1-6).

"Remember, I pray, the word that You commanded Your servant Moses, saying, 'If you are unfaithful, I will scatter you among the nations; but if you return to Me, and keep My commandments and do them, though some of you were cast out to the farthest part of the heavens, yet I will gather them from there, and bring them to the place which I have chosen as a dwelling for My name" (Nehemiah 1:8-9).

The Scriptures make it clear that turning is first of all a matter of the heart. That's why Jacob is a beacon for his people to follow.

"And behold, the LORD stood above it and said: 'I am the LORD God of Abraham your father and the God of Isaac; the land on which you lie I will give to you and your descendants. Also your descendants shall be as the dust of the earth; you shall spread abroad to the west and the east, to the north and the south; and in you and in your seed all the families of the earth shall be blessed. Behold, I am with you and will keep you wherever you go, and will bring you back to this land; for I will not leave you until I have done what I have spoken to you.'" (Genesis 28:13-15)

Jacob's Wrestling

Tests, scrutiny, examinations, and periods of being lowered by God are often encountered in our wilderness experience, even so they are part of our chastisement *"**As a man chastens his son, so the LORD your God chastens you**"* (Deuteronomy 8:5) so that we might learn the fear of the Lord and to walk in His ways. Torah portion *Eikev—because—*(Deuteronomy 7:12-11:25) is a proper sermon in the very sense of having a pedagogical component to it. Its words of rebuke to the children of Israel *"It is not because of your righteousness, for you are a stiff-necked people"* (Deuteronomy 9:5-6) echo the words of Ezekiel 36:32, 21-23 in that:

"Not for your sake I do this, says the LORD God, let it be known to you. Be ashamed and confounded for your own ways O house of Israel . . . but I had concern for My holy name, which the house of Israel had profaned among the nations . . .. Therefore I do not do this for your sake, O house of Israel, but for my holy name's sake . . . and I will sanctify my great name, which has been profaned among the nations, which you have profaned and the nations shall know that I am the LORD . . . when I am hallowed in you before their eyes."

Yes indeed, Israel inherits and receives because God promised, just for that very purpose. It is not for her righteousness Israel inherits the land, rather, she should regard herself as a stiff-necked people. Cleaving to God is the only way to the blessings of the Covenant in the Land of promise. Even the hunger and hardship during the wandering in the desert were part of God's fatherly discipline on behalf of His people. Suffering is thus transfigured into what the Rabbis called "chastisements of love"; in fact, *"God delivers the afflicted by His affliction"* (Job 36:15). But the most amazing thought I have not found in the same Torah portion, but in its *haftarah* of consolation (Isaiah 49-51), where it talks about the incredible and transcendent love of God for his nursing child, *"Even if these were to forget, I would not forget you."* Here, the great body of the Jewish people had lost hope of a national restoration. They thought that Israel's history was definitely closed. But the message is that *"EXILE* DOES NOT BREAK THE COVENANT OR SIGNAL DIVORCE" for God's mercy is more enduring than the strongest human affection.[1]

I believe that the story of the father of the twelve patriarchs of Israel reflects the transformation of the Jewish people in their procession of changing from Jacob to Israel. His name appears 350 times in the Bible and can refer to a number of entities, primarily the patriarch and ancestor, Jacob, but to the *United Nation*

---

[1] Hertz, Rabbi Joseph; The Soncino Press, **Pentateuch & Haftorahs** (The Soncino Press, LTD. 123 Ditmas Avenue, Brooklyn, New York 11218; copyright 1960; p. 794)

of Israel under David and Solomon, to *Judah* (the Southern Kingdom) or *Israel* in a broader sense. It follows from this that Jacob's identity is almost exclusively that of the progenitor of a **nation**.

After receiving a mighty revelation from God at a place he named Bet-El (House of God) where he received promises about a land and of numerous offspring that would prove to be the blessing of the entire earth, he sets forth on a long journey that turned his life upside down, taking him from being a supplanter and pretender to *"he who strives with God"* and *"a prince with God."* Thereby, he set forth to Haran arriving at his uncle Laban's home. He soon fell in love with Laban's daughter Rachel and worked for her father for seven years to obtain Rachel's hand in marriage, but then Uncle Laban substituted his older daughter, Leah, for Rachel at the wedding ceremony. Unwittingly, Jacob married Leah! Jacob was thus compelled to serve Laban for another seven years so that he could take his beloved Rachel as his wife as well. Jacob then had to serve Laban for another six years, during which he amassed a large amount of property; he then set out with his wives and children to return to the Land of promise. On the way back Jacob wrestled by the river Jabbok with a mysterious stranger, a divine being, and there received his covenant name of Israel and a new identity.

Like Homer's Odysseus, Jacob lived up to his identity throughout his story, although he had different attitudes after his transformation at Peniel. Then, just before journeying home, Rachel steals her father's idols. Some commentators, like Rashi, believed that by taking her father's Babylonian idols she intended to remove her father from idol worship as it is believed that Laban was an expert magician because he consulted oracles. Others, instead, believe that by bringing those idols she might have thought to draw strength from them in the hope that they would help her transitioning to her new life from home.

Whatever it is, the wandering Jacob resembles much of the story of the people and nation he stands as a representative. Like him, Israel is back in the Land of promise—yet traces of paganism are still found in the camp; sometimes they are oblivious to this fact. My question is, within this wrestling of the Jewish people of more than seventy years since the birth of the modern State of Israel up to now, is it possible that these resemble the seventy years of captivity and that now God is willing to break things open? Could it be that a *Kairos* (propitious moment) of time is about to be opened for a nation regathered? The facts and trends give reason and demonstrate that the blinders are getting ready to come out for the people of Israel and the spiritual captivity of the House of Jacob is going to be broken.

As a matter of fact, the re-establishment of the state or Israel in 1948 was the early beginning of the move of the Holy Spirit. Just consider the growth of the Messianic population and of "religious Jews" intent on the Final Redemption. A research made by One For Israel's Bible College (Israel) shows that in 1948 there were approximately ten million Jewish people around the world who had survived the Holocaust and about 600,000 were living in Israel, of those, only a couple of families believed in Yeshua as their Messiah—23 Messianic Jews to be precise! Then, in 1989 Israel's Jewish population had grown to 3.5 million, and by this point, the estimated number of Messianic believers had reached 1,200.

There were now 30 congregations. By 1999 there were 4.8 million Jews living in Israel, 81 Messianic congregations and an estimated 5,000 believers. In 2017, 300 congregations were counted. Today, it has become increasingly difficult to accurately identify the number of Jewish believers in Yeshua in Israel, but a conservative estimate is now (in 2020) to be more than 30,000. Israel Today, instead, observes that there are an estimated 100,000 Messianic Jews worldwide (that is an exceedingly conservative estimate).

Figuratively speaking, seventy years of captivity are now expired, and we are going to see more people in the land of Israel having divine revelation of who Messiah really is—the veil is being taken away. God is doing mighty things in other Middle Eastern countries like Jordan, Lebanon, and Syria where hundreds of people are receiving dreams and visions of Jesus and finding salvation in Messiah's deliverance. Is not God able to do the same with His people in Eretz Israel? Certainly so. For them it is going to be like Jacob's experience, in that God had to bring Jacob in a place that, if something would not happen, he would be dead. The same is going to be with corporate Israel. They will be drawn to a place of great transformation where their past, present, and future struggles will become the place of the greatest blessing ever. Theirs will be a corporate transformation which will culminate with an encounter with their long-awaited Messiah.

In the Old Testament it is common to find characters to be gradually transformed through life's experience. In ancient literature, including the Bible, for example, any pilgrimage brings a traveler into an encounter with God. Travel also produces change and growth in character and physical movement often provides new revelation. In the case of the children of Israel, theirs become a collective pilgrimage as it is about a story of a travelling community that finds itself in an epic journey that culminates in the formation of a sovereign nation in a promised land. When we consider the wrestling of Jacob at Peniel, the original Hebrew hints that the struggle was in the rolling on the ground which involves getting some dirt and dust until the struggling was over. Do we get the picture? Until Jacob wrestled with God, he couldn't get his transformation, so we're witnessing a similar transition from Jacob to Israel going on right now in the Jewish people, for it is in the wrestling that their eyes will be opened to be prepared to have a revelation of Messiah, a disclosure that will come in the midst of times of tribulation:

> *"For thus says the LORD: 'We have heard a voice of trembling, Of fear, and not of peace. Ask now, and see, whether a man is ever in labor with child? So why do I see every man with his hands on his loins like a woman in labor, and all faces turned pale? Alas! For that day is great, so that none is like it; and it is the time of Jacob's trouble, but he shall be saved out of it"* (Jeremiah 30:5-7).

Rescue at the Point of Weakness

To the Jewish community it is all about a journey that started from the Exodus out of Egypt, and from the return from Babylon, then, of an ongoing adventure story comprising defeats and triumphs, but of divine miracles of preservation as well. The climactic moment of struggle will find Israel resembling Jacob in his/their moment of weakness. While the House of Jacob at large has not come to a revelation of Yeshua the Messiah, we are to believe that this is going to be a future eschatological moment, boosted by a series of events that have their starting point in a scenario of a future demise of Damascus (Syria) according to Isaiah 17 (viz "The Oracle of Damascus"—see also, Zechariah 9:1-8), which says that *"In that day it shall come to pass the glory of Jacob will wane and the fatness of his flesh grow lean."*

Several commentators see the upcoming war between Israel and the forces of Damascus as the final phase of the Arab-Israeli war since 1948 in which Israel will be greatly diminished in her capacity to wage war and to defend herself—in that *the glory of Jacob will wane.* This might be due to a conflict that will be so intense to the detriment of Israel that this will be the moment that could be climactic in the struggle of the House of Jacob in anticipation to meet the Messiah (more on this topic in chapter 8).

Sir John Moore, a British army general of the Nineteenth Century, said that experience is not obtained in the daintiness of parade, but in warfare. When it comes to transformation, it could not have been better said than this. At the same time is with us, for God is never interested in winning the wrestling match so much as he is interested in the transformation of our heart in the wrestling. The angel had the power to touch Jacob's thigh with one finger and fix it for good, but he did not. This tells us of the spiritual dynamics in place. As far as the individual Jew is concerned, God is not satisfied until the third phase of the process is accomplished: **the salvation of the soul**. This explains why the intensity of the struggle gets tough at times, because the transformation process awaits any Jew who is preserved and alive at that time in the Land of promise.

Speaking about the redemption of Israel the Lord says, *"I am the LORD, in its time I will hurry it"* (Isaiah 60:22). This is quite a staggering statement because it is in reference to God's attribute of omnipotence in the redemption of His people. On this matter David Rubin has justly written:

> "The sages of Israel have taught us that the promised redemption will come in one of two ways. It will either come speedily and in a glorious way or it will come eventually in its time, but with terrible suffering. And how does it come speedily? When the people of Israel start to disengage from their secular ways, and start to walk in the ways of their God. As God's chosen people, every Jew, by choosing the path of Torah to whatever extent, can help to create a better world."[2]

It is by turning to God by means of walking in the ways of the Torah that redemption draws nigh. By the observance of the letter nobody is saved, however, because of the holy Scriptures (*which are able to make us wise unto salvation* - 2 Timothy 3:15), those gathered in the land will certainly be grafted back into the natural Olive Tree of Salvation.

Here, in the apex of the night Jacob spent in rolling on the ground, his name is changed to Israel[3], whose very word comes from the Hebrew verb *lisrot* (לִשְׂרוֹת), which means *to struggle, contend, fight* and El (אל which means *God*). In other words, "God reigns or prevails." In the biblical Hebrew there is more depth to the meaning of this word, that is, *to exercise influence, to prevail.* But there is even more depth to its meaning. The root word for Jacob יַעֲקֹב comes from עקב (**akov**), *dishonest, crooked* as in this verse: *"The crooked shall be made straight"* (Isaiah 40:4). The name *Israel*, on the other hand, can be read as Yashar-El. *Yashar* in Hebrew means *straight, honest, law-abiding* and El, means *God*. So, **Israel** can be read as: יִשְׂרָאֵל (Yashar-El) **Yashar** (*straight, honest, keeping the rules*) and **El** (God).

---

[2] David Rubin, *ibid*

[3] The word Israel (יִשְׂרָאֵל) appears 2563 times in the Bible.

On this, I have noticed that in the book of Isaiah the Lord uses interchangeably Jacob and Israel to refer to the corporate identity of His people. He uses Jacob to address them whenever he wants to remind them of their nature in the face of His unchanging faithfulness, but is keen in talking to them as Israel, as those being straight and honest as a result of His work of redemption. He also uses both in the same verse like in the instance of Isaiah 41:14: *"Fear not, you worm Jacob, You men of Israel. I will help you."* There is this continuous dualism going on in the life of one identity. Isaiah 44 is even more clear:

"Yet hear now, O Jacob my servant, and Israel whom I have chosen. Thus says the LORD who made you And formed you from the womb, who will help you: 'Fear not, O Jacob My servant; And you, Jeshurun, whom I have chosen'" (Isaiah 44:1-2).

Here the Lord employs a surname for Israel, Jeshurun, a poetical name used for the people of Israel, apparently expressing affection and tenderness. Alec Motyer writes:

"There is a designed tension between Jacob (*deceiver*) and Jeshurun (*upright*); the one looking back to the failure of the people, the other looking forward to what they will yet be by grace."[4]

Again, the same scenario of Isaiah 17 regarding the demise of Damascus is depicted in the book of Zechariah Chapter 9 which highlights Messiah's intervention and Israel's struggle to be ultimately saved by God Almighty. Interestingly enough, in the ensuing Chapter 10 the prophet speaks about the restoration of Judah and Israel gathered back in the land at the end of days where it is very clearly delineated as the diaspora (world-wide) and then the regathering in the last days.

"I will bring them back, because I have mercy on them. They shall be as though I had not cast them aside; for I am the LORD their God, and I will hear them" (Zechariah 10:6).

Let me summarize by quoting from Rabbi Zalamn

---

[4] Alec Motyer, ***The Prophecy of Isaiah*** (IVP, 1993)

Schachter:

"None of you could be where you are now if you hadn't struggled, if you hadn't done some God-wrestling, if you hadn't in some way responded to a call. And in answering the call, you accept that you are being deployed and sent on a journey. To what end?'[5]

Now we fully grasp the meaning of Jacob's change of nature in that Israel is the one whom God finally could reign and prevail, a honest and straight man in contrast to one who is crooked and uneven. But in the end, the wrestling in the ground ensues the final phase of the master plan, Aliyah to Yeshua.

≈ ≈ ≈ ≈ ≈

Prayer

Thank you, Father, for the story of the children of Israel. Their pilgrimage is our pilgrimage as we recognize that in the journey You have shaped and changed us into the people You have intended us to be. Help us to realize that if it were possible with us, You can surely transform Your people into the Israel you've always wanted them to be. Thank you for bringing them to their homeland but let us never be forgetful of their inner and outward struggle O Lord, as You are preparing Your people to welcome and meet You face to face!

---

[5] Rabbi Zalamn Schachter, in *Torah 1 – Genesis* by Rabbi Dr. Justin D. Elwell for Biblical Life College and Seminary

Chapter 7
The Adumbrative Language in Prophecy

*Oh, that the salvation of Israel would come out of Zion! When God brings back
the captivity of His people, let Jacob rejoice
and Israel be glad.*

(Psalms 53:6)

NOTHING LIKE THE INSPIRED WORD OF GOD CAN SUCCINCTLY EXPRESS A GREAT TRUTH IN A FEW WORDS AS THIS OPENING VERSE does, summing up the plan of God for those of Jacob gathered out of the nations into the Land of promise. It covers all that we have been discussing so far, yet adding one last component; namely, God will bring salvation right from Zion to the Jewish nation regathered from all over the world to live the last phase of their spiritual return to Him—the culmination of the **Holy Pilgrimage**.

As we have learned, the gathering of the Jewish people is in stages. The first one is in ***unbelief***, of which, the return under Zerubbabel constituted the beginning of the ascension movement of Aliyah, seen as the precursor of all the ensuing waves of return up until today. Thus, we have discovered that the promises on the return can be interpreted as on-going prophecies in the way toward their fulfillment; furthermore, that Ezekiel 36 stands tall amidst them all as far as the gathering of Jacob in unbelief for the purpose of the rebirth of God's chosen nation. As the children of Israel came to the end of their captivity in Babylon, their liberation was solved through divine redemptive action via the various edicts that allowed them to settle into their original homeland; nevertheless, the sin problem still affected them, to wit:

"And I scattered them among the heathen, and they were dispersed through the countries: according to their way and according to their doings I judged them . . .. For I will take you from among the heathen, and gather you out of all countries, and will bring you into your own land" (Ezekiel 36:19, 24 KJV).

The conundrum facing many today is the mystery surrounding Israel's current duress in light of God's ongoing covenant faithfulness. The **natural branches**, the Jewish people of natural Israel, were broken off that the **wild branches** be grafted in awaiting the prophetic culmination of both branches—*for God is able to graft them in again* (Romans 11:23).

> *"And they also, if they do not continue in unbelief, will be grafted in, for God is able to graft them in again. For if you were cut out of the olive tree which is wild by nature, and were grafted contrary to nature into a cultivated olive tree, how much more will these, who are natural branches, be grafted into their own olive tree? For I do not desire, brethren, that you should be ignorant of this mystery, lest you should be wise in your own opinion, that **blindness in part has happened to Israel** until the fullness of the Gentiles has come in. And so all Israel will be saved, as it is written: 'The Deliverer will come out of Zion, And he will turn away ungodliness from Jacob; For this is My covenant with them, When I take away their sins'"* (Romans 11:25-26).

God is first regathering His people in accordance with His plan (whether they believe in Him or not—i.e., regathered in unbelief) that they can possess the land. In His faithfulness to His promises, in His great mercy and compassion the Lord is still committing himself to bring them home. Moses foresaw that the children of Israel would sin, and in the Land of promise and forecasted that it would eventually force God to scatter them. In the midst of that, Moses also predicted the people's eventual return to their homeland.

> *"Now it shall come to pass, when all these things come upon you, the blessing and the curse which I have set before you, and you call them to mind among all the nations where the LORD your God drives you, and you return to the LORD your God and obey His voice, according to all that I command you today, you and your children, with all your heart and with all your soul, that the LORD thy God will turn thy captivity, and have compassion upon thee, **and will return and gather thee from all the nations, whither the LORD thy God hath scattered thee . . . .. And the LORD thy God will bring thee into the land***

which thy fathers possessed, and thou shalt possess it; and he will do thee good, and multiply thee above thy fathers" (Deuteronomy 30:1-5 KJV).

Today, Jacob is back in the Land of promise and awaits the final return of the rest of the brethren in expectation for the coming of Messiah—their final Redemption and that of the Messianic Age. Meanwhile, you and I are committed to decipher the times of which the prophecies to which the gathering of the Jews alludes. It was part of Jesus' teachings to His disciples to remind them of their responsibility in discerning the times and seasons. One day he taught a parable saying, *"Look at the fig tree and all the trees"* (Luke 21:29).

From the Scriptures we understand that the fig tree is a metaphor for Israel (Joel 2:21-25). Some have said that the budding of the fig tree speaks of the re-establishment of Israel as a nation which occurred in 1948, seeing it as a precursor of Christ's return. But there is not just one tree in view, but many of them. Jesus refers to trees in general (viz., *"all the trees of the field"*) and to what they do in the spring as the new leaves signal the return of summer, so the signs reveal His return.

It is also possible to consider that the flourishing of figs today in Israel is a Messianic sign in itself—the people are back in the land, the fig trees are abundant and plentiful, and the nation is now waiting for restoration to come in the guise of a spiritual revival. Virtually all His people will be welcoming their Yeshua, the Messiah. Instead, all the other trees stand for the other signposts helping us in deciphering the end of days.

The Exodus Motive in Prophecy

Returning to the many prophetic Scriptures regarding the gathering of the Jewish people, some refer to events which are placed within the brackets of a single prophetic utterance which is spoken in adumbrative language—having allusions to future fulfillment. So far, we have been considering several prophetic passages pointing to the return of the ancient people since the days of Ezra; however, inspiring and moving they may seem, perhaps the most incredible prophecy of the gathering is found in Isaiah 43. I remember vividly the day when Urs Kaesermann came from Switzerland to meet me in Italy for an interview about an opening of a position as a national representative for the international ministry of Ebenezer Operation Exodus. After exchanging introductions, Urs asked in haste, "Do you know the prophecy of Isaiah 43?" It seemed that all he came to say was this, as he was carrying out a most important assignment and to unload himself of a weight he was carrying. Whereupon I transparently answered "No!" Then Urs, with meticulously preparedness—utilizing a well-thought-out Power-Point presentation—unfolded before me the plan of God contained in Isaiah 43 regarding the gathering into the Land of promise of the Jewish people from the four corners of the earth. From that day on, Urs and I became friends for life and worked together in speaking tours and in numerous Aliyah projects in Italy and beyond. Here is the prophetic word of Isaiah:

> *"Fear not, for I am with you; I will bring your descendants from the east, and gather you from the west; I will say to the north, 'Give them up!' And to the south, 'Do not keep them back!' Bring My sons from afar, and My daughters from the ends of the earth"* (Isaiah 43:5-6).

Words fail me to express how much I consider Isaiah 43 to be perhaps my favorite chapter in the Bible. Not because of that evening meeting with my friend, but because it brings me back to the time when the Lord spoke to me audibly while reading these words when, young in the faith, all I wanted to do was to find a secret place of communion with Him while reading from His Word to seek His mind and heart.

For years, then, I did not want to hear anyone speaking from this passage since I did not want to lose the sacredness of that precious moment when the voice of the Lord resounded like mighty waters from the pages of Scriptures. Over the years, regrettably, I had to face the truth, that this passage, alongside many others on the return of the Jewish people, had been misinterpreted to mean the return from Babylonian captivity to the detriment of the whole plan of God. Instead, Isaiah is looking far beyond any threat that the Babylonian Exile may have imposed on the remnant of Israel, because a call to return from Babylon would not involve divine addresses to the four cardinal points which I have mentioned. Alec Motyer wonderfully renders the full meaning of the text in his commentary on Isaiah, to wit:

> "To confine these expectations to the return from Babylon reduces his high-flown eschatological conceptions to banality. Isaiah rarely, if ever, comes to grips with history without launching out into those visions which for him are the final solution to the historical predicaments of God's people. So it is here. He is about to mention (v. 14) but in case his hearers should cherish wrong views about that deliverance he draws the curtain further back to expose a world-wide regathering. I will bring your children . . . I will gather you indicates the continuity of the people of the eschatological day with those to whom Isaiah spoke."[1]

And this Isaiah does in the flow of prophetic utterances. He speaks of Israel's captivity and ends with their return home; he speaks of Israel being in sin but ends with a call to return to the Lord because of the redemption accomplished in the exodus. Moreover, the Lord wants His people to know that the deliverance from Babylon is patterned after the redemption from Egypt, saying, *"The LORD has redeemed His servant Jacob"* (Isaiah 48:20).

Yes, redemption is in the past, but now Israel can look with gratitude to their past deliverance knowing that the same One Who parted the waters is now able to make a way in the wilderness where there seems to be no way. Once again, Cyrus comes on stage in the prophecy of Isaiah reminding us that God chose him to make use of this Gentile king to further advance His purposes for the going out of His people from the four corners of the world (*"The LORD loves him...I even I, have spoken; Yes, I have called him, I have brought him, and his way will prosper"*—Isaiah 48:14-15). The context reveals that the Lord is different from all other gods in that He predicts and fulfills, and that His ***Cyrus-***

---

[1] J. Alec Motyer, ***The Prophecy of Isaiah*** (IVP, 1993)

plan will succeed against Babylon. Indeed, the Lord is still choosing other Cyrus ministries which work with Him in the Aliyah of His people. Still, it is Aliyah to the land to which God points at when He says:

> "***Who confirms the word of His servant*** [Cyrus's declaration of independence for the Jews] *And performs the counsel of His messengers Who says of Cyrus, 'He is My shepherd, And he shall perform all My pleasure, Saying to Jerusalem, 'You shall be built,' And to the temple, 'Your foundation shall be laid"* (Isaiah 44:26, 28).

To see how much God is involved in bringing home His people, we read that He will have all obstacles removed in the way of their return.

> "*Who says to Jerusalem, 'You shall be inhabited,' To the cities of Judah, 'You shall be built,' And I will raise up her waste places; Who says to the deep, 'Be dry! And I will dry up your rivers'"* (Isaiah 44:26-27).

Only the One Who created the heavens and the earth can promise to cover their return by opening a way to enable them to enter the Land of promise. So, Aliyah is very much a "holy" phase in the sequence of events climaxing to the salvation of the Jews. We need not ever underestimate what God is doing through the rebuilding of Israel with the *olim* (new immigrants) He is gathering home. You see, in the final "cosmic analysis" the very character of the Almighty is at stake—He keeps His Word— He will not renege on His Promise—He abides faithful, He cannot deny Himself!

The Exodus Motive in Salvation & the Greater Exodus

Other promises, instead, seem to focus on the immediate realization in the historical context in which the prophet conveys the message, yet there is a more complete fulfillment later of the same (adumbrative in nature—meaning *"prophetically foreshadowing; sketchy; faintly indicative"*). This tendency to speak of events that are separated by time, as though they were not, is called the law of *double reference.* In short, a prophecy of the Bible can be partially fulfilled early and then have a complete fulfillment later. In other words, two events, widely separated as to the time of their fulfillment may be brought together into the scope of prophecy. And the tendency of Scripture to reveal God's plan by way of double reference is consistent throughout the O.T. as in the case of the return of the Jewish people is concerned. It is metaphorically akin to the *"early* [former] *and latter rain"* (Jeremiah 5:21).

Commenting on the prophecy of Amos 9:13-15 through which the Lord speaks about the future return of the Jewish people to the land of Israel, to wit, *"And I will bring again the captivity of my people of Israel and they shall build the waste cities."*

Dr. Tom Horn and the late Cris Putnam observe that ". . . while this passage was a message of hope for the exiles, it is necessarily a case of 'already but not yet' as well. God states categorically that they will return to *'never again be uprooted'* (v. 15)."[2]

However, the timing of the last and greatest regathering is not clearly stated in the passage from Amos just mentioned, but it is by understanding and reading the times that we are able to appreciate God's unending care for His people.

"Hear the word of the LORD, O nations, and declare it in the isles afar off, and say, 'He who scattered Israel will gather him, and keep him as a shepherd does his flock.' For the LORD has redeemed Jacob, and ransomed him from the hand of one stronger than he" (Jeremiah 31:9-11).

Here the Holy Spirit inspired Jeremiah with adumbrative language pointing to the redemption of Jacob (the Jewish people)—the Holy Spirit does so within a prophecy related to the return of the Jews from captivity. In his classic text, **Daniel and Latter Days**, Robert Duncan Culver speaks about adumbration or adumbrative language[3] as a language faintly indicating or typifying

---

[2] Thomas Horn and Chris Putnam in **The Final Roman Emperor, The Islamic Antichrist, And the Vatican Last Crusade** (Defender, 2016)

[3] Robert Duncan Culver, **Daniel and the Latter Days** (Fleming H. Revell Company, 1954)

a yet future happening. In this case, the redemption of Israel, associated with the gathering from the diaspora who look to a yet future event which, as well, points to their spiritual salvation. In this regard one of the most incredible passages in the New Testament which is intended for the redemption of the Jewish people is found in Luke 1:68-75:

> *"Blessed is the LORD God of Israel,*
> *For He has visited and redeemed His people,*
> *And has raised up a horn of salvation for us*
> *In the house of His servant David,*
> *As He spoke by the mouth of His holy prophets,*
> *Who have been since the world began,*
> *That we should be saved from our enemies*
> *And from the hand of all who hate us,*
> *To perform the mercy promised to our fathers*
> *And to remember His holy covenant,*
> *The oath which He swore to our father Abraham:*
> *To grant us that we,*
> *Being delivered from the hand of our enemies,*
> *Might serve Him without fear,*
> *In holiness and righteousness before Him all the days of our*
> *life."*

Here we have Zechariah's blessing to God which speaks as if redemption has already occurred. It was the Spirit of the Lord Who made him see such a great salvation coming to Israel through the means of the atoning sacrifice of the Lamb of God. A study of the word *salvation* in the Tanakh reveals several senses in which it is used in connection with God; the first one is that God saves Israel His people from the hand of their enemies, then He promises to save them from their impurities. There is both salvation in physical terms as well as salvation as a spiritual condition. The spiritual salvation of which this passage alludes is through the promised Messiah. It is patterned along the lines of national liberation which occurred at the first exodus from Egypt and then Judah's deliverance from Babylon.

It is the opening of a road for Israel that may serve the One Who redeemed her without fear. Fear is one other reason why the Lord saves the Jewish people from the hands of their enemies when He does it by taking them out of the nations where antisem-itism is rampant. Antisemitism has been defined as "hatred of Judaism and ethical monotheism, followed close by the Chosen People idea."[4] Indeed, it is the hatred against all Jews which hides a real hatred against God, His Son, and His Word. Someone rightly suggested that "You cannot love Jesus whom you have not seen (who was/is Jewish) if you don't love the Jewish people whom you have seen."[5] (Incidentally, Yeshua, the man, is returning as the "Root of Jesse, the Son of David"—yes, returning as the "Lion of the Tribe of Judah"—*ipso facto* He's still Jewish!)

In its myriad of manifestations, like anti-Zionism for example, antisemitism is a hatred against the Jews because they bring upon themselves the Name of God. Whether they are secular Jews or religious ones, it doesn't matter; they are the target of the evil spirit of Haman, who, as of old, still has plans for extermination. I could personally testify regarding an evil spirit the day when I approached a man to hand him a Christian yearly devotional. He was known as a violent man, so I prayed to the Lord to give me the courage to go and speak to him kind words, but the moment he realized that I was there to show Jesus' compassion, he turned against me with fury, throwing a river of words against me wishing me to die like the Jews in the ovens of Auschwitz.

Had he known what my role was in helping the Jews fulfilling their God-given destiny, I would have understood the reason of his hatred, but he did not. As he spewed from his mouth a river of filth against me and the Jews, I could feel the venom of a nasty and threatening spirit coming out of him. Antisemitism can be felt and perceived because it stems from a real spirit at work. Not just amongst the nations of the world where antisemitism is being expressed, but in some Christian leaders and teachers who are devoted to anti-Israel and who are anti-Zionist in their theology. However, God is able to turn what Satan has meant for evil and

---

[4] Prager and Telushkin, ***Why the Jews? The Reason for Antisemitism.*** New York: Simon and Shuster, 1983.
[5] Mike Evans: ***Why Christians Should Support Israel,*** 2011.

has reserved a future and a hope for His people. So, the exodus theme provides the pattern of the coming acts of the Lord in the history of His people to deliver, save, and bring to a desired end what He has planned to do with them.

Isaiah 43:21 renders it magnificently by saying, *"The people that I have formed for Myself, they shall declare My praise."* Even the captivity and the subsequent return have their part to play in the grand finale awaiting His people, until the day comes, when a perfected people will at last perfectly recount the praise of their Lord. In fact, the Exodus is the only historical event which prefigures eschatological redemption in which we, those saved from among the Gentiles, recognize the story of our own redemption. In fact, the Exodus from Egypt does not only provide a pattern for our liberation, but the Red Sea event confirms the whole phenomenon as a work of salvation.

Jesus Christ has brought us release through the waters of His death, burial, and resurrection. In his outstanding series on ***Systematic Theology***, J. Rodman Williams, speaks about the Exodus that Jesus accomplished for us at the cross:

> "On the mount of transfiguration when Moses and Elijah appeared, they spoke of Jesus' 'departure' (literally exodus—hence deliverance) which he was to accomplish at Jerusalem (Luke 9:31). Accordingly, at the cross Christ accomplished that Exodus, that vast deliverance and release."[6]

Indeed, the Exodus provides a pattern for our spiritual Exodus, a type through which we identify our personal experience. The word *type* comes from the Greek *typos*, a synonym of *resemblance, likeness*, and *similarity*. David Baker defines *type* as "A biblical event, person or institution which serves as an example or pattern for other events, persons or institutions."[7] In other words, the relationship between events, one initial and the other in the future, is a typology.

---

[6] J. Rodman Williams, ***Renewal Theology***, page 362 Vol. I
[7] David Baker, "Typology and the Christian use in the Old Testament," cited in ***Hermeneutics*** by Henry Virkler.

Along this line, let me amplify it by saying that there is another adumbrative meaning to the final return of the Jews which culminates in a singular Greater Exodus at the time of the Church's regathering. Author and researcher Chad J. Schafer firmly asserts that the sequence of the First Exodus shall be repeated again prior to the second coming of Yeshua, the Messiah. In other words, all the events that took place in Egypt will be prophetically rehearsed upon the whole world where the Greater Exodus will be patterned after the First Exodus.

This time it will be the gathering of God's people, of the Commonwealth of Israel (Ephesians 2), of those who partake of the New Covenant (Jews and Gentiles), and of National Israel (sealed on earth, Revelation 7:1-8) in the presence of all nations. In this perspective, the end of the age can be compared to the timing of the Greater Exodus. I find his conclusion fascinating to say the least and extremely in line with the typology of the Exodus. Here I would like to quote from Chad's text because he gives the missing link to what we need to refer for a complete comprehension of the Exodus motive:

> ". . . prior to the First Exodus, the children of Israel were 'sealed/preserved' from the Ten Plagues upon Pharaoh's Egypt—even so Revelation 7:1-8 indicates that upon the earth the Twelve Tribes of Israel shall once again be preserved from the Wrath of God and the Lamb as the Seventh Seal is opened in Revelation 8:1. With this understanding before us it follows that we should understand the events which took place in Egypt and the order in which they occurred. All those events will again be prophetically rehearsed upon the whole world— the Greater Exodus will be patterned after the First Exodus."[8]

Prior to the First Exodus, the children of Israel were preserved from the Ten Plagues that fell upon Pharaoh's Egypt—even so, Revelation 7:1-8 indicates that upon the earth the Twelve Tribes of Israel shall once again be preserved from the wrath of the Lamb as

---

[8] Chad J. Schafer, "The Greater Exodus" in ***One In Messiah*** (Commonwealth Of Israel Foundation, 2019)

the Seventh Seal is opened in Revelation 8:1.[9] At that future time, they shall not wander in the desert for forty years but shall enter directly into the promised land, led by the second Joshua/Yeshua. It will be a time of the final "**corporate**" liberation!

What we can see here is that the Scripture clearly states this final corporate Exodus shall occur just prior to the wrath of God and the Lamb; prior to the pouring out of the bowls of judgement being upon those who "*dwell upon the earth.*" It will be:

> ***"Immediately after the Tribulation of those days** the sun will be darkened, and the moon will not give its light; the stars will fall from heaven, and the powers of the heavens will be shaken. Then the sign of the Son of Man will appear in heaven, and then all the tribes of the earth will mourn, and they will see the Son of Man coming on the clouds of heaven with power and great glory. **And He will send His angels with a great sound of a trumpet, and they will gather together His elect from the four winds, from one end of heaven to the other"*** (Matthew 24:29-31).

The Greater Exodus shall be led by His Angels. God's corporate people shall be gathered from every land, and I should think the miracle which parted the Red Sea shall be repeated one hundred-fold from all the face of the earth. The pragmatics of this, from man's standpoint, shall be of no consideration. It will be miraculous. They shall be gathered to the land and those who are faithful and of an upright heart and have accepted Yeshua shall be translated at His appearing.

What I'm saying here is this: Israel and the Church (aka "*the elect from among the nations*"—Ephraim so scattered, swallowed up, assimilated) are not separated in the ultimate plan and purposes of the ages, they are distinct, yes, but not separated for they are attached to the same root (Yeshua) and enjoy the same covenant in fullness at the coming of the Son of Man in glory. From this we understand that the Greater Exodus is comprised of both events leading up to the final regathering of the Jewish people to

---

[9] Chad J. Schafer and Doug Krieger, ***The World In The Bondage Of Egypt . . . Under the Triumphal Arch of Titus,*** (Tribnet Publications, 2016)

the land of Israel **and** the implications of this in-gathering to those called out from among the Gentiles –"*Now brethren, concerning the coming of our Lord Jesus Christ and our gathering together to Him*"— (2 Thessalonians 2.1). This is too incredible to comprehend to its fullest, but I do believe as the prophetic clock keeps ticking, the Holy Spirit will shed light into this wonderful subject of the final and Greater Exodus. I hasten to add that the final Exodus is a type of the divine harvest at the end of the age described in Isaiah 27:12-13, to wit:

> *And it shall come to pass in that day that the Lord will thresh, from the channel of the River to the Brook of Egypt;* ***And you will be gathered one by one, O you children of Israel***. *So it shall be in that day:* ***The great trumpet will be blown;*** *They will come, who are about to perish in the land of Assyria, and they who are* ***outcasts*** *in the land of Egypt, and shall worship the LORD in the holy mount at Jerusalem.*

This is the plucking up and gathering of all of the Lord's people, the conclusive ingathering, the time when "All Israel" (meaning all the children of Israel – both Houses – that of Judah and that of Ephraim) shall be saved—for when the "*fullness of the Nations has come in, THEN ALL ISRAEL shall be delivered*" (Romans 11:25-26); at the sound of the last great trumpet. As it states in Romans 9:6:

> "*But it is not that the word of God has taken no effect . . . for they are not all Israel who are of Israel, nor are they all children because they are the seed of Abraham; but 'In Isaac your seed shall be called.'*"

Here the differential is striking: ALL ISRAEL are those, not of the flesh (i.e., "*the seed of Abraham*") but of the "*faith of Abraham*"—for Abraham was justified prior to circumcision and was "*justified by faith*" (Romans 4) before God. Abraham placed his faith in the Seed, in Christ (Galatians 3:15-18), in Isaac, the Son of Promise.

Motyer once again does justice to the eschatological context of this prophecy:

"Isaiah relates the eschaton to the map of his own world. From the ends of the earth, and even from the supreme oppressors themselves (Egypt the first, Assyria the contemporary), there will be those whom the atonement trumpet calls to Zion."[10]

We will now look into the last and final phase of the pilgrimage in the next chapter.

≈ ≈ ≈ ≈ ≈ ≈

Prayer

Lord, we are beginning to see that there is more than we thought there was, that our story is intertwined with that of Israel regathered to its Land from the four corners of the world. From beginning to end the Exodus of the children of Israel mirrors our salvation and we are grateful to You, Lord, for our destinies meet in the Greater Exodus at the end of this present age. Show us more of your plan, O Lord, that we may appreciate all that we share with Your people Israel—so much so that You on that day shall take the "Stick of Ephraim and the stick of Judah and make them ONE STICK" in Your hand! Amen.

---

[10] J. Alec Motyer, ibid

Chapter 8
Called to Salvation

(With Contribution from Douglas W. Krieger)

"Then you shall know that I am the LORD, when I bring you into the land of Israel, into the country for which I raised My hand in an oath to give to your fathers."

(Ezekiel 20:42)

THE NOTION AND PHILOSOPHY EMBRACED BY THE GNOSTICS CLAIMED THAT THE "PHYSICAL WORLD" WAS ALTOGETHER INFERIOR TO THAT OF THE MA-terial world. When God said, *"And it was good"*—i.e., His creation—He meant what He said—plain and simple. The "spirit of Antichrist" that has come into the world abhors the birth and ultimate transfiguration of mankind; especially, the following:

> *"For many deceivers have gone out into the world who do not confess Jesus Christ as coming in the flesh. This is a deceiver and an antichrist . . . whoever transgresses and does not abide in the doctrine of Messiah does not have God. He who abides in the doctrine of Christ has both the Father and the Son"* (2 John 7, 9).

> *"Things visible and invisible"*—makes no difference—*"all things were created for Him and by Him"* (Colossians 2:16).

Those who deny the materiality of today's Israel, likewise, find themselves embracing the alleged rejection of the physicality of the promised land to a specific people group; and, normally, to buttress their argument of the same they quote Scripture relative to *"But the hour is coming, and now is, when the true worshipers will worship the Father in spirit and truth; for the Father is seeking such to worship Him. God is Spirit, and those who worship Him must worship in spirit and truth"* (John 4:23-24). Well then, that should take care of those who ascribe to an "extreme biblical literalism"—all the while eschewing Jesus' words regarding the Temple as a ***House of prayer for all people***—Matthew 21:13; Mark 11:17; Isaiah 56:7; Jeremiah 7:11. Let me make

129

a bold statement borne out in Scripture (Psalms 2): Denial of Israel's materiality is a denial of Messiah as the Son of Man and a rejection of His character and second coming in glory as the Deliverer Who shall "come out of Zion!"

The 70 AD "Abomination of Desolation" brought the immediate end to the sacerdotal rites of the Temple; however, we should ask: "How can you call this the 'Abomination of Desolation'—or the yet futurity of the same (Matthew 24:15; 2 Thessalonians 2:1-12) when that which is irrelevant or unholy can be "abominated" or "made desolate?"

Theologically denigrating the physical creation as altogether void of spirituality is a most subtle subterfuge of the enemy of our souls. Yes, the "heavenly New Jerusalem" descends therefrom—to the earth, not the ionosphere. How can you reconcile Ezekiel 40-48 with Revelation 21? The Holy City of Ezekiel 40-48 is the same Holy City, the New Jerusalem of Revelation 21; even so, there is only One Bride of Messiah—the notion that Old Testament saints are betrothed to Jehovah as the Wife of Jehovah and New Testament saints are set apart as the Bride of Christ makes our God, Who is ONE, a polygamist! May we conclude, then, that the Holy City, the New Jerusalem, is "multi-dimensional"—much like the resurrected body of our Savior Who could instantly appear and disappear—indeed: *"Then He* (Jesus) *said to Thomas, 'Reach your finger here, and look at My hands; and reach your hand here, and put it into My side. Do not be unbelieving, but believing . . . for a spirit does not have flesh and bones, as you see I have"* (John 20:27; Luke 24:39).

One final thought—why would there be a contestation between Satan and the Archangel Michael (Jude 1:9) over the very body of Moses? Yes, we humans tend to venerate our heroes, even to the point of worshiping at their bodily shrines—but that, I do not think, was why this Scripture finds itself in the inspired canon. It is not just a matter of how we address the powers of darkness but, more so, the physicality at stake . . . apparently, Moses' body meant something to God!

The Land of promise issue is, therefore, very significant—Aliyah and Klitah—as we understand that this is one of the greatest miracles as it evokes the redeeming power of God in redemptive history placing an ultimate seal upon His incontrovertible Word. In the same way, loyalty to Torah and to the whole Word of God is a true advantage for the Jew, that should and does count for something of immense propriety.

Romans 3:1-2 explicitly says:

"What advantage then has the Jew, or what is the profit of circumcision? Much in every way! Chiefly because to them were committed the oracles of God."

However, at the end, if that advantage is not transformed into a salvific deliverance that divests itself of anything of its own righteousness, it avails nothing. About this, Paul writes with much heart-felt conviction, exclaiming:

"For I bear them witness that they have a zeal for God, but not according to knowledge. For they, being ignorant of God's righteousness, and seeking to establish their own righteousness, have not submitted to the righteousness of God" (Romans 10:2-3).

Hence, I have already stressed that moving to the Land of promise cannot be salvific *per se.* It is also true that the salvation of the full House of Jacob still remains a matter pertaining to God—we must not forget that *"salvation comes from the LORD"* (Jonah 2:9 NIV). For the people of Israel, it is displayed in clear, simple terms, to wit:

"For I will take you from among the nations, gather you out of all countries, and bring you into your own land. Then I will sprinkle clean water on you and you shall be clean; I will cleanse you from all your filthiness and from all your idols. I will give you a new heart and put a new spirit within you; I will take the heart of stone out of your flesh and give you a heart of flesh" (Ezekiel 36:24-26).

With such a great salvation we have reached the nexus, the apex, of the phases of the pilgrimage so far examined; yet our focus here is on the crescendo leading up to the final destination. In all things, from the incipit to its consummation, it has been the Holy One of Israel Who oversees the **Holy Pilgrimage**, the going-up all the way to this crucial prophetic moment. The climactic events leading up to the unveiling of Yeshua to His brethren requires nothing but YHVH to govern the final phase that will see His people saved unto an everlasting deliverance—a full salvation. The God who began a good work, will also bring it to pass. The God who started the pilgrimage will see it accomplished on such a glorious day. His truthfulness has moved Him to substantiate His purposes confirming that He would never abandon them before their fulfillment. He is YHVH and will never give His glory to another (Isaiah 48:11). Indeed, He used various means to reach His goals in bringing the exiles out of captivity as noted with King Cyrus, but be it known, all acts of redemption, albeit carried out by human instruments, always reflect the imprint of Him Who superimposes His will from heaven. To that end, the whole theme of Isaiah revolving around the chapters of hope (Isaiah 40-66)—even though these portions look back on Israel's sin and at the Cyrus-plan for the liberation from their captivity—has as its central subject the ministry of the suffering Servant, namely Yeshua the Messiah and Redeemer, who comes into the scene at a time of history to announce that His work includes bringing Israel back to the Lord (Isaiah 49:6). So, the Redeemer figure (*goel* in Hebrew) is dominant to the salvation of the House of Jacob. The Torah, we emphasized, albeit necessary and important as it is, can only serve as a tutor to bring the child to the real teacher and schoolmaster to whom it belongs (therefore, it is mandatory that it be *"spiritual and holy"*—Romans 7:12; 3:31), for it is only the Redeemer Who can identify Himself with the need to liberate His people. The resolution of the plight of His people comes from Him. He is the Servant, the covenant figure sent first to Israel, the one who was chosen to bring back Jacob to Him, the spiritual restoration of the people. *"The remnant will return, the remnant of Jacob, to the Mighty God"* (Isaiah 10:21). This supernaturally preserved company are brought back to the Lord through the ministry of the Servant, who has been sent to restore and to bring back those who were alienated from Him, to recover the Jewish people again to the pure worship of YHVH. In Isaiah 49:6 light is shed upon the ministry of the Servant Whose service to His people was, *"To raise up the tribes of Jacob, and to restore the preserved ones of Israel."* It is interesting to note that the word *restore* in the Hebrew is *Lehashiv* (לְהָשִׁיב Strong's H#7725) which means *to return, to bring back, to allow to return*; it is the same verb from which we derive the word *shub* (turning, making *teshuvah*).

It is the Servant's prerogative causing the remnant to return to Him. In addition, the word *preserved* comes from the Hebrew *netzirei* (נְצִירֵי Strong's H#5341) a derivative of *branch*, inferring that it means the branches of Israel, the descendants of Jacob, those who are kept, preserved, applicable to those who are preserved for purposes of mercy and grace out of the common mass that is corrupt and unbelieving; notwithstanding, a remnant will return.

Considering the premises our question remains the same: What then will He use to restore and save His people? Will He do it just because they are of the stock of Jacob? Will traditions or dogma of the Oral Law and Rabbinical teachings suffice? Definitely not. I am sad to see that many are they, among the supporters of Israel who tend to skip the very climax of Jacob's pilgrimage—the salvation of the soul—but prefer to flirt with *"dual covenantalism"*—i.e., the Jews of today are brought (now) into right standing with the Almighty through the Mosaic Covenant; whereas Christians are brought to right standing via the *"Blood of the Everlasting Covenant"* (and some say the New Covenant) juxtaposed to the Old Covenant (which is still viable under "dual covenant" dispensationalism).

They go to the extent to say that because the Jews have a special relationship with God through the revelation given to them at Sinai, they will be welcomed into Heaven even if they deny Yeshua as the Messiah. This belief is known as Dual Covenant Theology. Founder and Pastor of King of Kings Ministry in Jerusalem, Wayne Hilsden, wrote a paper on "One Covenant for All (Dual Covenant Theology)," saying,

"There are two major errors in the church today in relation to Israel. One is 'replacement theology'. Yet, among some Christian Zionists there is another heresy even more serious and detrimental to God's purposes. It is often referred to as 'dual covenant theology.' In essence, those who teach a dual covenant theology believe there are two distinct ways to salvation: for the Jews, salvation is obtained by obedience to the Law of Moses. For Gentiles, salvation is obtained through the 'New Covenant,' by putting one's trust in the shedding of Jesus' blood on the cross and receiving God's free gift of atonement and eternal life."

So, the question awaits its answer. By what means will God save His people, the Jews? As Motyer comments on the way of God's salvation,[1] "There is no separate salvation for separate groups . . . Zion's salvation is the world's salvation." God will use nothing but the same old message, He will do what He has been doing since the cross, sending the Holy Spirit to convict, and providing a LAMB for atonement! He will be merciful to the Jews in the same way He has been merciful to us (*for by grace you have been saved* – Ephesians 2:8) whereby the cross will forever stand in remembrance of the blood of the atonement. The result of the "Passover Lamb of God" relative to all the Jews who came before the cross looked forward to the Lamb of God, Who provided them His offering for sin; whereas all those since the cross, the death, burial, and resurrection of Christ, look back to that all-inclusive sacrifice for their deliverance and salvation.

The third and last phase of the plan of God for the Jewish people is the most crucial one because it leads to their redemption. I've entitled it **ALIYAH TO YESHUA** because Yeshua is the end, the object, the finality of Aliyah as well as it is for the Torah (*"For Christ is the **end** [telos—end result] of the Law for righteousness to everyone who believes"*—Romans 10:4). Therefore, Aliyah to Yeshua is the final manifestation of their call to a **Holy Pilgrimage**, their progressive ascent from the natural to the spiritual.

---

[1] J. Alec Motyer, ibid

Accordingly, leading up to Yeshua implies a detailed prophetic timeline that would take Jacob up through his radical transformation receiving a new name, despite all his struggles and wrestling.

Here we need to realize that the things which characterize this culminating phase of the pilgrimage of the House of Jacob will literally take place during the Revelation (the Apocalypse) consisting of events surrounding the second coming of Messiah. We need spiritual eyes to understand, especially in light of what the apostle Paul taught to the Romans about Israel being blinded in part. He wrote this after explaining our ingrafting into Israel.

What this speaks to is the partial blindness afflicting the Jewish people—in point of the divine plan they were blinded to Messiah's identity; and similarly, the Gentiles were blinded as well to many other things, *"For now we see through a glass, dimly"*—1 Corinthians 13:12; so much so that all of us simply know in part. Then when the veil is lifted, I dare say, it will be lifted on both sides. The knowledge of the purposes of God is generally increasing and the comprehension of this wonderful plan is going to grow more and more. They are blinded in part (Romans 11:25) so they are in partial blindness, yet they apparently see something, so do we, for "blinded in parts" does not mean "blinded in full."

Prophetic Wars and Mass Aliyah Waves

The progression towards the unveiling of Messiah to the Jewish people is well elucidated by ***The Visions, Prophecies, and Messianic Scenario of Zechariah,***[2] which help us in unfolding and unraveling this enormous Gordian Knot of the prophetic Scriptures. The book of Zechariah clearly shows us with unques-

---

[2] This is the magnus opus of D. W. Krieger and one of the best commentaries on the book of Zechariah ever written: ***Unsealing the End of Days, the Visions, Prophecy & Messianic Scenario of Zechariah***, https://www.amazon.com/Unsealing-End-Days-Messianic-ZECHARIAH-ebook/dp/B087LWGN2K/ref=sr_1_4?dchild=1&keywords=Douglas+krieger&qid=1592145197&sr=8-4

tionable prophetic elucidation that between the first and the second coming of Messiah (first as the suffering servant and second as the glorified Son of Man, whose name is the Branch) the destiny of Israel and the Jewish people are in play. In particular, as far as it concerns the subject at hand, in Zechariah 7-8 there is a cosmic view of the reoccurring theme of Israel's scattering among the nations and her ultimate regathering in which Eretz Israel is prominently featured (Aliyah to the Land):

> "**'Yes, I scattered them** *with a whirlwind among all the nations which they had not known . . .* [only to regather them]. *I am zealous for Zion with great zeal; with great fervor I am zealous for her. Thus says the LORD,* **I will return to Zion** *and dwell in the midst of Jerusalem. Jerusalem shall be called the city of truth, the mountain of the LORD of hosts, the holy Mountain. Behold,* **I will save my people from the land of the east and from the land of the west, I will bring them back**, *and they shall dwell in the midst of Jerusalem. They shall be my people and I will be their God, in truth and righteousness"* (Zechariah 7:14; 8:2-8).

Here we see the Almighty's choice of Eretz Israel, which is without dispute, and God's commitment to bring his ancient people back as He has set them apart for a witness and a testimony to all the Nations. I believe that without Israel in the land there cannot be a testimony. Her prophetic engagement starts with the regathering of the House of Jacob to the land as Messiah could not come without a regathered people.

Zechariah 9 introduces what some commentators say to be the countdown to the reign of the Son of David, highlighting the Burden of Damascus. In other words, there is something that functions as a trigger that initiates the Messianic scenario introduced here in Zechariah 9. It alerts us to the soon coming of Messiah in glory. Prefigured by Zechariah 9 and Isaiah 17, the Burden or Oracle against Damascus is what will lead to the pseudo Peace Treaty, the most welcomed, but deceitful, Covenant with Death, Agreement with Hell (Isaiah 28:15), which shall be an agreement between the Antichrist and world leadership with Israel's consent. This Oracle of Damascus initiates a trilogy of conflicts (we will elaborate later) culminating in the coming of the Messianic Era, and the establishment of David's throne upon the earth.

It (the "Damascus Oracle") will also introduce the prophetically impactful Seventieth Week of Daniel (the last seven years of the present age). It will unveil the revelation of the Man of Sin, the Son of Perdition, the Antichrist. The Hebrew prophets have pointed out this particular war (viz., the "Oracle of Damascus") shall result in Syria's complete destruction with the city of Damascus being uninhabitable, *Damascus will cease from being a city* (Isaiah 17:1). It is very probable that Israel shall be victorious in this final and seventh conflict of all the Arab-Israeli wars since 1948, but she will be greatly diminished in her capacity to wage further war, nor shall she be able to defend herself after the conflict: *"Now in that day the glory of Jacob will fade, And the fatness of his flesh will become lean"* (Isaiah 17:4 NASB).

As a result, Israel's glory will fade because of the loss of her splendour due to the conflict with her enemies resulting in Damascus' demise. In Isaiah 17 and Zechariah 9 we find an amazing and accurate assessment in deciphering who these enemies are. The *"cities of Aroer"* (the land east of the Jordan River); the *"Fortress of Ephraim"* (lit., Ramallah, the Palestinian Authority in Samaria); Damascus (Syria); *"Tyre and Sidon"* (Lebanon); Ashkelon, Gaza, Ekron, Ashdod, Philistines (south of Israel and literally ancient Philistia, now Gaza).[3]

Behind some of these forces there could be Iran, Israel's modern archenemy. In fact, today Iran is the most dangerous country in the Middle East, not just because of its nuclear program, but also through her conventional weapons and support for terror activities against Israel. The IDF (Israel Defense Forces) believe that Iran's influence reaches into the first of the three circles of threats against Israel; the first being small terror groups on Israel's borders, like Hamas; the second being larger threats, like the Syrian

---

[3] Doug Krieger, *The Two Witnesses Volume II*, pp. 282-283, Tribnet Publications 2014.

army and Hezbollah; and the third being countries that do not share a border with Israel, like Iraq.

It is believed to support and finance Israel's enemies in the first circle and chiefly Hezbollah, it influences and supports Hamas and the Islamic Jihad, and it is behind attempts at terror actions against Israel in a variety of dimensions and arenas, near and far. All this to say as far as the massive account of the Gog-Magog War described in Ezekiel 38-39, this doesn't mean that the next round of confrontation will be less confrontational—it is simply the final war prior to the Gog-Magog conflagration.

Commentators, pundits, and analysts are all saying and envisaging that due to the annexation by Israel of parts of the West Bank (with reference to the Peace to Prosperity plan of the Trump administration presented in 2020) Israel will undergo a massive outpouring of fury from the Palestinians and their allies. The process of annexation envisioned in Israel's plan to extend its sovereignty to the Jordan Valley, for example, could represent the crossing of the red line in the eyes of the abovementioned conglomeration of foes whereupon the entire Middle East could erupt in flames until the day when all this will most assuredly result in the demise of Damascus (i.e., the Oracle of Zechariah 9 and Isaiah 17).

Here we have Jacob in the heat of the struggle (Ref. Chapter 6 of this text) for his transformation in the final preparation in meeting Messiah. This belligerent constellation of nations would make Israel exceedingly vulnerable to the attacks by other Islamic States in the aftermath of the Oracle of Damascus—which, again, will greatly weaken Israel—although she will prevail in that conflict. Occurring on the heels of the Damascus demise will be the subterfuge of the "Treaty of Death and Sheol."

The Antichrist could enforce this pact upon Israel (included in the "many" nations which will sign in on the agreement), as per Daniel 9:27 where it reads that: *"Then he shall confirm a covenant with many for one week"*. Delving deeper into the Hebrew text provides valuable insight into the nature of this treaty. In fact, the phrase *"he shall confirm a covenant"* in the original Hebrew (בְּרִית וְהִגְבִּיר) has a different connotation, that of *prevail, to have strength, to be strong.* **In essence, the text suggests that the Antichrist will literally impose a future 'peace plan' on Israel.** The common teaching that Israel would readily agree to a final peace deal is a misconception; the reality may be far more complex and resistance. From a realistic perspective, a genuine peace agreement is something that Israel will never accept. The fundamental obstacle is that any viable plan would necessitate significant territorial concessions, a condition that conflict directly with Israel's enduring security doctrine and current political consensus.

Secretary of State, John Kerry, under the Obama Administration, attempted to partition Israel during the failed 70-nation Paris Peace Accords; however, this alignment of nations persists to this day (2017-2020)[4]—thus, a prototype of this has already taken place eerily mirroring the principalities over the 70 nations in Genesis 10 and their ultimate demise under divine disbursement and confusion at the Tower of Babel in Genesis 11.

Out of this conspiratorial consortium of deceit will prophetically result in the following:

"Why do the nations rage [lit. "throng tumultuously"]*, and the people plot a vain* [lit. "worthless or empty"] *thing? The kings of the earth set themselves, and the rulers take counsel together, against the LORD and against His Messiah, saying, 'Let us break their bonds in pieces and cast away Their cords from us.' He who sits in the heavens shall laugh; the Lord shall hold them in derision. Then He shall speak to them in His wrath, and distress them in His deep displeasure: 'Yet I have set My King upon My holy hill of Zion.' 'I will declare the decree: The LORD has said to Me, 'You are My Son, today I have begotten You. Ask of Me, and I will give You the nations for Your inheritance, and the ends of the earth for Your possession. You shall break them with a rod of iron; and shall dash them to pieces like a potter's vessel.'" Now therefore, be*

---

wise, O kings; be instructed, you judges of the earth. Serve the LORD with fear; and rejoice with trembling. Kiss the son, lest He [lit. "the Lord"] *be angry, and you perish in the way, when His wrath is kindled but a little. Blessed are all those who put their trust in Him"* (Psalms 2:1-12).

You see, this anger, hatred, and rage perpetrated by Satan, who accused Joshua the High Priest (Zechariah 3:1-2), targets Zion's Holy Hill—the people of Israel—but in actuality their infuriating anger is against Messiah. It is the ultimate manifestation of rebellion against the God of Israel, His Messiah, the Anointed One, the Son—unless He is "kissed" His anger will surmount against the kingdoms of this world and their intentions shall be exposed as they center their capricious and devilish attacks against the "apple of His eye." He shall confound His enemies as they seek to destroy His peculiar treasure!

This is the period in which the efforts of many, motivated by the willingness to help the Jewish people of the diaspora making Aliyah, will turn into overnight operations. Pretty much like at the times of the Aliyah Bet. Historical research and fonts of various origins, including public domain documents, and other fonts, attest to the fact that Aliyah (as we intend it today) began in a totally different way compared to what we are accustomed. In fact, Aliyah has always been connected to seasons of suffering and persecution of the Jewish people caused by dangerous times while precipitated by a violent tide of antisemitism. This was the case of the *pogroms* of the late 1800s, let alone the aftermath of WWII and the Holocaust.

In his remarkable research into the rescue of the Jews since WWII, journalist, and researcher Tad Szulc[5] writes that prior to Israeli independence in 1948, legal migration was referred to as Aliyah Alef (Alef stands for A or number one in Hebrew). This had its incipit in the movement of Russian Jews to the Holy Land in 1882 prompted by anti-Semitic persecutions and the gleam of

---

[5] Tad Szulc, *The Secret Alliance, The Extraordinary Story of the Rescue of the Jews Since WWII* (1991)

nascent Zionism ideas. It was the *first wave of Aliyah.*[6] However, the clandestine immigration has been wider in its scope than the legal one, namely, the Aliyah Bet (*Bet* is the second letter of the Hebrew alphabet and stands for number two). In other words, his research clarified that the birth of the State of Israel was rendered possible by immense pressure created by the migrations set in motion in postwar Europe by the *underground* Israeli operatives (the so-called *brichah*). Various organizations were thus simultaneously engaged in this illegal immigration into the new-born State of Israel.

We also need to realize that since the early days of the birth of the State of Israel, the immigration has always been restricted by limits imposed on the number of people able to immigrate under restrictions imposed by the British government—the first such immigration restrictions imposed on Jewish immigration. Restrictions were so severe that at times 700 to 1000 Jewish people per year were given permission to enter Palestine. This is another story, however, even today the Israeli government allots a budget for the covering of Aliyah for only a certain number of people per year. On the other hand, the Aliyah Bet was secret and underground but necessary, as it guaranteed the entry of thousands of people in contrast to the official and restricted avenues of entry to the Land. The Aliyah Bet was the illegal immigration to the land of Israel under the British Mandate's laws during WWII which included the Holocaust.

The Aliyah Bet was organized by the Yishuv[7] (lit. settlement) from 1934 until the declaration of the State in 1948. During Aliyah Bet's fourteen years of activity, 115,000 Jews made Aliyah to the Land of Israel. They came by sea, but also by land and by air to defy the Mandate (the famous Exodus boat brought four-and-a-half-thousand). So, it was because of the Aliyah Bet that the State

---

[6] In the book *"Israel, the Nations and the Valley of Decision"* (Harald Heckert, 2013 - CVI), **Philip Holmberg** wrote an excellent article in which he quotes the various waves of Aliyah stemming from the first one of 1882.

[7] http://palmach.org.il/en/history/database/?itemId=5028

of Israel could grow and thrive amidst all the wars of liberation. Today, the same factors of risk are combining, precipitating a coming "perfect storm" for other waves of Aliyah, both official and non-official as well.

The goal of this book is not of digging deep into the ramifications of the context in which future Aliyah will take place, for all of us understand that the final return of the Jewish people will occur in turbulent times and amidst wars and conflicts.

Let me once again use King Cyrus and quote from Isaiah 45 to explain what I believe will happen, because when carefully considered, there we see another trait of Cyrus' calling that deserves our attention. I am very puzzled by the words of the Lord about King Cyrus, which, to my view, hold a very important message in regard to those now engaged in helping the Jewish quest for their homeland. When the Lord, prophesying about Cyrus says, *"I will give you the treasures of darkness and hidden riches of* secret places" (Isaiah 45:3), He has in mind another specific purpose besides that of raising financial support for the return of the Jews from Babylon. In the Hebrew, *Treasurers of* **darkness** (אוֹצְרוֹת חֹשֶׁךְ – Strong's H#2822) has a particular meaning, like *although God created darkness and uses it to judge His enemies, He enlightens the darkness of His people*, bringing them out of desperate situations, observing secret actions, and giving insight and freedom. Besides, **hidden** *riches of secret places* (מִסְתָּרִים וּמַטְמֻנֵי – Strong's H#4301) refers to *a secret storehouse* and **places** (מִסְתָּרִים Strong's H#4565) stand for places of refuge. In other words, this establishes the biblical basis of an underground, or "not in the front" kind of activity.

"That you may know that I, the LORD, who call you by your name, am the God of Israel . . . I will gird you" (Isaiah 45:3, 5). Only the Lord can enable us to do what He has allowed us to see in His word. No plans or strategies could substitute the Lord's girding. *"He shall build My city and let My exiles go free, not for price nor reward"* (Isaiah 45:13).

In other words, Cyrus' calling goes beyond his decree of freedom for the Jews to go back to their and of promise (*Aliyah Alef*) for there is more here that we have not seen so far. It encompasses a series of non-conventional modes of activities embedded in the words "*Secret Places*" and "*Not for money nor reward*" (*Aliyah Bet*). Mindful of that fact, Christians who hid Jewish families during the Holocaust endangered their own lives and the lives of their family members.

If I may be permitted, I remember that the Lord is calling numbers of faithful believers worldwide who are willing to walk the extra mile in order to fulfill their obligation towards the Jewish people in their way towards freedom. Among the nations, God has sovereignly called people all over the world to assist in hiding and moving Jews out and up to Eretz Israel. It does not come from fancy dreams; it is a clarion call for those who have a listening heart and a willing mind:

> "*Take counsel, execute judgment;* **make your shadow like the night in the middle of the day; hide the outcasts, do not betray him who escapes**. **Let My outcasts dwell with you**, *O Moab;* **be a shelter to them from the face of the spoiler. For the extortioner is at an end,** *Devastation ceases, the oppressors are consumed out of the land*" (Isaiah 16:3-4).

This is a heartfelt invitation from the Lord to make the cause of the fugitive pilgrims their own *raison d'être* and calling. The NASB is even more emphatic in its translation: "*Be a **hiding place** to them from the destroyer*" (Isaiah 16:4 NASB). This is what precisely addresses Isaiah 58:7 talking about the fasting that pleases the Lord: "*And that you bring to your house the poor who are cast out.*" It is in the heart of God specific to true religion—bringing relief and shelter to those who are escaping persecution and rampant anti-Semitism.

A further look at prophecy is found in the revelation of Ezekiel 38-39. This can assist us much in configuring the times of the greatest mass Aliyah wave yet to come. In this regard, going back to the prophetic sequence of events, the internal and external conflicts of Israel that will cause the Oracle of Damascus, culminating in the commencement of the Seventieth Week of Daniel which would ensue in a major conflagration - aka the Gog-Magog War described in Ezekiel 38:1-23 to 39:1-16 which will take place in Israel: *"After many days you will be visited . . . In the latter years you will come into the land"* (Ezekiel 38:8; 39:12-14). It will be at a time when the House of Jacob is regathered and dwells safely in the land:

> ***"In the latter years you will come into the land of those brought back from the sword and gathered from many people*** *on the mountains of Israel, which had long been desolate; they were brought out of the nations, and now all of them dwell safely"* (Ezekiel.38:8).

> *"You will say, 'I will go up against a land of* ***unwalled villages****; I will go to a peaceful people, who dwell safely, all of them* ***dwelling without walls****, and* ***having neither bars nor gates"*** (Ezekiel 38:11).

Unwalled villages, dwelling without walls, having neither bars nor gates clearly depicts a situation of complete quietness, security, and peace at a time when Israel will have gained her security within its newly redesigned borders. I am wholly persuaded that the so-called **One State Solution**[8] is coming soon. This will be a result of difficult times where internecine wars surrounding the Oracle of Damascus with a constellation of forces within and without Israel, will collide in the commencement of the Gog-Magog Conflagration.

How could the regathered people of Israel live in this condition of safety from the attacks within and live without walls and barriers that divide the sectors of Judea and Samaria, Gaza and the south had it not been for exerting sovereignty over these territories? It would not be possible without Israeli administration. It will be a time of distress for both parties involved, and for Israel,

---

[8] Caroline B. Glick, ***The Israeli Solution: A One State Plan for Peace in the Middle East*** (Crown Forum, New York, 2014)

especially, even if it will apparently gain territory as *"In that day it shall come to pass the glory of Jacob will wane and the fatness of his flesh grow lean"* (Isaiah 17:4).

So, the ensuing Gog-Magog War will be ignited by a principality over the region called *Gog* "the chief *principality*" (Ezekiel 38:3) over the spiritual *"powers"* of Magog (lit. "the allies of Gog") who will provoke and influence nations surrounding Israel (excluding those who had been involved in the Oracle of Damascus). Now, under Gog's jurisdiction they will wage war against Israel. These nations will form two confederations, giving way to the formation of the King of the North, comprised of the peoples of modern-day Turkey (Meshech, Tubal, Gomer and Togarmah) along with the modern state of Iran (Persia) and, finally, joined with ancient Cush (aka Ethiopia or, the land between the rivers—i.e., the Tigris and Euphrates Rivers—ancient Assyria/North Iraq).

A "pincer movement" of nations will join with the King of the North (Turkey, Persia, and ancient Cush—the "land the rivers divide" or portions of Iraq) as well as the King of the South, including Egypt, North African Islamic States (aka, Put or Libya), and Libya/Tunisia/Algeria/Morocco and Sudan. This is not the same war mentioned in Revelation 20:8 when Satan is loosed at the end of the Millennium and gathers Gog-Magog from the four corners of the earth to oppose Israel, but the war which occurs on the heels of the Oracle of Damascus (the war with Syria and her proxy powers in which Damascus will cease to be a city and become *"a ruinous heap"*).

The Oracle of Damascus War and the Gog-Magog War will precede the revival of the Third Temple at the commencement of the Seventieth Week of Daniel; however, the Messianic (Fourth Temple) fulfillment mentioned in Ezekiel 40-48 will commence upon the return of Messiah at the close of the 1,290[th] Day mentioned in Daniel 12:11.

It appears that after the Gog-Magog Conflict, the forces aligned with the Merchants of Tarshish (the Western Powers) will defeat the Kings of the North and South and will straight forward hear of *"rumors from the east and north will trouble him"* (aka, the Willful King now appears to march forth to annihilate many in the east and north [Daniel 11:40-45]). Some have conjectured—with good reason—that this will commence, throughout the remainder of Daniel's 70th Week and is known as the "Armageddon Campaign."[9]

The Gog-Magog War, however, will be so fierce it will take seven months (210 prophetic days) to cleanse the dead corps (perhaps due to radiation issues), *"For seven months the house of Israel will be burying them, in order to cleanse the land"* (Ezekiel 39:12).

As of this writing, I wish to bring to our immediate attention the present so-called "Abraham Accord" signed at the White House on 09/14/2020 with the USA, Israel, the United Arab Emirates and Bahrain which shall establish diplomatic relations between Israel and the United Arab Emirates and Bahrain.

It is abundantly clear that Ezekiel 38:13 is in view here. *"Sheba, Dedan, the merchants of Tarshish, and all their young lions will say to you (viz. to Gog-Magog), 'Have you come to take plunder? Have you gathered your army to take booty, to carry away silver and gold, to take away livestock and goods, to take great plunder?'"*

The "economic intent" behind this alliance of nations—siding with Israel in the Gog-Magog Conflagration—finds itself in direct conflict with—in particular—the King of the North anchored by the nation states now comprising Turkey and Iran (in the main). Doug Krieger has for nearly 20 years asserted that the entire Saudi Arabian Peninsula—along with all its independent nations states (including Saudi Arabia, Kuwait, Qatar, Bahrain, the UAE, Oman, Yemen)—constitute ancient Sheba and Dedan. Krieger contends that all of them, for economic reasons, will oppose—allied with the

---

[9] *Things to Come*, Dwight Pentecost, Dunham Publishing Company, Findley, Ohio, 1962, pp. 345-357.

Western trading nations—these formidable Kings of the North and South in accordance with Daniel 11:40-41 . . . allow me:

> *"At the time of the end the king of the South shall attack him* (i.e., the Willful King of Daniel 11:36—who is an archetype of the future Antichrist . . . yet to be the Beast); *and the king of the North shall come against him like a whirlwind, with chariots, horsemen, and with many ships; and he shall enter the countries, overwhelm them, and pass through. He shall also enter the Glorious Land, and many countries shall be overthrown; but these shall escape from his hand: Edom, Moab, and prominent people of Ammon. He shall stretch out his hand against the countries, and the land of Egypt shall not escape. He shall have power over the treasures of gold and silver, and over all the precious things of Egypt; also, the Libyans and Ethiopians shall follow at his heels. But news from the east and north shall trouble him; therefore, he shall go out with great fury to destroy and annihilate many. And he shall plant the tents of his palace between the seas and the glorious holy mountain; yet he shall come to his end, and no one will help him"* (Daniel 11:40-45).

These enigmatic and intensely adumbrative prophetic statements in Daniel place the nexus of the Gog-Magog War upon the Willful King/Antichrist as the central focus of the attack by these Kings of the North and South; whereas, in Ezekiel 38-39 the focus of the attack is Israel; thus, sadly so, Israel finds herself allied with an allied force hardly her ultimate friend but is indeed her archenemy!

The ultimate placement of the Willful King's headquarters in the Beautiful Land is accompanied by future assaults upon the "rumored" antagonists of both the East and North (not the king of the North this time but a state much further north—perhaps Russia and the East being China?). The commencement of the Armageddon Campaign is wrought by the Willful King vs. the rumored states of the East and North. Please note that the West is seemingly obfuscated from these Kings of the North, South and eventually the opposition to the Willful King found in the East. The Three Prophetic Wars MAP will assist in the clarification of these prophetic conflicts—wherein the Oracle of Damascus has for the past eight years commenced, pending culmination:

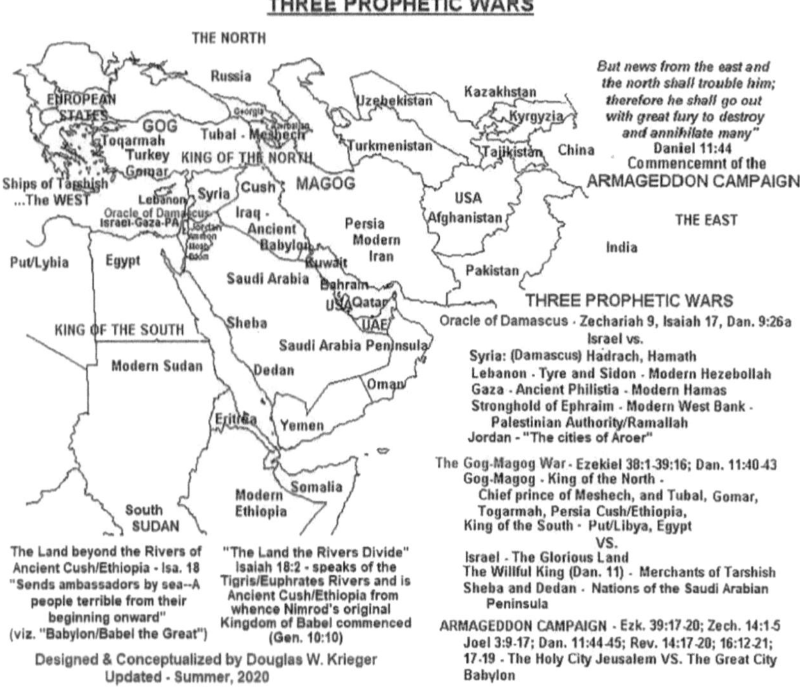

Figure 16 - Map of the "Three Prophetic Wars"

The Lord Himself will miraculously intervene to defend Israel and will destroy the opposing forces while destroying the power of Gog, the principality:

"And you, son of man, prophesy against Gog, and say, 'Thus says the LORD God: 'Behold, I am against you, O Gog . . . I will knock the bow out of your left hand and cause the arrows to fall out of your right hand. You shall fall upon the mountains of Israel, you and all your troops and the peoples who are with you; I will give you to birds of prey of every sort and to the beasts of the field to be devoured. You shall fall on the open field; for I have spoken,' says the LORD God . . . And I will send fire on Magog and on those who live

in security in the coastlands. Then they shall know that I am the LORD. So I will make My holy name known in the midst of My people Israel, and I will not let them profane My holy name anymore. Then the nations shall know that I am the LORD, the Holy One in Israel" (Ezekiel 39:1-7).

It will be a trigger for an incredible spiritual awakening of Jews in Israel where God's Spirit will begin to move upon the remnant as a result of God's mighty intervention on Israel's behalf.[10]

Isaiah 44 offers us a picture of the last days outpouring upon the House of Jacob.

"Thus says the LORD who made you and formed you from the womb, who will help you: 'Fear not, O Jacob My servant; and you, Jeshurun, whom I have chosen. For I will pour water on him who is thirsty, and floods on the dry ground; I will pour My Spirit on your descendants, and My blessing on your offspring'" (Isaiah 44:2-3).

This describes a revival of the Spirit of God descending like streams and floods. Albert Barnes comments on this saying: "This refers, doubtless, in the main, to the period after their return from the captivity, and to the general prevalence of religion then."[11]

Notwithstanding, the third (Oracle of Damascus, the Gog-Magog War, and the Armageddon Campaign) will ensue almost immediately AFTER the Gog-Magog War and persist, even in "times of trouble" up through the final 3 ½ years of the 70th Week of Daniel unto the 1,290th Day when "Desolations" shall cease (Daniel 12:11). It is during this time that revival will break out in both Houses – the House of Judah and the House of Ephraim (aka, the Ekklesia).

The culmination of this Armageddon Campaign is found in Ezekiel 39:17-20 and is entitled the "GREAT SACRIFICIAL MEAL" and is referred in the book of Revelation as "SUPPER OF THE GREAT GOD" (Revelation 19:17-19). This is, quite biblically, judgment day, when the Wrath of God and the Lamb is poured

---

[10] Steve Urick, ***Nowmillenial Dispensationalism***, Author House, 2009
[11] Albert Barnes, ***Isaiah*** (Baker Books, 1998)

out upon Babylon the Great and where the Beast and False Prophet are *"thrown into the lake burning with fire"* (Revelation 19:20) and Satan is bound for 1,000 years (Revelation 20:1-3).

Thus, at the conclusion of these three end-time wars we read in Ezekiel 39:22:

> *"So the house of Israel* **shall know** *that I am the LORD their God* **from that day forward.***"*

In the Hebrew, the verb *shall know* means to properly ascertain by seeing. In other words, on the heels of God's incredible intervention, Israel will begin to experience God for having seen Him in action on their behalf as never before. Moreover, the miraculous intervention would be made manifest among the nations as a powerful witness to God's everlasting purposes on behalf of His people. Not only this, for God's end-time witnesses to His everlasting covenant relationship will be the House of Jacob itself, through a massive regathering back to the Land of promise.

> *"The Gentiles shall know that the house of Israel went into captivity for their iniquity; because they were unfaithful to Me, therefore I hid My face from them. I gave them into the hand of their enemies, and they all fell by the sword. According to their uncleanness and according to their transgressions I have dealt with them, and hidden My face from them."* ***"Therefore thus says the LORD God: 'Now I will bring back the captives of Jacob***, *and have mercy on the whole house of Israel; and I will be jealous for My holy name'"* (Ezekiel 39:23-25).

In this context it is as if God will say, NOW I WILL BRING BACK THE REMNANT OF JACOB. This is the point in the prophetic sequence from which I believe and expect to see one of the greatest mass Aliyah ever seen since the creation of the State of Israel.

> *"After they have borne their shame, and all their unfaithfulness in which they were unfaithful to Me, when they dwelt safely in their own land and no one made them afraid. When I have brought them back from the peoples and gathered them out of their enemies' lands, and I am hallowed in them in the sight of many nations,* **then they shall know that**

I am the LORD their God, who sent them into captivity among the nations, but also brought them back to their land, and left none of them captive any longer. And I will not hide My face from them anymore; for I shall have poured out My Spirit on the house of Israel,' says the LORD God" (Ezekiel 39:26-29).

I am absolutely amazed by these prophetic words announcing a world-wide regathering of the Jews in front of the world. They will be God's end-time witnesses to the powers, leaders, and nations of the earth that there is a God in heaven whose name is the LORD God of Israel.

The mass Aliyah ensuing from the Gog-Magog war will also be fostered by the announcement of the soon to be resumed daily sacrifices in the newly built Third Temple in Jerusalem. It is quite hard trying to describe the excitement mixed with a sense of urgency of the hour that will pervade the minds of those Jews who will make haste in returning to Israel during those days, but it will be an awesome sight to behold.

In any case, the mass influx of Jewish people into the Land of Israel, whether it will start in part prior the Oracle of Damascus, but most certainly after the Gog-Magog war (no doubt at the commencement of Daniel's 70th Week), will spark revival in the nation of Israel and throughout the world. A similar thing happened at the time of the outpouring of the Holy Spirit in the early 1900s which coincided with the first waves of Aliyah soon after the Zionist movement[12] was birthed. Ezekiel prophesied that at the time of the last days' ingathering a great revival will spark.

"And I will sanctify My great name, which has been profaned among the nations, which you have profaned in their midst; **and the nations shall know that 'I am the LORD,'** *says the LORD God, when I am hallowed in you before their eyes"* (Ezekiel 36:23).

---

[12] Theodor Herzl was the founder of the Modern Zionist movement. In his 1896 pamphlet "Der Judenstaat," he envisioned the founding of a future independent Jewish State during the 20th Century.

*"Thus I will magnify Myself and sanctify Myself, and **I will be known in the eyes of many nations. Then they shall know that I am the LORD"** (Ezekiel 38:23).*

"Then the nations shall know that I am the LORD, the Holy One of Israel" *(Ezekiel 39:7).*

Figure 17 - Alex Levin's – "The Third Temple"

Salvation is Coming out of Zion

To me it is clear. God always works simultaneously with His people and the nations. The two are walking hand-in-hand in the plan of God for deliverance and salvation.

Of course, the prophetic context depicting Messiah's intervention on behalf of Israel and Israel's struggle to be ultimately saved by God Almighty is paralleled by what Zechariah 10 shows, moving right into the restoration of the house of Judah gathered back in the land at the end of days, very clearly delineated as the world-wide diaspora, and then the regathering in the last days.

"I will strengthen the house of Judah, and I will save the house of Joseph. I will bring them back, because I have mercy on them. They shall be as though I had not cast them aside; for I am the LORD their God, and I will hear them" (Zechariah 10:6).

After that, Zechariah 11 flashes back to Israel's desolation in their overall 2,000-year history and the false shepherds juxtaposed to the Shepherd of Israel (the Messiah) and then chapter 12 speaks of the Coming Deliverance of Judah and their ultimate mourning for the *"pierced one"* on that day wherein *"I will seek to destroy all the nations that come against Jerusalem"* (Zechariah 12:9)—wrought by Messiah Himself.

Allow me now to look into the timing of the prophetic sequence where Israel will be saved. The ancient Jewish sages and Rabbis confess with one voice that salvation comes to Israel in the hour of their greatest extremity. This is far from supposing that the enemy will not have cruel success and prevail for *"a season and a time"* (Daniel 7:21, 25; Revelation 11:2; 13:5). The ancient Rabbis described Israel's last woes by such terms as, "the birth pangs of Messiah," or, "the footsteps of Messiah."

Throughout the writings of the sectaries of Qumran (the people of the Dead Sea Scrolls) and many of the Rabbinical writings of the Christian period, the view was commonplace that the final redemption comes only at the end of a brief but unequaled time of severity (Jeremiah 30:7; Daniel 7:25; 9:27; 12:1, 11). Furthermore, on this theme, there is one Scripture that I believe has never been adequately unpacked, but that sums up and underscores the entire mystery of the faith, to wit, *" ... **when the power of the holy people has been completely shattered**"* (Daniel 12:7. See also Deuteronomy 36:26).

I believe that here Daniel is speaking about a corporate entity at the end of the age that sees us believers in Yeshua, called out from among the Nations, His elect, together with the Jewish people—but that's a matter for another book. However, there it is, that's where Christ is revealed, at the end of our natural strength and power. That is where the dead are quickened and nowhere else. He alone knows how to take them there, as He will also take His elect from among the Gentiles which will manifest His strength that lies at the end of our strength (Revelation 12:10).

> *"For the deliver shall come out of Zion, and he will turn away ungodliness from Jacob, 'for this is my covenant with them when I take away their sins'"* (Romans 11:26; Isaiah 59:20-21; 27:9).

We need to understand that the Deliverer/Redeemer will come out of Zion to deliver and to save Israel. Messiah is the Deliverer who shall roar out of Zion—*"I will place salvation in Zion, for Israel my glory"* (Isaiah 46:13). It is right there in a place of intense struggle that the Deliverer will come out of Zion. Let us look at what might be the prophetic sequence of events leading up to this mighty deliverance.

Firstly, where does the Lord start to save His people?

In Zechariah 12:7 we read:

> *"The LORD will save the tents of Judah first so that the glory of the house of David and the glory of the inhabitants of Jerusalem shall not become greater* (magnified) *than that of Judah."*

The *Tents of Judah* being saved first, and their honor being held higher? Yes, the Tents of Judah will be the first to be delivered. Judah is a clearly delineated geographical location, central to Israel being the tribal territory right around Jerusalem. That is exactly what the nations are now saying that Israel has not the right to expand Jerusalem and the West Bank—to the east as well.

These Tents could well represent the settlers' commitment to the land, the many caravan communities, the tents, and mobile homes, surrounded by 1.3 million Muslims who have pledged to destroy Israel. There certainly is something incredibly special about these people from Judea and their commitment to the covenant land. Then, the Lord will proceed to defend Jerusalem. *"In that day the LORD will defend the inhabitants of Jerusalem"* (Zechariah 12:8).

It is there that, in respect to the Jewish people, the Lord says:

"And I will pour out on the house of David and on the inhabitants of Jerusalem the Spirit of grace and supplication" (Zechariah 12:10).

The Unveiling of Yeshua

Here is the climactic moment when Messiah will be unveiled before His own people because of the outpouring of the spirit of grace and supplication. *"Then they will look on Me whom they pierced."* **Whom they pierced** in Hebrew is past tense however it is personified as *the pierced one* (Zechariah 12:10). The nail prints in His hands, as the suffering servant are immediately recognizable by the Jewish remnant of the House of David. We can catch a glimpse of the effect that the revelation of the name of God might have had on those who were spectators at the crucifixion of Jesus on the cross when a sign was put over the cross with an inscription *"Jesus of Nazareth the King of the Jews."*

In John 8:28-29 we read:

"Then said Jesus unto them when you have lifted up the Son of Man then shall you know that I AM he."

I AM is another way of saying the holy name of God.

When Pilate wrote Jesus' epitaph, the particular wording he chose displeased the religious leaders who got mad and demanded that the inscription be changed. Pilate knew that the Jewish people are taught to look for signs and acrostic. What we do not notice in the English translation is that the acrostic made up of the first letter of each word spells out Yahweh (YHWH). So, by looking at the inscription over the head of Jesus they could decipher the most sacred name of God, just like Pilate said it would be:

יהוה *Yeshua, HaNatzrei V'Melech Hayehudim* –
(Jesus the Nazarene and King of Kings).

But at which point will the mourning take place? Their grief and mourning upon seeing Him will be Jesus' words coming to pass: *"You shall see me no more till you say, 'Blessed is He who comes in the name of the Lord!'"* (Matthew 23:39). God's ancient covenant people will look to Jesus and repent before He comes back. Jesus clearly prophesied it as He wept over Jewish Jerusalem. In other words, Jesus said He would not return until He is welcomed by His own people in Jerusalem. Peter preached the same message to the Jews in the temple:

"Repent therefore and be converted, that your sins may be blotted out, so that times of refreshing may come from the presence of the Lord, and that he may send Jesus Christ, who was preached to you before" (Acts 3:19:20).

The people of Israel have an appointment with Yeshua, and believe it or not, they are turning to Him now in greater numbers than at any time since the book of Acts.

The meeting point is in Zion, *"The Redeemer will come to Zion, and to those who turn from transgression in Jacob,' Says the LORD"* (Isaiah 59:20). It is there wherein God said: *"You shall know that I, the LORD, am your Savior and your Redeemer, the Mighty One of Jacob"* (Isaiah 60:16).

The mourning and weeping found in Zechariah 12:11-13 brings us to Messiah's unveiling of Himself to Judah in the most personal, intimate, even tender manner.

"In that day there shall be a great mourning in Jerusalem, like the mourning at Hadad Rimmon in the plain of Megiddo. And the land shall mourn, every family by itself: the family of the house of David by itself, and their wives by themselves; the family of the house of Nathan by itself, and their wives by themselves; the family of the house of Levi by itself, and their wives by themselves; the family of Shimei by itself, and their wives by themselves."

The Bible says that every family by themselves shall mourn and weep. What a sight it will be! This is altogether reminiscent of **Joseph's** revealing of his identity to his brethren during the intensity of the famine; it is akin to the time of *Jacob's trouble* and the persecution of God's people at the time of the end (Ref. Genesis 44:1-14). In fact, I would say that the story of Joseph is a type and parable of the comings of Jesus to Israel.

It is in the seven-years of famine that after two years of the famine (Genesis 45:6-10) Joseph's brethren came to him from the land of Canaan seeking provision and ultimate deliverance. The prophetic implications seen in the seven-years' famine will see Joseph revealing Himself to His brethren (the Jewish people). There will be famine, pestilences, and tribulation all over the earth, yet there is salvation and provision through Joseph, the type of Messiah and Savior. As Doug Krieger explains:

"For nigh these 2000 years has He been in the House of Pharaoh providing for the Gentiles His bountiful provisions—until all fully realize that only Joseph can save them."[13]

The phrase, *"Then the remnant of His brethren shall return"* in Micah 5:3, is so profoundly evocative of Joseph's family reunion at the moment of his revelation to his brethren who had formerly rejected and sold him. At the time of the regathering and possession of the land, Israel will be regenerated by the Spirit of

---

[13] Douglas Krieger, **Commonwealth Theology** (Tribnet Publications 2018)

God so as to have a living relationship with Him. The hiding of God's face from the nation of Israel as a whole, ends with the pouring out of the Spirit. But Judah's spiritual regeneration will not be until *"They shall look upon me whom they have pierced"* (Zechariah 12:10 KJV).

This most holy and precious moment will take place at the terminus of the 1290 days found written in Daniel 12:11, *"And from the time that the daily sacrifice is taken away, and the abomination of desolation is set up, there shall be 1290 days."*

These **1290 days** are both 30 days beyond the 1260 days of the latter half of Daniel's final week, allowing for both the rapture of the Church and the terminus of the full 70th week (2,520 days or 7 prophetic years or 360 * 7 = 2,520 days) as well as the **30 days** of the outpouring of the wrath of God and the Lamb for a total of 2,550 days.

Even so, this is the time of the commencement of the final "45 days" unto the 1335th day or the "45 days" beyond the 1,290th day. It seems complicated, I understand, but it is actually very linear and absolutely scriptural.

Therefore, *"Blessed is he who waits and comes to the 1335 days"* (Daniel 12:12). Indeed, *"For I tell you, you will not see me again until you say, '**Blessed** is he who comes in the name of the Lord'"* (Matthew 23:39). **This is what I mean when I say the unveiling of Messiah to His brethren.**

Moreover, the prophetic Scriptures allow us to expand on the scenario surrounding the unveiling, whereby the first verses of Zechariah 13 present a millenarian scene in which a fountain shall be opened up for the house of David and for the inhabitants of Jerusalem for their uncleanness.

"In that day a fountain shall be open for the house of David and for the inhabitants of Jerusalem, for sin and for uncleanness . . . It shall be in that day, says the LORD of hosts, 'that I would cut off the names of the idols from the land, and they shall no longer be remembered. I will also cause the prophets

and the unclean spirit to depart from the land" (Zechariah 13:1-2).

This is a direct reference to all of those who have prophesied falsely that YESHUA was NOT the Messiah, the Son of the living God—they shall on that day be confounded, exposed as false prophets, when the revelation of the true Prophet shall cause the prophets and the unclean spirit to depart from the land. It will be a day when these phony prophets are no more, only the genuine Prophet will stand! The ***pierced one*** can now display the wounds in His hands.

> *"And will say to him: 'What are these wounds between your arms? Then they will answer, 'Those with which I was wounded in the house of my friends'"* (Zechariah 13:6).

This passage is astonishing; there is no way that it does not move you because it is about Yeshua unveiling Himself to His brethren by showing them the wounds between His arms. I believe this is perhaps the most stunning moment in prophetic time! This is when:

> *"The Deliver shall come out of Zion, and he will turn away ungodliness from Jacob, 'for this is my covenant with them when I take away their sins . . . and all Israel shall be saved"* (Romans 11:26; Isaiah 59:20-21; 27:9) . . . *"But on the Mount Zion there shall be deliverance"* (Obadiah 17).

Rachel, the End of Captivity and the Coming of Messiah

In Jeremiah 31 it depicts Rachel, Jacob's wife and the matriarch of Israel, weeping for her children as they were taken into captivity in Babylon.

> *Thus says the LORD:*
> *"A voice was heard in Ramah,*
> *Lamentation and bitter weeping,*
> *Rachel weeping for her children,*
> *Refusing to be comforted for her children,*
> *Because they are no more."*
> (Jeremiah 31:15)

Rachel is mourning in Ramah, a village north of Jerusalem in the land of the tribe of Benjamin. There is no doubt that the Holy Spirit chose to insert into the prophetic record this place because of its significance. In Jeremiah 40:1 it tells us:

"The word came to Jeremiah from the LORD after Nebuzaradan commander of the imperial guard had released him at Ramah. He had found Jeremiah bound in chains among all the captives from Jerusalem and Judah who were being carried into exile to Babylon."

Simply put, when Jerusalem was destroyed by the Babylonians, those taken captive were assembled in Ramah before being moved to Babylon. It was like a staging area for the exiles in waiting to be carried to their final destination. It would be from here Rachel (considered the Matriarch of Israel) would be seen weeping before this despairing sight of the children of Israel being dragged away by the armies of Babylon (her day of remembrance is on 10-11 Cheshvan—the very day the Rabbis accord the coming of Messiah to Israel).

For Rachel it is as though her children are being dragged away from her with no hope for the future. It must have looked very much like those traumatic scenes from films about the Holocaust as families were separated at the train station, parents and children never again to see one another. No wonder that Rachel could not be comforted.

In the New Testament, Ramah is mentioned in Matthew's Gospel (Matthew 2:17-18); where it is stated that Jeremiah's prophecy about Rachel received a second accomplishment in the slaughter of children carried out by King Herod in order to eliminate the Messiah.

"Then what was said through the prophet Jeremiah was fulfilled: A voice is heard in Ramah, weeping and great mourning, Rachel weeping for her children and refusing to be comforted, because they are no more."

Joseph Benson's Commentary on the New Testament confirms that in relation to Herod's cruel edict . . .

". . . extended itself to all the neighboring places, and in particular to this same Ramah, a town of Benjamin, which lay near to Bethlehem, the prophet's words are, with great propriety, applied to this melancholy event likewise, and are represented as receiving a second accomplishment in the bloody slaughter of these infants. And when it is considered that the Jews who were carried captive were not slain, but lived many of them to return again, as the Prophet Jeremiah foretold, to their own border, it must be allowed, that the prediction was much more literally fulfilled on this latter than on the former occasion. This application of the prophecy by the evangelist affords a sure proof that a passage of Scripture, whether prophetical, historical, or poetical, may, in the language of the New Testament, be said to be fulfilled, when an event happens to which it may with great propriety be accommodated."

In Jeremiah 31 we have read that Rachel cries for her children, but she will not be comforted. She constantly mourns over the exile of her children, and the Almighty comforts her with these words:

> *"Thus says the LORD:*
> *'Refrain your voice from weeping,*
> *And your eyes from tears;*
> *For your work shall be rewarded, says the Lord,*
> *And they shall come back from the land of the enemy.*
> *17 There is hope in your future, says the Lord,*
> *That your children shall come back to their own border.'"*
> (Jeremiah 31:16-17)

The Jewish commentators say:

"Literally, 'return to their border' refers to the return of the Jewish people to the Land of Israel. But, more deeply, it refers to the return of our people to our natural spiritual environs: Judaism and our ancestral Jewish nature. These are the borders that truly circumscribe the uniqueness of our people. Amazingly, numerically, the value of the Hebrew word for border' (*g'vul* / גבול) is exactly the same as the value of the word for 'mother' (*eim* / אם); both equal 41. How much more beautiful are the words of the prophet who promises our return to our border, our mother Rachel."[14]

In a moving example of symbolism, this very verse is often sung with emotion at Ben Gurion Airport as new Jewish immigrants arrive in Israel. Once again Aliyah is in view here and as Anglican minister David Ould suggests on this very point:

"The balm for Rachel's tears lies in the very promises that surround the report of her distress. It seems like the end of everything, but it is not. For with God nothing is impossible and His great plans to prosper His people cannot be thwarted. The context of Rachel's tears is the promise of great hope grounded in the love and mercy of God. This is enough to bring comfort to even the most distressed of mothers."[15]

This is an incredible picture of restoration at the end of days concerning the return of the House of Jacob within their borders in anticipation of the coming of Messiah. Besides, the promise of the Son Who will set His people free from the hand of those who hate them (Luke 1:67-75), makes real the adumbrative meaning of Jeremiah's prophecy in that the One who saves His people is also He Who brings to fulfillment all that He has promised on their behalf.

It is with this sense of great expectations the Jews have set a day in their calendar to commemorate Jewish Mother's Day and Rachel on the 11th of Cheshvan. The month of Cheshvan is the eighth month of the Hebrew calendar of the religious year.[16] In the course of history Cheshvan has been a time that has brought much suffering for the Jewish people (i.e. Hitler's Kristallnacht, the infamous pogrom that initiated the Holocaust), but some

---

[14]https://www.chabad.org/theJewishWoman/article_cdo/aid/580778/jewish/Jewish-Mothers-Day.htm
[15] https://davidould.net/fulfilled-rachel-weeping-for-her-children/
[16] The Hebrew calendar is based on both the lunar and the solar cycles. There are twelve months in the Hebrew calendar: Nisan, Iyar, Sivan, Tammuz, Av, Elul, Tishrei, Cheshvan, Kislev, Tevet, Shevat, Adar. The average value is about 29.5 days, months alternating between 29 and 30 days in the Hebrew calendar.

maintain the month of Cheshvan will eventually lose its bitterness because it will be the time in which Messiah will come back to a newly built temple in Jerusalem. Simply put, they say it is relevant because the date of 11ᵗʰ Cheshvan marks the date of the commemoration of Israel's Matriarch, the mother of both Joseph and Benjamin, Rachel, the wife of Jacob (Genesis 46:19)—she died in Bethlehem (Genesis 48:8)—and her tomb is there to this day.

Rachel is seen throughout rabbinical literature to be weeping for her children as they were taken away into Babylonian captivity, but the very date of her death, 11 Cheshvan, is generally seen as the coming date of the Messiah to Israel. In connection with this it is interesting to note this is the only month in the Hebrew calendar where there are no festivals—divinely-appointment times—with neither feast nor fast. That is why the sages have reserved it for Messiah and His coming to Israel.

In other words, Rachel's weeping for her children, from Bethlehem, as Judah was taken into captivity will be over at the coming of the Messiah. It is a rabbinical tradition, I understand, but it is fascinating to know that, according to this rabbinical view on eschatology the coming of Messiah is inherently connected with Rachel's weeping for her children on the way to their captivity in prophetic anticipation of their return on the road of their **Holy Pilgrimage**. Here, it is impossible to overlook the Scriptural fact that Yeshua, their Jewish Messiah, was born in Bethlehem—the very place where Rachel is buried—for it was He Who would make of the two (Jews and Gentiles) one new man, so making peace (Ephesians 2:14-17).

The Unveiling of Messiah

Could it be that the end of Rachel's weeping is fraught with another possible adumbrative meaning of the blessed day of the unveiling of Yeshua to the children of Israel? I believe so. There is more than that, for the prophetic order of the events most likely seems to indicate the day of the coming of Messiah for His national Israel—the unveiling of Yeshua—to be precisely at the conclusion of the Seventieth Week of Daniel and after the out-pouring of the wrath of the Lamb, and at the commencement of the 45 days of blessing[17] found in Daniel 12:12 wherein we read:

> ***Blessed is he*** *who waits and comes to the one thousand three hundred and thirty-five days."*

Let me succinctly explain. Daniel is willing to know the end of all things whereupon the angel reveals to him that from the middle of the Seventieth Week (3 ½ days or 3 ½ years into the 70th Week) the sacrifices in the newly reconstructed temple will be put to a halt by the Antichrist who will be revealed *"so that he sits as God in the temple of God, showing himself that he is God"* (2 Thessalonians 2:4).

> *"My LORD, what shall be the end of these things?"*
> *"And from the time that the daily sacrifice is taken away, and the abomination of desolation is set up, there shall be one thousand two hundred and ninety days"* (Daniel 12:8, 11).

This is the abomination of desolation: *"Therefore when you see the '**abomination of desolation**,' spoken of by Daniel the prophet, standing in the holy place whoever reads, let him understand"* (Matthew 24:15); whereupon the image of the beast will be set up in the holy place; thus, Daniel's prophetic revelations will be validated since *"desolations will continue"* until 1290 days later (Daniel 8:11-14) or 30 days past the latter half of the week's additional 1,260 days. The end of the desolation will come after 1,290 days, the sum of 1,260 days of the second half of the week + 30 days extension beyond the latter half of the Week known as the period of *Great Tribulation* equaling to 1,260 days or 42 months or 3.5 years of time; again, with the final 30 days being the time of the *Wrath of God and the Lamb* (Revelation 6:16-17; 16:1, aka Judgment Day—Joel 2).

---

[17] Doug Krieger speaks of "45 Days of Blessedness" to indicate the period of 45 days beyond the 1290th day, or 30 days beyond the terminus of the Seventieth Week of Daniel. For a detailed prophetic road map of these final days see the books ***The Testimony of Jesus*** (Tribnet Publications 2015); ***Signs in the Heavens and on the Earth . . . Man's Days Are Numbered & he is Measured*** (Tribnet Publications, 2014); ***The Two Witnesses Vol. II*** (Tribnet Publications, 2014).

Then Daniel is told to wait to be blessed on the 1335th day after the middle of the week. This adds an additional 45 days unto the end of the seven years' period, the Seventieth Week of Daniel.

"Blessed is he who waits and comes to the one thousand three hundred and thirty-five days" (Daniel 12:12).

It follows that the additional 45 days unto the 1335 days constitute the days of blessings in which Messiah will reveal Himself to His people in fullness—the coming of the Son of Man in glory. Joseph, the type of Messiah, shall reveal Himself fully during these 45 days of blessedness in which both the *"elect from among the nations"* and the House of Judah (i.e., ALL ISRAEL) shall sit together at the Marriage Supper of the Lamb as *"Blessed are those who are called to the marriage supper of the Lamb!"* (Revelation 19:9). This incredible setting and scenario will ensue during the commencement of the coming on earth of Yeshua, the Messiah, with all the saints (Jude 14) after the 30 days of the wrath of God upon the earth. In light of these prophetic postulates, I strongly affirm the time of the salvation of the Jews will be the time of their complete engrafting and will be synchronized precisely at the time of the unveiling of Yeshua during these 45 days of blessing as per Daniel 12:12 which commences the 45 days of blessing allotted to the coming of the Messiah; again on 10/11 Cheshvan—could this be the date of His coming again in glory? Thus, *"Blessed is he who waits and comes to the 1,335th Day,"* being the literal second coming of Christ, our mutual Messiah. The sequence is undeniable. At the terminus of the Seventieth Week Israel shall be delivered from the wrath of her enemies, then they shall look on Him and shall be saved.

The whole period known as Jacob's Trouble leads up to the unveiling of Yeshua. Furthermore, and it certainly can be so argued, *"all Israel will be saved"*—means full deliverance! This deliverance is wholly dependent upon: *"The DELIVERER* (i.e., the Messiah) *will come out of Zion, and He will turn away ungodliness from Jacob; for this is My covenant with them, when I take away their sins"* (Romans 11:2-27)—delivered physically and most certainly, delivered from sin. Therefore, it would appear that this deliverance is salvific in nature but has embedded within its statement the physical deliverance of Judah at the close of the age. It indeed represents the last scene of the final drama of history, when the deliverer will come with *"Healing in His wings"* (Malachi 4:2), after that *"The kingdoms shall be the LORD's"* (Obadiah 1:21).

This allows me to expand and further look into the dynamics involved at the moment of the Second Coming of Yeshua at the terminus of the 1335th day by considering a final element that is normally overlooked, that is the dimensional shift that will take place on that incredible day. As pastor and best-selling author, Carl Gallups, presents in his outstanding book, ***"Gods of the Final Kingdom,"***[18] the *unveiling* will be at the time when the Bible says that the sky will roll up like a scroll, the stars falling from the sky, the elements disappearing and all of a sudden something is wrapped up, it looks like something that is burned up and everything is disappearing from this side of history.

> *"All the host of heaven shall be dissolved, **and the heavens shall be rolled up like a scroll**; All their host shall fall down as the leaf falls from the vine, And as fruit falling from a fig tree"* (Isaiah 34:4).

> *"And the stars of heaven fell to the earth, as a fig tree drops its late figs when it is shaken by a mighty wind. Then the sky receded as a scroll when it is rolled up, and every mountain and island was moved out of its place"* (Revelation 6:13-14).

> *"You, LORD, in the beginning laid the foundation of the earth, and the heavens are the work of Your hands. They will perish, but You remain; And they will all grow old like a garment; **Like a cloak You will fold them up, and they will be changed**"* (Hebrews 1:10-12).

One of the cataclysmic things that is going to happen in the very last days, right before Jesus is going to unveil His final kingdom—while He will put His feet on the Mount of Olives—is the

---

[18] Carl Gallups, ***Gods of the Final Kingdom*** (Defender Publishing 2016)

phenomenon of everything rolling up like a scroll. It all speaks of a massive celestial shift when the veil will be lifted. The point is that there are multiple dimensions of reality—even God does not live in our dimensional universe as He is not confined within the concept of space and time like we know it.

In other words, as Pastor Gallups suggests, at the restitution of all things there is going to be a cosmic dimensional shift. It will occur at the rolling up of our present dimension when the veil is dropped. Simultaneously, people will cry out for the rocks to fall on them and exclaim: *"How can we hide from the face of God and His wrath for the wrath of the Lamb has come?"* (Ref. Revelation 6:12-17).

Given these fascinating premises, I was able to answer the on-going question I've been asking myself for years, and that many are still asking: How will the Jewish people, who have been marked on their foreheads and forthwith preserved throughout the latter half of the Seventieth Week of Daniel—the Great Tribulation period—who are found alive can simultaneously see Yeshua coming to save them out of Zion? With the lifting of the veil, all things are possible with God, for *"Behold, He is coming with clouds, and every eye will see Him, even they who pierced Him. And all the tribes of the earth will mourn because of Him. Even so, Amen"* (Revelation 1:7). The canopy is therefore completed with the grafting in again of the House of Jacob into their natural Olive Tree of Salvation, and in that day, it shall be that *"all IS-RAEL shall be saved."*

God's timeline, His sacred calendar, does not skip a beat—our "times and seasons" are in His hands. Remember, 10/11 Cheshvan commences the 45-days of blessing. Then upon what day do the 45 days conclude? Right: forty-five days bring us to 24/25 Kislev which is calculated as: 20 days left in Cheshvan + 25 days in Kislev = 45 days. This date is amazingly the Feast of Dedication which had not taken place at the time of Daniel's writing but many years later under the Maccabees—known as the Festival of Lights and better in the Christian Scriptures as the Feast of Dedication

as found in John 10:22-39 where Jesus *"walked in the temple"* –
to wit:

> *"Now it was the Feast of Dedication in Jerusalem, and it was winter. And Jesus walked in the temple, in Solomon's porch. Then the Jews surrounded Him and said to Him, 'How long do You keep us in doubt? If You are the Christ, tell us plainly.'"*

The "heated exchange"—if you would and should recognize as such—is where Jesus *"declared Himself as God in the Temple of God"* (precisely preempting the sordid activity of the yet future manifestation of the Antichrist in 2 Thessalonians 2) because, the astute Jewish authorities knew full-well what He was saying when they said: *"For a good work we do not stone You, but for blasphemy, and because You, being a Man, MAKE YOURSELF GOD"* (John 10:33).

Therefore, it shall be at a yet future Feast of Dedication wherein He shall plainly tell His brethren, according to the flesh, He is, most definitely, their Messiah, their Joseph, their Deliverer. Then shall commence the Messianic Age when Daniel's seven-fold prophecy shall be fulfilled as the Messiah and the Messianic Temple inaugurates the Messianic Era!

> *"To finish the transgression,*
> *To make an end of sins,*
> *To make reconciliation for iniquity,*
> *To bring in everlasting righteousness,*
> *To seal up vision and prophecy,*
> *AND TO ANOINT THE MOST HOLY PLACE."*
> (Daniel. 9:24)

≈ ≈ ≈ ≈ ≈ ≈

Prayer

Lord, You have never wanted us to be ignorant of the mystery of Israel and of the things surrounding their time of redemption, for whatever pertains to the House of Jacob needs to be of our concern because you have elected us out from among the nations to include us within the very Commonwealth of Israel. Thank you for revealing to us that the pilgrimage of your people is a holy thing as it has to do with their final salvation, the return of Yeshua, our coming together into the heavenly and celestial City, and Satan's demise. Lord God Almighty, we await the time when Rachel's weeping shall utterly cease and Your Temple's manifestation shall be dedicated where the Nations shall yearly celebrate the Feast of Tabernacles and where You, as the King of Israel shall rule in righteousness from Your Throne in Jerusalem! Even so, come Lord Jesus!

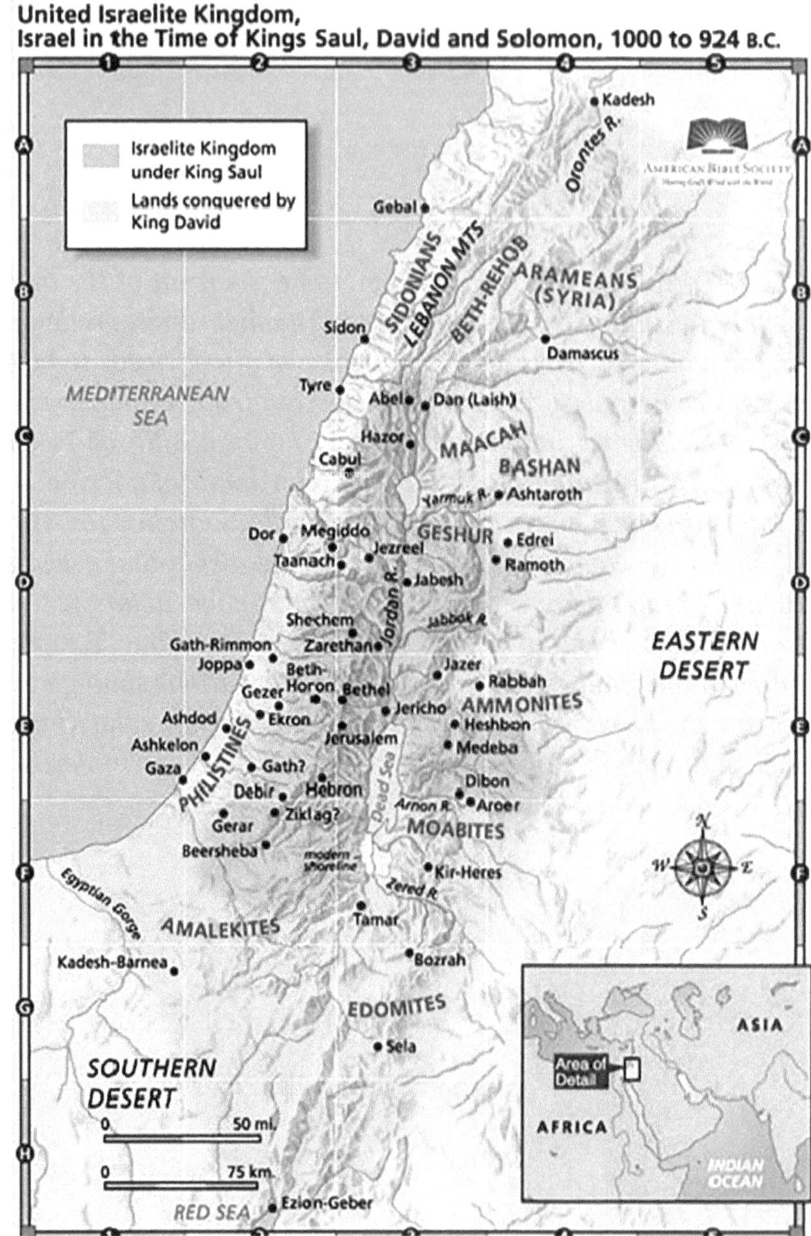

Figure 18- The United Israelite Kingdom

Chapter 9
Called to Family Reunion

"In the latter days you will consider it."

(Jeremiah 30:24)

IN HIS SOVEREIGNTY, THE LORD HAS ARRANGED THAT THE CALL TO A HOLY PILGRIMAGE OF THE HOUSE OF JACOB—TO ERETZ ISRAEL, TO THEIR GOD by means of *teshuvah* and to Yeshua their Messiah—will have definitely been a matter of consideration in these last days. The prophet Daniel wrote that in the last days *"Many will go back and forth and search anxiously* [through the scroll], *and knowledge* [of the purpose of God as revealed by His prophets] *will* [greatly] *increase"* (Daniel 12:4 AMP).

The generation we are living in is the one referred to in the above passage from Daniel. To expound, I wish to take the concept of "need to know" proper of the Intelligence Community, where in specific security clearances you may be handed orders and classified information and told to not open them until you reach your destination (which will be for your eyes only). That means I am not supposed to open them until I arrive at the right place at the right time and they are not meant for anyone else to see. Spiritually speaking, we are living in the generation with a prophetic "need to know."

We are at the right place and at the right time in history where access to our Hebraic Heritage and to prophetic understanding is now available, like never before. The secret still lies in the running to and from the Book, the key to the riches hidden in dark places.

There is More

Most Christians who look at Israel as their prophetic compass are like Daniel of Chapter 9. They are wonderful people, dedicated to prayer and fasting, called to make a difference with intercession, beloved of God and approved by men, except for the fact that they have not yet found the missing link that would enlighten

171

them to see the whole spectrum enabling them to be far more powerful instruments in the hands of the Lord. In other words, they do not see that there is more to it that they realize. Daniel, as well, was intent and busy in praying for His people according to the findings from the scrolls of Jeremiah which would point to the Babylonian captivity coming to an end.

". . . in the first year of his reign I, Daniel, understood by the books the number of the years specified by the word of the Lord through Jeremiah the prophet, that He would accomplish seventy years in the desolations of Jerusalem. Then I set my face toward the LORD God to make request by prayer and supplications, with fasting, sackcloth, and ashes. And I prayed to the LORD my God, and made confession, and said, 'O LORD, great and awesome God, who keeps His covenant and mercy with those who love Him, and with those who keep His commandments, we have sinned and committed iniquity, we have done wickedly and rebelled, even by departing from Your precepts and Your judgments . . . .. We have not obeyed the voice of the LORD our God, to walk in His laws, which He set before us by His servants the prophets. Yes, all Israel has transgressed Your law, and has departed so as not to obey Your voice; therefore the curse and the oath written in the Law of Moses the servant of God have been poured out on us, because we have sinned against Him. And He has confirmed His words, which He spoke against us and against our judges who judged us, by bringing upon us a great disaster; for under the whole heaven such has never been done as what has been done to Jerusalem. As it is written in the Law of Moses, all this disaster has come upon us; yet we have not made our prayer before the LORD our God, that we might turn from our iniquities and understand Your truth . . . .. Now therefore, our God, hear the prayer of Your servant, and his supplications, and for the LORD's sake cause Your face to shine on Your sanctuary, which is desolate. O my God, incline Your ear and hear; open Your eyes and see our desolations, and the city which is called by Your name; for we do not present our supplications before You because of our righteous deeds, but because of Your great mercies. O LORD, hear! O LORD, forgive! O LORD, listen and act! Do not delay for Your own sake, my

God, for Your city and Your people are called by Your name"' (Daniel 9:2-19).

He was so focused on them returning to the Land. This so much pleased the Lord as he was greatly beloved for his passionate desire to help his countrymen. Then, seemingly out of nowhere, the angel Gabriel himself showed up bringing to him a revelation of titanic proportion compared to the one he had just received (Daniel 9:24-27). In fact, because of his prayers and dedication to the welfare of his people, Daniel was given an expanded mind into the future while still absorbed and focused on the **70 years** prophecy of Jeremiah: he received the greater revelation of the **70 weeks** (destined to his people and to Jerusalem):

"Seventy weeks are determined
For your people and for your holy city,
To finish the transgression,
To make an end of sins,
To make reconciliation for iniquity,
To bring in everlasting righteousness,
To seal up vision and prophecy,
And to anoint the Most Holy.
"Know therefore and understand,
That from the going forth of the command
To restore and build Jerusalem
Until Messiah the Prince,
There shall be seven weeks and sixty-two weeks;
The street shall be built again, and the wall,
Even in troublesome times.
"And after the sixty-two weeks
Messiah shall be cut off, but not for Himself;
And the people of the prince who is to come
Shall destroy the city and the sanctuary.
The end of it shall be with a flood,
And till the end of the war desolations are determined.
Then he shall confirm a covenant with many for one week;
But in the middle of the week
He shall bring an end to sacrifice and offering.

> *And on the wing of abominations shall be one who makes deso-*
> *late, even until the consummation, which is determined,*
> *Is poured out on the desolate"* (Daniel 9:24-27).

The incredible thing about Daniel is that he received all this secret intelligence in one prayer session only! The message from Daniel 9 came home: there is always more than we realize. It is as if God were saying to him, "Daniel, the seventy-years' period of captivity is but a launch pad to an even greater set of 'seventies' of which you have never thought. You are looking at the here and now, but there is more in My master plan for your people. Their end is not yet, there is more in store for them, and I want to show you the plan for the ages which has your people as leading figures. Know that I have determined the beginning and the end of their story and I want to use you to reveal it to all future generations because you have sought for the truth with all of your heart." It is in this context of expansion of the divine knowledge—*"In the latter days you will consider it"*—that the full restoration unto salvation of the Tents of Jacob (the House of Judah) is reserved for the latter days. As it was for Daniel, so the Lord looks around to seek for people whose hearts are stayed on Him to reveal His heart and purpose.

End of the Breach–Restoration of the Brotherhood

Albeit great is Israel's restoration, the House of Jacob does not stand alone in the eyes of the Lord, but parallels with the restoration of the brotherhood, which is the reparation of the longstanding feud that occurred at the "Breach of Jeroboam"[1] during the time when Israel became a divided kingdom. Mark this well, the never-ending breach is about to come to an end.

To understand its implications, we need to go back when at the death of Solomon his son Rehoboam, contrary to the elders' wise advice, exerted his authority to increase the treasuries of Judah by imposing upon the Northern Ten Tribes an additional ulterior weight or yoke. Jeroboam, who by divine choice was to

---

[1] Dr. Gavin Finley in: http://endtimepilgrim.org/jeroboam.htm

become king over ten of the Twelve Tribes of Israel, fled to Israel when he heard that Solomon his master had conspired to kill him as he did not want him to become king. Jeroboam returned to Israel as soon as he heard that Solomon had died, complained to Rehoboam, in front of the assembled people about the expropriation of labor and the imposition of high taxes levied upon Israel by his late father; therefore, Jeroboam asked Rehoboam to lighten the burden upon the people. Whereupon Rehoboam responded to the Northern Tribes, after consultation with both the elders of Judah (who cautioned him NOT to levy such additional burdens upon Israel) and then with his youthful contemporaries—who recommended much harsher treatment upon the Northern Tribes, telling them that not only would he not lighten their burden, but he would increase it. The reaction of the people should not have come as a surprise to King Rehoboam. So, the kingdom became divided and split into two houses administered via two kings. The split was a rebellion by Israel against the House of David (the cities of Judah), because of the harshness of Rehoboam, and *"So Israel has been in rebellion against the house of David to this day"* (1 Kings 12:19). Moreover:

> *"There was none who followed the house of David, but the tribe of Judah only"* (1 Kings 12:20). *"What share have we in David? We have no inheritance in the son of Jesse. To your tents O Israel! Now, see to your own house O David! ... Let every man return to his house"* (1 Kings 12:16, 24).

From that moment Israel split into the two separated houses, Judah and Benjamin with the Holy City of Jerusalem continued on in the south; whereas, under Jeroboam the Ten Northern Tribes went their own way establishing an independent kingdom called Israel—later to be referred to as Samaria, Jezreel, and, especially the tribal designation as Ephraim. In the historical sequence, extending over 800 years (cir. 1445 BC to 712 BC), the Ten Northern Tribes (Israel) were conquered by the Assyrians and led into captivity (745-712 BC). They were scattered throughout the nations and largely assimilated among those very nations to become the so-called "Ten Lost Tribes."

After this, Judah, was likewise led into captivity into Babylon some 130 years later (cir. 722 BC to 586 BC). Then after 70 years (607/8 BC to 537 BC) Judah returned to the Land of Israel—specifically Judea. The Ten Northern Tribes (Israel) were still occluded among the nations—*"Israel is swallowed up; now they are among the Nations"* (Hosea 8:8).

Now, the good news. According to Ezekiel 37, in the last days this family feud would come to an end as the Lord declared through Ezekiel, *"Son of man, these bones are **THE WHOLE HOUSE OF ISRAEL"** (Ezekiel 37:11). Please, carefully note, the *"Whole House of Israel"* in its context clearly speaks to the House of Israel and the House of Judah—a divine recognition of their distinction with the prophetic intent: NOT their separation.

Here we have a picture of oneness and inseparable completion. Then, with the use of a symbolic imagery the Lord prophesied that the two houses would be reunited as two sticks becoming ONE stick in the "hand of the Lord." Precisely, the stick of Judah would be taken in the hand of the LORD with the Stick of Joseph, which is in the hand of Ephraim . . . *"and they will be one in My hand"* (Ezekiel 37:19).

> *As for you, son of man, take a stick for yourself and write on it: '**For Judah** and for the children of Israel, his companions.' Then take another stick and write on it, '**For Joseph, the stick of Ephraim**, and for all the house of Israel, his companions.' Then join them one to another for yourself into one stick, and they will become one in your hand. "And when the children of your people speak to you, saying, 'Will you not show us what you mean by these?'— say to them, 'Thus says the LORD God: '**Surely I will take the stick of Joseph, which is in the hand of Ephraim, and the tribes of Israel, his companions; and I will join them with it, with the stick of Judah, and make them ONE STICK, and they will be ONE in My hand.'"* (Ezekiel 37:16-19).

I wish to point out here there are many astute biblical scholars, researchers—both Christian and Jewish—who have either concluded that the so-called "Ten Lost Tribes" . . .

(1) Remain forever lost among the Gentiles.

(2) Were merged into Judah during all these captivities and became Jews themselves, while tangentially maintaining their tribal designations.

(3) Are still being "hunted down"—researchers using modern technologies such as DNA and/or followed up by additional archaeological evidence.

(4) Have been identified among various European nationalities and perhaps other locations among tribal entities in Southwest Asia, Africa, even Pacific Islanders or the Japanese!

However, and notwithstanding the myriad of conjectures as to Israel's whereabouts, there is a far more biblical resolution to the issue. The book of Genesis provides the background to this incredible prophecy which sees Ephraim as a separate stick in the hand of the Lord in connection with Joseph. It is recorded in the incident in which Jacob adopts the sons of Joseph as he imparts the blessing over them. Before blessing Joseph's sons Jacob stands on the promise of God for his life: *"I will make you a multitude of people"* (Genesis 48:4). Rabbi Dr. Justin D. Elwell correctly says:

> "Ephraim and Manasseh are part of this family and dynasty of blessing that goes back from the living God on to their grandparents. They are the first children born in exile and the blessing goes to the child of remembrance. Ephraim and Manasseh were not eligible to be tribes counted among the sons of Israel because they were not direct sons of Jacob, but in the New Testament, we know that when the Lord calls he establishes no matter if we are born in the house or if you are brought into the house, you have the same position in the end."[2]

So, Jacob says, *"Let my name be named in them"* (Genesis 48:16), "May they be worthy of having their names coupled with my own, and those of my ancestors Abraham and Isaac."[3] Jacob blesses Joseph's seed with a double portion to bring them into the Commonwealth of Israel. In adopting Joseph's two sons by Os'nat

---

[2] Rabbi Dr. Justin D. Elwell in *Torah 1 – Genesis* (Syllabus, pp. 66-67 and Audio Lesson)
[3] Hertz, Rabbi Joseph; The Soncino Press, *Pentateuch & Haftorahs* (The Soncino Press, LTD. 123 Ditmas Avenue, Brooklyn, New York 11218; copyright 1960; p. 182)

the Egyptian (Genesis 48:8), Jacob embraces the promise for a *K'hilah-a kahal amim* (the Hebrew for assembly of peoples). He insists that Ephraim will become a *kahal amim*. The blessing opens the door for the adoption of Gentile nations in the days following Messiah's death.[4] In essence and in inescapable biblical fact (not just a metaphor) we gentiles are from Ephraim with a Savior from Judah. It is what I call the **blessing of inclusion** into the Commonwealth of Israel. It all began at the end of Jacob's life when he looked upon Joseph and his two children (Manasseh and Ephraim) and said to him, *"Behold I will make you fruitful and multiply you, and I will make you a MULTITUDE OF PEOPLE"* (Genesis 48:4). Dr Feinberg sheds light into this instance in his commentary in that there is a great significance in adopting Joseph's two children by Os'nat, the Egyptian, because by doing so, Jacob embraces the promise for an ***assembly of people.***[5]

Ezekiel speaks about the stick of Joseph which is in the hand of Ephraim. Now, with Jacob about to bless Joseph's inheritance there is a transfer of heritage in view with worldwide repercussions for the son receiving the blessing would, as well, receive the inheritance. So, Joseph brought the two (Manasseh and Ephraim) near to Jacob for the blessing. Then Jacob stretched out his right hand and laid it on Ephraim's head, who was the younger, and his left hand on Manasseh and gave the blessing saying, *"And let them grow into a **multitude** in the midst of the earth"* (Genesis 48:16).

Displeased about the reversal of his sons' birthright, Joseph attempted to manipulate his father's hands, but eventually the seed of **Ephraim** (which in Hebrew means *fruitful*) was destined to become that fruitful multitude of nations. *"I know my son, I know. He [Manasseh] also shall become a people, and he also shall be great; but truly his younger brother [Ephraim —*

---

[4] Jeffrey Enoch Feinberg, PhD; ***Walk GENESIS!*** pp. 212, 224 (Lederer Books, a division of Messianic Jewish Publishers, Clarksville, Maryland, 1998).
[5] Ibid.

fruitful] *shall be greater than he, and his descendants shall be-come a **multitude of nations**"*—from the Hebrew מְלֹא־הַגּוֹיִם - *melo hagoim* – Strong's H#4393; H1471 (Genesis 48:19). Eventually, Ephraim was destined to inherit the rights of the firstborn and is blessed with populousness. This extended blessing would become the **fullness [i.e., "completeness"] of the Gentiles** (Romans 11:25). In reference to this expansion of Ephraim into a multitude of nations Hosea says *"Aliens would swallow it up. **Israel is swallowed up now they are among the gentiles** like a vessel in which is no pleasure. For they have gone up to Assyria like a wild donkey alone by itself **Ephraim** has hired lovers"* (Hosea 8:8-9).

To be swallowed up means *to be wholly assimilated*, so that now they are among the nations. It happened when God gave a certificate of divorce to the Northern Ten Tribes saying: *"You are NOT my people"* (Hosea 1:9); thenceforth, they were swallowed up of the nations. They never blended into Judah during the Babylonian captivity whereby they became Jews. The so-called Ten Lost Tribes have been scattered among the nations after five Assyrian kings trampled them asunder during their invasions between 745 BC and 712 BC at the time of the final siege of Samaria by the hand of King Sennacherib.

Doug Krieger has, on several occasions, written that over the course of nigh 33 years, the Assyrians brought into captivity somewhere between 10 to 15 million Israelites of the Ten Northern Tribes (based on historical demographers and in relation to the 1,100,000 "men of war" counted among the Ten Northern Tribes by King David, cir. 1000 BC—1 Chronicles 21:5). Yes, some of them returned with Judah when Judah was taken captive into Babylon, but only a small number returned.[6]

When Jesus said, *"Other sheep I have which are not of this fold, them also I must bring"* (John 10:16), He had in view this amazing family reunion. Are we getting the picture here? God, in

---

[6] Doug Krieger, ***Unsealing The End of Days, the Visions, Prophecy & Messianic Scenario of Zechariah*** – p. 358 (Tribnet, 2017)

His sovereignty, has orchestrated during the end-time drama, by the closing of the present age, that the *exiles*, the captives among the nations (the House of Ephraim) and the House of Judah (Jacob) will be reunited as ONE STICK in the hand of the Lord.

Here, it is important to echo at that time of the writings of the Hebrew prophets the Northern Tribes had not yet returned, still the Lord promises to gather them from the nations. In this connection I'd like to quote Dr. Michael Heiser from his ground breaking work, **The Unseen Realm**, because he throws further light into the latter part of Ezekiel 37 (normally left out) and brings the entire concept to the proper level of our understanding, thus, demonstrating the analogy of Scriptures from a well-balanced standpoint. He explains:

> "Part of the reason Jews expected a military deliverer in their Messiah is that the prophets had taught that the regathering of all tribes of Israel and Judah went hand in hand with the appearance of a great messianic shepherd-king."[7]

The passage at hand describing the restoration of all the tribes by the hand of a mighty deliverer is the following:

> *"Thus says the LORD God: Behold, **I am about to take the stick of Joseph (that is in the hand of Ephraim) and the tribes of Israel associated with him. And I will join with it the stick of Judah, and make them one stick, that they may be one in my hand.** When the sticks on which you write are in your hand before their eyes, then say to them, Thus says the LORD God: Behold, I will take the people of Israel from the nations among which they have gone, and will gather them from all around, and bring them to their own land. And I will make them one nation in the land, on the mountains of Israel. And one king shall be king over them all, **and they shall be no longer two nations, and no longer divided into two kingdoms. My servant David shall be king over them, and they shall all have one shepherd.** They shall walk in my rules and be careful to obey my*

---

[7] Michael S. Heiser, ibid – p. 364

statutes. They shall dwell in the land that I gave to my servant Jacob, where your fathers lived. They and their children and their children's children shall dwell there forever, and David my servant shall be their prince forever. I will make a covenant of peace with them. It shall be an everlasting covenant with them. And I will set them in their land and multiply them, and will set my sanctuary in their midst forevermore." (Ezekiel 37:19-26)

On the biblically balanced approach to the regathering, Dr Heiser insists:

"In terms of biblical theology, this expectation was fulfilled in the inauguration of the kingdom of God and at Pentecost. Not only was the reclamation of the disinherited nations launched at that event, but it was accomplished by means of pilgrim Jews from all the nations in which they had been left in exile, now converted to faith in Jesus, the incarnate Yahweh, and now inheritors of the Spirit and the promises of the new covenant. As Paul said in Galatians 3, anyone who followed Christ was a true offspring of Abraham, Jew, or Gentile. Jews from every nation of exile had returned to the land to serve as catalysts for a greater regathering, the apostolic mission of the Great Commission."[8]

I find it fascinating to say the least because it opens the way to a better understanding of the imagery of the Exodus theme throughout the Bible, whose central meaning is that of deliverance and of salvation. The ***Dictionary of Biblical Imagery*** states:

"The exodus motif was used by prophets and poetic writers to transfer the significance of the original Exodus to new situations requiring deliverance, obedience, identity or belief. As great as the deliverance of Israel in the Exodus was, Christ's salvation is greater (Hebrew 2:1-4), salvation of which the exodus is the forerunner."

---

[8] *"Who Are Gog and Magog, and What's So Evil About the North?"* Michael S. Heiser – Wed, November 29, 2017 – Articles @ https://blog.logos.com/2017/11/gog-magog-whats-evil-north/ - Retrieved on 08.05.2020.

Israel and the Church (*Ekklesia*—Ephraim, and the "rest of mankind/Edom" if you would – based on Acts 15:16-17 and Amos 9:11-12) are in transition; however, the Exodus theme cements and bolsters the reunification of the Household of God. It is in the Exodus with its binary facets wherein Judah and Ephraim meet. There is a physical regathering and a spiritual regathering at play.

No More Disorientation & Confusion Over Our Identity

What subsequently amazes me is that Isaiah, as well, confirms the reconciliation whereby light is shed upon another facet of truth where he says that at *last **"the envy of Ephraim shall depart**, And the adversaries of Judah shall be cut off; **Ephraim shall not envy Judah, And Judah shall not harass Ephraim"*** (Isaiah 11:13). This will be the climactic reunion between the two as they will comprise the one elect or chosen people. Before that happens, a number of considerations need to be taken. First of all, we need to realize that the enmity between the Jews (Judah/Jacob) and Gentiles (Ephraim) had four components.

(1) The Gentiles were envious of the special status accorded by God to Israel in the Torah.
(2) The Jews were proud at being chosen.
(3) The Gentiles were resentful of that pride.
(4) There were mutual dislikes of each other's customs.

All of this is coming to an end in the latter days (the "time of the end") as God is restoring all things. I have personally observed this in my own experience, having alluded to this phenomenon in previous portions of this text—i.e., I am a first-hand witness of it.

Speaking of the envy of Ephraim about Judah, allow me to digress here and share from my own experience what I have learned. Several years ago, my wife and I took part in a conference in a European country with international guests and people from different nations attending. The speakers were wonderfully gifted people of God; very humble, down to earth and sound in teaching, but as it is the norm in large gatherings, we came across people we had never met. I remember when at coffee break a peculiar looking lady approached us who turned to my wife saying she had received something from the Lord to tell her. With an expression of excitement, she whispered, "The Lord revealed to me that you have Jewish origins," claiming she had a particular gift of discerning the Jewish identity of people in general. She did this in the hope of moving us to excitement, while on the contrary we were moved to less than enthusiastic, to her evident displeasure.

What I want to say is that these kinds of people normally start in sincerity, then move in naïveté, and ingenuity for some time, but inevitably finish by becoming a fertile breeding ground for those who cunningly try to buy as many people as possible into the error of their sectarian and narrower position, especially twisting and obscuring the true dynamics between our Hebraic Heritage and Christian identity. What I have found in my years of experience is that many sincere believers tend to look at the *Jewishness* side of things with envy springing from an inferiority complex, as so well-depicted by Isaiah in the verse above, which will be only solved (in their view) by embracing a Jewish cultural lifestyle as a means whereby one can be fully accepted by God.

Please do not misunderstand me. I wish to make clear my ministry is totally interwoven with the Jewish people and with the State of Israel. I work with the Jewish people. I try to love them as God requires me to do; I have a special affection in my heart for Jerusalem—from where the Lord called my wife and me to serve Him on behalf of the Jewish people. Moreover, I am in love with the Land of Israel. I have made efforts to learn how to handle the Hebrew language, both in reading, writing, and speaking and among my best friends there are many with Jewish heritage. I have been to Israel more than twenty times (in less than ten years) and will continue to visit the Land regularly as long as I can.

Furthermore, by God's grace, I will defend the right of the Jews to their Land and help them to make Aliyah; speaking on their behalf until death will "graduate" me from this earthly clod. What I want to underscore here concerning the words of Isaiah which I have just mentioned, regarding the jealousy of Ephraim towards Judah, represent a reality which I have been witnessing to for many years—most definitely, there is a reason for this focus. It all comes from either overlooking or obfuscating our mutual participation (viz. between Judah and Ephraim), whereby Ephraim was called out from the nations for the express purpose to be joined with the House of Judah, into the Commonwealth of Israel, the Household of Faith, the entirety of the House of Jacob. What I have noticed over the years is this: hardly anyone dares to tackle this subject because it seems to be too complicated or difficult to understand in the eyes of many, but it is not.

It is one of the simplest truths of the New Testament, yet one of the most neglected ones. In general, regarding our **participation** in the Commonwealth of Israel there is a lot of confusion and disorientation which comes from the false assumption regarding the status of the Church being an ***entity separated*** from Israel or subsuming the Jews, claiming the Church is exclusively Israel. No wonder this broken relationship has been kept in both theological and physical separation.

This is a deep error and seriously misleading because it is based upon a medieval Church tradition going back to Augustine, Constantine, and, most certainly, Origen, even to some of the earliest of the so-called Early Church Fathers, let alone the adjudged heretic, Marcion (cir. 144 AD). Nonetheless, the Church as an entity separated from Israel is not founded upon any biblical truth whatsoever.

The erroneous theological concept that the "Church is a mystery hidden in Christ in eternity past" as an exclusively separate revelation given through Paul having absolutely nothing (aside from types and shadows) to do with the "Ekklesia in the Wilderness" (Acts 7:38) is a tragic misinterpretation, or distorted hermeneutics. The *"elect from among the nations"* are brought into the Commonwealth of Israel"—not separated therefrom!

Virtually, my entire text affirms this theological reality. Similarly, the "we in the Church" vs. "those Jews of Israel" attitude, is evidence of a broken relationship. The "us and them" approach is very definitely being taught from worldwide pulpits in the majority of evangelical circles. In fact, this has become so entrenched as to create a neat separation of paths and destinies where the mainline Bible prophecy teachers proclaim that the CHURCH has a separate role and a separate destiny from ISRAEL and the Jewish house, including their Nation and their Judaism—begrudgingly surmising that in the Eschaton (after the Millennial Reign of 1,000 years, yet future) we might find ourselves together as one People—that will take heaven to pull that one off—even then, the Jews will remain a separate people.

This system of interpretation has produced an unbridgeable chasm between Jews and Gentiles to the extent there is both distinction but irreparable separation. Moreover, those who adhere to this belief system are hostile to their members who show an interest in *Hebrew roots*—imaging and contriving all manner of heresies among those who wish to discover those peculiarities of the House of Judah/Jacob. Consequently, this persistent error in our theology has fueled the blood feud between the "Church" and "Jewish Israel" to this day.

All this feuding has blurred our vision of such divine duality between Israel and His Ekklesia (aka "the Church"). But as I have always believed, the Lord has called us to be *"repairers of the breach,"*—the breach that comes from an ancient animosity going back to a rebellion in Israel that happened nearly three millennia ago, the breach between Rehoboam of Judah and Jeroboam of Israel which divided the Tabernacle of David, creating a split into two separated kingdoms (Israel - North, Judah - South). It is time to put right all historical wrongs and for Christians to bridge the gap that our forebears created.

Do You See it Brethren?

What saddens me most is, despite scores of books published on the subject, the plan of God for Israel—notwithstanding countless conferences and seminars allegedly tackling the topic (which is absolutely good and just to do)—languishes! Our status of co-participation and equality with the house of Judah/Jacob within the Commonwealth of Israel is theologically resisted, diminished, and obfuscated. Some do so for malice, others out of ignorance, and some are simply oblivious—it is not on their radar.

> *"Therefore remember that you, once Gentiles in the flesh—who are called Uncircumcision by what is called the Circumcision made in the flesh by hands— that at that time you were without Christ, being aliens from the **commonwealth of Israel** and strangers from the covenants of promise, having no hope and without God in the world. But now in Christ Jesus you who once were far off have been brought near by the blood of Christ"* (Ephesians 2:11-13).

A word search for **Commonwealth** provides us with its significance for it connotes *polity, community* or the *State* and is corporate in nature—*politeia*—(Strong's G#4174), the relationship that a citizen shares with the State. It brings together Jews and Gentiles in accordance with Romans 9:22-24, which has a profound meaning:

> *"**Even us** whom he **called** not of the Jews only, but also of the **Gentiles"*** (*ethnos* –Strong's G#1484– multitude or nations).

Therefore, what Paul tries to portray in Ephesians 2 concerns those who once were aliens (we Gentiles) who have now been welcomed into a different kingdom—a **United Kingdom**—into which they are no longer slaves or second-class citizens, but can now bask in a position of equality, taking their place and enjoying their new citizenship proper within the Commonwealth.

To enter into the Commonwealth of Israel is to be blessed with the same blessings destined to those who were near because of their status as children of Abraham by lineage—". . . *beloved for the fathers sake"* (Romans 11:28). The statement that the apostle Paul lays out in Ephesians 2 is truly clear. Every person saved, born-again under the blood of Christ, people from every nation race or tribe, yes, even people drawn out of the *goyim* (nations), moved from their previous state *as aliens and strangers and foreigners* to full-blown legal citizenship in the Commonwealth of Israel. In short, from far, from a position of jealousy, if you wish (Isaiah 11:13), we have been brought near to a position of **CO-EQUALITY**! At the time we come to be in Christ, we are simultaneously put into the Commonwealth of Israel. This understanding is what removes the jealousy of Ephraim vs. Judah, without diminishing our love and service for the House of Judah/Jacob. Granted, rightly perceiving our POSITION in the *Commonwealth of Israel* aims at dismantling both Replacement Theology's summation of Jewry and Dispensationalism's implacable separation of the Jews, as both systems abrogate the relationship between Israel and the *Ekklesia*.

In fact, *"He Himself is our peace, who has made both one, and has broken down the middle wall of separation"* (Ephesians 2:13). Ah, yes, but you claim that is only "IN CHRIST." True, but that heavenly reality is just as viable as being within the Commonwealth of Israel! The work of the one who has become our Shalom (peace) is such that the wall that separated us has been broken down. In Hebrew, the middle wall of the boundary fence which separated us is *m'chitzah*, which means, literally, *"that which divides something in half."* Dr. David Stern rightly confirms what Paul said regarding the Gentiles: "They are no longer separated but can now join the Jewish people and be One with them as God's people through faith in the Jewish Messiah, Yeshua".

Therefore, the partition is down, now the Gentiles can join. The Messiah *". . . has broken down the m'chitzah which divided us by destroying in his own body the enmity occasioned by the Torah, with its commandments set forth in the form of ordinances"* (Ephesians 2:15 - The Complete Jewish Bible). This enmity between Jews and Gentiles had four components. The Gentiles were envious of the special status accorded by God to Israel in the Torah. The Jews were proud at being chosen. The Gentiles were resentful at that pride.

Finally, there was mutual dislike of each other's customs. In particular, Jewish customs were different from those of the Gentiles because of the Jewish people's response to the Torah, with its commands set forth in the form of ordinances, later developing into "dogma." Simply put, the enmity or hatred sourced in this dogma has nothing to do with the Torah. In other words, Yeshua did not abolish the Torah in its entirety, but the *takkanot* (rabbinic ordinances and dogma) relating to the spiritual separation of Jews and Gentiles, most definitely erected this hateful barrier, the *"wall of separation."* Nevertheless, the middle wall of the spiritual temple is done away with forever.[9]

> *"To create in Himself **one new man**, from the two"* (Ephesians 2:15).
>
> *"That he might reconcile them both to God in **one body**"* (Ephesians 2:16).
>
> *"Now, therefore, you are no longer strangers and foreigners, but fellow citizens with the saints and members of the **household of God"*** (Ephesians 2:19).

Can you imagine? We were once aliens; now, the sons of the stranger are brought near and included in the great community of faith, **God's Assembly**, with co-equality—distinct yet not separated—partaking of the covenant and blessings promised to Israel. This new spiritual status enables us to freely enjoy the special privileged position of those who have obtained a kingdom and a priesthood.

We who were once Gentiles have now been, through the Blood of Christ, brought into the Commonwealth of Israel, clearly meaning that such a Commonwealth of Israel pre-existed before we ever arrived. Spiritually speaking, now we partake with the Old Testament saints as much as we fellowship with any other believer in the here and now. It's a positional blessing, I dare say, where our citizenship grants us access to a broader fellowship because we have come to *"Mount Zion and to the city of the living God, the heavenly Jerusalem, to the general assembly and church of the first born who are registered in heaven"* (Hebrews 12:22-23).

---

[9] David. H. Stern, **Jewish New Testament Commentary** (1992, Jewish New Testament Publications)

What a positional blessing we have obtained through the Blood of Christ! Yet not everyone sees it or is up to it despite the remarkable words of Peter:

> *"But you are a chosen generation, a **royal priesthood, a holy nation, His own special people**, that you may proclaim the praises of Him who called you out of darkness into His marvelous light; who once were not a people **but are now the people of God**, who had not obtained mercy but now have obtained mercy"* (1 Peter 2:9-10).

Even the word *Church*, as understood in the strictest New Testament sense of the word refers to *"the called out from among the nations"* (aka the Gentiles or *'ethnos'* – Romans 9:24; Acts 15:14)—not simply a physical building or "house of worship." *"God at the first visited the Nations/Ethnos to take out of them a people for His name"*—in addition to the "called" out ones from among the progeny of Abraham, the Jews of Judah, to be *"a people for His name."* The term used for *Church* does not appear in the Testaments; the normative word is the Greek word in the New Testament: ***Ekklesia*** (Strong's G#1577 – used for both **assembly** and for Church). The *Ekklesia* are the elect, the *"called out"* Jews and the *"called out from among the nations"*—together they constitute the One Body, the One New Man, the Household of God.

There is Hope in the Balance of Truth

More illumination from the Scriptures has come to us in these last years in favor of a balanced view which sees the Assembly as an *organic* entity, through seeking the proper knowledge of its components, because God wants us to have a biblically based organic faith wherein Commonwealth of Israel Theology offers to us the keys to interpret this holistic vision while meeting the expectations of any diligent student of the Bible.

In his groundbreaking book ***Commonwealth Theology***,[10] Doug Krieger has *de facto* delineated a new paradigm that combines a theology that does not replace nor subsumes the

Figure 19 – "Commonwealth Theology" By Douglas W. Krieger

Jewish people—yet makes scriptural sense in that the identity of the "Church" in her relationship to the promised New Covenant is intrinsically linked with Israel (aka, Judah and Ephraim). In other words, Krieger postulates that there is DISTINCTION YES (between Israel and the Church) because we see the Jewish people as the House of Jacob (aka Judah) which comprises both believing and unbelieving Jews wherein there is NO SEPARATION, because of their mutual citizenship in the Commonwealth of Israel.

Additionally, unlike any other position, this paradigm affirms that there is no separation from Judah (or the House of

---

[10] Douglas William Krieger, ***Commonwealth Theology, An Introduction*** (Tribnet Publications 2018)

Jacob, the Jews, the broken off branches, those gathered in Eretz Israel in unbelief) and the House of Joseph, Ephraim (the Christians). We, the *elect from among the nations*, have not fully seen our heritage with Judah (ours is a Hebraic heritage), while Judah (most ethnic Jews) have not yet seen His full deliverance of our common calling.

Preparatory to the understanding of the nuts and bolts of the balanced view of Commonwealth Theology, the reader will have to recognize that for centuries the Church (aka, His Ekklesia) has been busy only with herself to the exclusion of the physical progeny of Abraham; thus, completely dismissing the Jewish element of her faith: are not we nurtured from Jewish soil after all? Even though the Church was born out of the Jewish people (this is the internationalization of the gospel going to the nations in fulfillment of the promise made to Abraham), Judah is given short shrift . . . hardly contemplated by the Church as an integral part of the divine equation.

Yes, we affirm Paul's understanding that in Christ there is neither *"Jew nor Greek, there is neither slave nor free, there is neither male nor female; for you are all one in Christ. And if you are Christ's, then you are Abraham's seed, and heirs according to the promise"* (Galatians 3:28-29); however, none of these juxtapositions eliminates the blatant fact that we still "are" Jews, Greeks, slave, free, male or female. What we from among the Gentiles have done is to assert our "Greek" status above that of our "Hebrew" origins! The balanced view of Commonwealth Theology does a new thing, it looks at the future to the time when **ALL ISRAEL** will comprise both the multitude of nations as Ephraim—along with Edom, the "rest of mankind"—and unbelieving ethnic Jews who will experience salvation in Messiah. It sets the record straight, demonstrating that the Church has a responsibility to regard the unity of her components—with the increase in the knowledge of God's purposes over which we now bear special responsibilities. In Commonwealth Theology you will finally see **"ISRAEL"** formed as **THE STICK OF JUDAH** (the Jewish people, both believing and unbelieving) and **THE**

STICK OF EPHRAIM (the *elect from among the nations*).

This clarifies the identity within "**The Commonwealth of Israel**" comprises both believing and unbelieving Jews and the called out from among the nations. In other words, we, as the Stick of Ephraim have a prophetic destiny with the Jewish people (the Stick of Judah) and both of us constitute the whole House of Israel. This paradigm enters the theological arena thereby amending the endless distortions and doctrinal inaccuracies, as well as theological misconceptions which have so long attempted to disinherit both Jews and Christians excluding one another from their common inheritance in the Commonwealth of Israel. The end result of this "mutuality" is that the tenets of Commonwealth Theology provide evidence whereupon the reconciliation of Judah and Ephraim, the repairing of the breach, is *de facto* coming to its conclusion.

How do we know that? Well, if you are careful enough to observe the signs of the times you certainly can concur and conclude we are living in the days of prophetic regathering—the final revival. *Can these bones live*? YES, together they most definitely shall arise a mighty army before the Lord as the breath of the Spirit of God is breathed into them!

As the Jewish people are regathered from the four corners of the world to the Land of Israel, we are witnessing another ingathering taking place—the prophecy of the reunification of the Two Sticks, where both Houses (Judah and Ephraim) are being called home into the "Household of God" (Ephesians 2:19) with each part bearing a prophetic role to fulfill.

Thus, our inclusion into the Commonwealth of Israel brings to our attention the ongoing fulfillment of the prophecy of the Two Sticks being reunited while at the same time repeatedly emphasizing these two components stand as distinct but not separated in the economy of God. Personally, I have been many years engaged in supporting the reunion of the natural branches of the Olive Tree (the ethnic Jews - the Stick of Judah) to their own Land of Israel in fulfillment of a regathering in unbelief (Ezekiel 36) in view of their ultimate salvation; I had been a strong advocate of Commonwealth Theology *without even knowing it*—and convinced, today, many of you reading this for the first time are now being confirmed in your understanding of the same! The practice of anticipating and embracing our prophetic destiny with Judah, looking at the time of our unity in Messiah (when *"All Israel shall be saved"*) gives tremendous credit to the developing of a theology that centers around this final consummation. Prior to this fulfillment, Israel and the Church currently have a prophetic role to play awaiting their most glorious hour when they will be summoned by God to prophesy together during the final drama of history known as Daniel's Seventieth Week. I strongly believe that coming to appreciate our identity in this Messianic Community (The Commonwealth of Israel) will make our quest come to the end; consequently, a much fuller understanding of the phrases found in Revelation 14:12: *"Here is the endurance of the saints who keep the **commandments of God** and the **faith of Jesus**."*

I believe that this balanced approach is one of the greatest advancements in our understanding of the purpose of God in this, perhaps, the latest decade as it really represents a well-balanced view, a wondrous prophetic statement in that unbelieving Jews/National Israel shall one day come into full prophetic fulfillment at the end of days. This is to say that PROPHETIC JUDAH/JACOB/NATIONAL ISRAEL IS ALREADY WITH US IN THE COMMONWEALTH OF ISRAEL BECAUSE EVEN IN UNBELIEF THEY HAVE A MOST PECULIAR PROPHETIC DESTINY FOR WHICH GOD ALMIGHTY IS GATHERING THEM BACK INTO THEIR LAND OF PROMISE.

In other words, we do anticipate, in faith, their grafting in again into the one common root which bears both the natural and wild branches.

Understanding our **collocation**[11] in the Family of God has become quintessential to our enjoyment of the blessing of being in the Commonwealth of Israel because the goodness of the Lord is not only that He cleanses us of our sins—forgetting the past—but that He has lifted us up to a place of honor calling us His people, sharing with us the promises originally belonging only to Israel; only to the House of Judah—for the House of Israel was given a "certificate of divorce" (Jeremiah 3:8). We have not replaced Israel in the plan of God, we only have been awakened to our original but renewed wedding covenant—we have become a new corporeity and citizenship that finds its fulfillment in the soil of Hebraic roots. I know for sure that it is not done intentionally.

Simply put, the Commonwealth of Israel (Jews and Gentiles meeting and sharing the same status in the Household of God) is out of the equation, perhaps because this was not yet the time for the Body of Messiah to apprehend this positional truth? One thing is most certain: if you see it from another angle it is called the One Olive Tree of Salvation—which bespeaks the same thing corporeity and citizenship "organically expressed." The grafting in of the wild branches substantiates the Commonwealth of Israel, the spiritual citizenship of ALL Israel. Our inclusion or collocation brings us near the universal Assembly of the Saints (from both Old Testament and New Testament) through the mediator of the New Covenant. Therefore, the image of the TWO having become ONE, the ONE NEW MAN, and the ONE BODY is a way to explain the multi-diversity of the Ekklesia. From whatever side, you arrive at the same expression, view.

---

[11] Collocations are partly or fully fixed expressions that become established through repeated context-dependent use. Such terms as 'crystal clear', 'middle management', 'nuclear family', and 'cosmetic surgery' are examples of collocated pairs of words. Collocations can be in a syntactic relation (such as verb-object: 'make' and 'decision'), lexical relation (such as autonomy), or they can be in no linguistically defined relation. Knowledge of collocations is vital for the competent use of a language: a grammatically correct sentence will stand out as awkward if collational preferences are violated. This makes collational an interesting area for language teaching. (Source: Wikipedia, Retrieved on 08.05.2020)

It follows that having come close to the Household of God, it allows us to widen our circle, enlarge the stakes of our tent and refocuses our vision.

Gentile Christians who have come to faith in the God of the Hebrew Scriptures (i.e., the "Prophetic Scriptures"—Romans 16:26) have been grafted into God's family Tree of Salvation and covenant relationship—together with the Jewish people we have become fellow citizens in the Commonwealth of God's eternal Israel . . . we are no longer aliens. We are now naturalized citizens of this Commonwealth. We are Abraham's children and heirs according to the promises made by God to Abraham. Christian Scriptures permit believers in Yeshua to join the Jewish people and the Nation of Israel as part of the greater Household of God, sharing both the blessings and the responsibilities of biblical faith so that now, they—those having been shown mercy—have the greater responsibility for establishing the means of coming alongside the Jewish community in true fraternal relationship because the *"elect from among the nations"* have been the greater source of division through its overt persecution of the Jewish people for the past two millennia.

WHERE DO YOU SEE YOURSELF DETERMINES WHO YOU ARE IN THE PLAN OF GOD! Our understanding and appreciation of our citizenship in the *Commonwealth of Israel* can be beneficial to our ministry, and in various ways, the least of which is the fact that the Lord has given us ample opportunity to be a living example of the *collaborative witness* of Gentiles and Jews operating together for a common goal (Aliyah); consequently, believers everywhere, by looking at us, might be enfranchised with a sense of belonging to the *Commonwealth of Israel* with ownership of the vision in the restoration of Israel at the same time. Through any practical work of helping the Jews making Aliyah, it assuredly bespeaks of our full participation in the Commonwealth of Israel. By this example other people may come to see themselves as partners in the restoration of Israel by supporting the Aliyah of the Jewish people.

The Tabernacle of David

Yes, it goes deeper than that, for it is about living in a new spiritual dimension. God, in fact, does not save us just to give us a status but He comes to us having something in view, our participation in the rebuilding of the Tabernacle of David. He proclaims in Amos 9:11 "*I will raise up its ruins, and rebuild it as in the days of old*"—yet He will do so with human instrumentality, just as He always has done by "stirring up the spirit" (Haggai 1:14) of those called to rebuild the ruins of His Tabernacle once again. I believe this is the additional component to the whole plan of the Almighty. In Acts 15 the apostle James uses the prophecy of Amos to be significant of the coming in of the Gentiles into the blessings of David. From Acts 15 we understand our God promised this through the prophet Amos He would build again "*The Tabernacle of David*," by taking out from among the Gentiles a people for His name.

"*After this I will return **and will rebuild the tabernacle of David**, which has fallen down; I will rebuild its ruins, and I will set it up; **So that the rest of mankind may seek the Lord, even all the Gentiles who are called by My name**,' Says the Lord who does all these things*" (Acts 15:16-17).

In Volume II of the Trilogy on Divine Habitation (**The Tabernacle of David**) Dr. Kevin J. Conner confirms:

"James, the apostle, by a word of wisdom, quotes from the Amos passage and applies it to the coming in of Gentiles into the Messianic Kingdom and the movement of God among the Gentiles. The Church would be composed of Jews and Gentiles. It should be remembered that the New Testament Apostles are the infallible interpreters of the Old Testament Prophets. The Old Testament Prophets foretold the coming of the Gentiles into Messiah's Kingdom . . . God did visit the Gentiles in the house of Cornelius to take out of them a people for His name, as Peter had already testified":

"***On that day I will raise up The tabernacle of David***, *which has fallen down, and repair its damages; I will raise* *up its ruins, and rebuild it as in the days of old;* **That they may possess the remnant of Edom, and all the Gentiles who are called by My name,**' *Says the LORD who does this thing"* (Amos 9:11-12).

I cannot turn a blind eye to my Italian origin and say that I am very proud of my ancestry when I remember that it was to the House of Cornelius, the Italian Band, to whom the gospel of the grace of God was initially opened—in point of fact it was this House of Cornelius which was the center of Peter's remarks at the Acts 15 "Jerusalem Council."

Also, in Acts 15 it speaks not only of the remnant of Ephraim (so implied in the unity of the United Kingdom seen in the Tabernacle of David), but likewise, "*so that the rest of mankind*" (Amos 9:12) may seek the LORD, even all the Nations (aka "Gentiles") who are "*called by My name.*" This allusion by James bespeaks of Amos 9:12:

> **'"That they may possess the remnant of Edom, And all the Gentiles who are called by My name,'** *Says the LORD who does these things"* (Amos 9:12).

Commenting on this passage from Amos, **The Pulpit Commentary** (pp. 177, 178) sheds light into the meaning of Edom vs. "*The rest of mankind*" of Acts 15, to wit:

"The Septuagint (LXX) gives us this: '*That the remnant of man may earnestly seek the LORD,*' regarding Edom as a representative of alienation from God and altering the text to make the sense more generally intelligible. '*Which are called by my Name*' ("*Over whom My Name has been called*"'– Septuagint)". This is closer to the Hebrew, but the meaning is much the same, viz. all those who are dedicated to God and belong to Him being by faith incorporated into the true Israel of God.

God has let us in so that we could have communion with Him as David did. He went in before us to demonstrate it was possible to gaze on the glory of God in the Sanctuary of the Tabernacle. Even greater would have been the glory that the Lord would have bestowed on us, the living Tabernacle of His presence. If you were David gazing on the glory inside the tent, what would you remember after you left? The tent of the manifested glory of God? It is the gazing on the glory that allows the King to be enthroned—observed as the One dispensing grace upon the United Kingdom of David.

When we look at Jesus, we cannot but see Him as the peacemaker between the two, *so making peace.* Jesus Himself becomes the very gate to the Family, the Household of God. So, not only do we come close to one another, but to the most precious pearl of great value, the Root of the Olive Tree of Salvation, the entrance to the spiritual family, the mediator of the New Covenant.

The Healing of the Envy

Returning to the Isaiah 11:13 passage: ***"the envy of Ephraim shall depart . . . Ephraim shall not envy Judah."*** I remember one evening after speaking about God's plan for Aliyah and the Jews at an open camp meeting in Italy, I was approached by a good friend of mine who said to me, "You speak so well, you must be a Jew." Well, I would not mind that at all; I believe it was a particularly good compliment as I really wish I had the in-depth knowledge of the biblical Hebrew of a Rabbi, but that's the reality of some people today as they perceive a golden image of forbidden mystical aura around this subject.

Perhaps in ignorance and not purposely, nevertheless it is there. To teach that God has a plan for Israel is absolutely right and due, but it is a part of the big picture. The result is that I have witnessed scores of Christians coming out of Replacement Theology only to find themselves after a while into **OPPOSITION THEOLOGY**, a term I have coined to define *the anti-Church behavior that has caused partitions between groups of Israel-only-people on the one hand and on the other hand, all others, to the detriment of a balanced view between the teachings of the First Covenant and the New Covenant in the Ekklesia of Jesus Christ.*

All of the above happens because of an inferiority complex. However, if people would just take time to investigate the Scriptures for their benefit (remember Daniel 9 – there is more) they would discover with amazement all things given to the Jews, were extended through the New Covenant to the Gentiles as well. Then the Ekklesia would progressively find its lost path and the peace so much wanting, thereby bringing them back in the camp. As Dr. Garr points out very well in his book when he says that in seeking to reclaim our biblical Hebrew heritage:

> ". . . we must be careful that we do not establish a new elitism that brings judgment and condemnation upon those who do not understand these concepts. If we are to adopt a truly Judaic mindset, we will maintain tolerance for others, and we will shun the development of yet another creed that establishes another orthodoxy and further divides the body of Christ."[12]

I am much confident that as the Word of God declares, one day ***"the envy of Ephraim shall depart .... Ephraim shall not envy Judah,"*** but that also ***"Judah shall not harass Ephraim"*** (Isaiah 11:13). On the latter, *"Judah shall not harass Ephraim,"* we need to ask why those within this part of the House of Jacob have been hostile to us believers. In simple terms because we have never done anything to approach them; we've never considered them; we have stolen their promises and relegated them (i.e., the Jews) to a theological ghetto by separating them from us.

We saw in the early chapters where many are those who have embraced the call to repair the longstanding breach by acting out in love according to the declarations of the Hebrew prophets wherein one day Gentile believers would willingly take part in the process of the restoration of the Jews to the Land of Israel. So, the envy and the hostility are coming to an end. More people will perceive a clarion call to go back to the complete Bible (it was A. W. Tozer that once said that 'it takes a whole Bible to

---

[12] John D. Garr, ***Our Lost Legacy***, chapter 19 (Golden Key Press, 2006)

make a whole Christian'). Thus, the Ekklesia Jesus is building, in order to withstand the *"gates of Hades"* will awaken from her slumber to embrace her roots, partake of its nourishment, get back to the apostolic way—then signs would follow, revival will come, and many children will come back to its tents while all carnal ministries will cease to exist.

Sadly, the scarcity of sound teaching in the Body of Messiah has caused many to leave her shores to embark upon a journey which has brought them to places where they still hunger for more. Another personal note. Besides my first period in London (England) where I met the Lord in 1994, I was born and bred in Italy (as a believer) in the main, within a Pentecostal denomination, where the motto was, *"All the Gospel—the Full Gospel"* as if to say, "We hold all of the Truth." It did not take me long to find out their claim was spurious, to say the least. As years went by, it became evident that essential pieces of God's mosaic were missing to give credibility to that claim put at the forefront. This was one reason why I was inspired to pursue the missing components of the One True Faith and to become a seeker of what I felt was "balanced truth."

Thus, need for a paradigm shift in the original teaching I was given if I were to somehow recover the old paths, the ancient ways, in which to dwell. There is more to teaching on the love of God for Israel only—*"I will bless him who blesses you, and curse those who curse you"* (Genesis 12:3). On the starting block I would put a balanced view of the **engrafting** or **inclusion** into the Family Tree of Salvation, which would open the way to the understanding of the Hebraic Heritage of the Christian Faith. It is all about our position as Gentiles obtained when born again into the Household of God. The envy of Ephraim is ceasing as the Lord is shedding light into our participation as partners with the Jewish people in the covenant promises of the New Covenant—even in those whose vision extends but to Genesis 12:3.

By teaching the supreme truth embedded in His Ekklesia whereby our engrafting into the Family Tree of Salvation is championed, we become restorers of *"streets to dwell in"* (Isaiah

58:12). Looking back at **Abraham** is paramount in understanding the **Inclusion** and in helping in the task of getting back our **lost status as citizens in the Commonwealth of Israel**. The key to understanding the *"root and the branches"* metaphor in Romans 11 lies in looking at the Jews called the *natural branches* because they boast a lineage derived from both paternities: they are the children of Abraham and the children of Abraham by faith (when they believe in Yeshua). The Gentiles, on the other hand, are called the *wild branches* because they are children of Abraham only by faith, not by birth. So, it is faith that determines the **Inclusion**, not ethnicity (Galatians 3:1-18)[13]

Therefore, when Gentiles are saved by Israel's Messiah, He brings them into His eternal covenant. Jeremiah 30-31 paves before us the entire plan of God concerning this great restoration with Jacob (the House of Judah) being gathered to the Lord. His mercy has been shown to the House of Ephraim (the Gentiles) whereby both Houses are included in the New Covenant—for they have always been so included (Jeremiah 31:31: *"Behold, the days are coming, says the LORD, when I will make a new covenant with the house of Israel and with the house of Judah"*). It is through the new birth they take on their new identity in the Commonwealth of Israel (Ephesians 2:11-13). As Dr. Gavin Finley states:

> **"Nowhere** in the Holy Scriptures does God **ever** speak of two covenant peoples. **Nowhere** in Holy Scripture do we see one salvation plan for Israel and another for the Church. All who have been saved, or ever will be saved, are saved by the same plan of salvation. They are saved by grace through faith in Israel's promised Sacrifice Lamb."[14]

One Body, One Flock

This is what is needed, a comprehensive understanding of the

---

[13] Douglas R. Shearer, **Calvin on the Ropes**, 2009

[14] Dr. Gavin Finley, MD, in http://endtimepilgrim.org/elect.htm. Dr. Gavin Finley is a pioneer of Commonwealth Theology and the editor of the website www.endtimepilgrim.org, a ministry dedicated to helping us in understanding the mystery of the Commonwealth of Israel.

mystery as explained in Ephesians. First of all, there is one passage which rivets my attention as I read about the ONE BODY. In fact, the entire exposition by Paul has to do with the Gentiles becoming fellow citizens, no longer aliens, and PART OF THE SAME BODY, the Body of Messiah, which is the True Israel. Paul well-said **THERE IS ONE BODY** (Ephesians 4:4). The Holy Spirit opened my understanding while reading this and associated it with "then **ALL ISRAEL** *shall be saved*" found in Romans 11:26.

Perhaps we should change our paradigm on the way we have seen the "*All Israel*" up till now?[15] Unless we understand Torah and the way Paul taught us with his rabbinical background, we will never be able to connect the mysteries Paul is trying to bring forth from the "Prophetic Scriptures." In Ephesians 3, when Paul talks about MYSTERY, he is going into Torah teaching while explaining it. There are things that in Christ the people of old could not comprehend (such as the new birth as the greatest miracle of all). So, what is this mystery?

Simply put, that the Gentiles should be fellow heirs of the same body (Ephesians 3:6). In all Systematic Theology you have two bodies, two houses (Israel and the Church kept separated), but in Jesus there is One Body. Just because someone is Jewish does not mean they are part of that One Body. This is the Remnant grafted into the One Olive Tree (that is why we are connected with Israel). Then, to make all see what the fellowship of the mystery is altogether essential (Ephesians 3:9). In other words, what is my connection in that mystery?

The New Testament provides ample proof of this reality. I remember years ago the Holy Spirit enlightened me expanding this concept while reading John 11:52. In this instance, the High Priest, Caiaphas, prophesied with John, the Beloved, extending

---

[15] There is great book by Chad J. Schafer and Doug Krieger which delves into this aspect of ALL ISRAEL. It pretty much has to do with the two houses of Israel—Judah and Ephraim. The book is called ***The World in the Bondage of Egypt . . . Under the Triumphal Arch of Titus*** (Tribnet Publications 2016)

his prophecy beyond the immediate:

*"'You know nothing at all, nor do you consider that it is expedient for us that one man should die for the people, and not that the whole nation should perish.' Now this he did not say on his own authority; but being high priest that year he prophesied that Jesus would die for the nation, **and not for that nation only, but also that He would gather together in ONE the children of God who were scattered abroad**"* (John 11:49-52).

When I saw this, I exclaimed: "It is right there in plain sight; how could I have not seen it before, we are ONE?" Yet, there are many today who when they read John 11:52 *"Not for that nation only, but also that He would gather together in one the children of God who were scattered abroad"* either consider those "scattered abroad" are only Jews, since they conjecture "all Jews" constitute all Twelve Tribes or generic believers in Messiah from all the nations (including the Jews) who have received the New Covenant given to the Church as a result of the Kingdom's rejection by the leadership of the Jews at the time of Jesus' earthly ministry. However, what John said in these passages (John 11:47-53) is utterly profound. Let me repeat, John said that *"Now this he* (Caiaphas) *did not say on his own authority; but being high priest that year he prophesied that Jesus would die for the nation"* (i.e., for Judah) . . . then John doubles down and declares: *"And not for that nation only, but also that He would gather together in one the children of God who were scattered abroad."*

What could John have meant by this additional statement? The nation in the eyes of Caiaphas simply meant the Jews of Judea, but John amplified it to include not only the Jews of Judea but all Twelve Tribes scattered abroad as did James, the half-brother of Jesus in James 1:1, *"James, a bondservant of God and of the Lord Jesus Christ, To the twelve tribes which are scattered abroad."* The recognition of these so-called "lost tribes" (i.e., Ephraim, the Ten-Northern Tribes of Israel taken into captivity) *"He would gather together in one the children of God who were scattered abroad."* We simply cannot isolate these prophetic statements made by John from those rehearsed by Paul in his epistle to the Romans when Paul quoted from Hosea regarding the Gentiles inclusion into the Household of Faith:

". . . and that He might make known the riches of His glory on the vessels of mercy, which He had prepared beforehand for glory, even us whom He called, NOT OF THE JEWS ONLY, BUT ALSO OF THE GENTILES? As He says also in Hosea: 'I will call them My people, who were not My people, and her beloved, who was not beloved.' 'And it shall come to pass in the place where it was said to them, 'you are not My people,' there they shall be called sons of the living God'" (Romans 9:23-26).

And, this, Paul said in direct reference to Israel-Ephraim who had been divorced and were no longer His people!

I have also come to apprehend that the mystery is solved in the words of Jesus in John 10:16 where he says, *"And other sheep I have which are not of this fold; them also I must bring, and they will hear My voice; and there will be **ONE FLOCK** and one shepherd."* Like in the days of Jesus, He is still operating among His children as He wants people to open their eyes that they might see the reality of the one flock. One day He said, *"You do not believe because you are not of MY SHEEP"* (John 10:26). Jesus talks about one flock and ONE sheepfold. To me it is perfectly clear. When I read Romans 9:24 I see another glaring evidence that ***"Even us whom He called, not of the Jews only*** *(The House of Jacob/Judah),* ***but also of the Gentiles"*** (The House of Ephraim, those who were swallowed up of the nations).

Those whom He called are none other but the Ekklesia Yeshua is building in the here and now, the assembly of the called out (comprised of both Jews and Gentiles)—the *"gathering of the Lord."* And again, just after this incredible statement Paul goes on describing the Gentiles/Nations by quoting directly from Hosea:

"I will call them My people, who were not My people, and her beloved, who was not beloved. And it shall come to pass

in the place where it was said to them, 'You are not My people,' there they shall be called sons of the living God" (Romans 9:25-26; Hosea 2:23; 1:10).

In other words, Paul directly identifies Ephraim's presence within the context of the Gentiles/Nations wherein they were assimilated, swallowed up.

But it is in the New Covenant's elucidations in both Jeremiah and in Ezekiel described as *"an everlasting covenant with them"* (Ezekiel 37:26) which we see the two becoming as one. This *"covenant of peace"* mentioned in Ezekiel, is in point of fact, the very NEW COVENANT—SO MAKING PEACE then and there. Yes, Ephesians 2:15—for there is but one New Covenant Peace!

". . . that He might reconcile them both to God in ONE BODY through the cross, thereby putting to death the enmity". . . "to create in Himself **one new man** *from the two, thus making* **peace"** (Ephesians 2:15-16).

First, the New Covenant promise was exclusively made *"with the HOUSE OF ISRAEL and WITH THE HOUSE OF JUDAH"* (the two houses) which are then addressed in Jeremiah 31:33:

"But this is the covenant that I will make with **THE HOUSE OF ISRAEL** *after those days, says the LORD: I will put My law in their minds, and write it on their hearts; and I will be their God, and they shall be My people."*

Here we can see the TWO HOUSES as **ONE and only ONE House of Israel.**

As per the New Covenant I do not see different Covenants as dispensationalists affirm keeping apart Israel and the Church thus creating a dichotomy. Nor do I see, as John Nelson Darby taught, that the Ekklesia of our Lord Jesus simply enjoys the "spiritual blessings of the New Covenant but not the New Covenant promised," exclusively to Israel (as per his understanding of who constituted Israel). The list of those who keep the Jews ghettoized is exceedingly long.[16]

Suffice it to say that disassociating Ephraim from the Nations/Gentiles is theologically incorrect, for they were assimilated and lost among the nations but now through the blood of His Cross those who were **afar off** have been brought nigh and are no longer strangers but are considered *"members of the Household of faith!"* They are "Citizens of the Commonwealth of Israel" and are, therefore, no longer aliens. Moreover, the original promise of the New Covenant (Jeremiah 31:31-36; Ezekiel 36:26-27) and its spiritual blessings were and still are committed to both Houses of Israel (the Twelve Tribes of Israel), and all the more in that Ephraim's dispersion among the nations was God's ultimate intention of expressing the entry of the Gentiles into the Commonwealth of Israel. This is the greatest expression of the call to a family reunion.

Expressed in another way, Jacob's call to family reunion is but a shadow of the UNITY we are called to keep in the Body of Christ. Jesus prayed for unity of all believers down to our present day:

> *"I do not pray for these alone, but also for those who will believe in Me through their word; that they all may be ONE, as You, Father, are in Me, and I in You; that they also may be ONE in Us, that the world may believe that You sent Me. And the glory which You gave Me I have given them, that they may be one just as We are one: I in them, and You in Me;* **that they may be made perfect in ONE**, *and that the world may know that You have sent Me, and have loved them as You have loved Me"* (John 17:20-23).

"That the world may know"—on this earth, in the here and now, not in the sweet by-and-by. When this UNITY of which Jesus

---

[16] For a comprehensive and extended treatise on the erroneous theological system that keeps Israel and the Church separate please read the groundbreaking work of Douglas Krieger, **Commonwealth Theology**, Tribnet Publications, 2018 @ https://www.amazon.com/Commonwealth-Theology-Douglas-W-Krieger/dp/1977951643/ref=tmm_pap_swatch_0?_encoding=UTF8&qid=1592055967&sr=8-7

earnestly prayed for will be reached here on earth, then the *Ekklesia* will be given herself to a prevailing witness to principalities and powers in the heavenly places of the manifold wisdom of God. She will be ready to meet her Bridegroom whereupon it will be as Jesus said, *"Many will come from east and west, from the north and the south, and sit down with Abraham, Isaac and Jacob in the kingdom of heaven"* (Matthew 8:11; Luke 13:29). The best is yet to come!

≈ ≈ ≈ ≈ ≈ ≈

Prayer

Father, we long for the day when all of your Royal Family will be together—for You have said: ". . . the scepter shall not depart from Judah." Now we see in part, but Oh, what is coming, when we will experience perfect fellowship within the Household of Faith! We will be sitting and dining with Abraham, Isaac, and Jacob and then we will turn our eyes upon You, the only One worthy of all glory, who died and rose again to purchase, through Your redeeming blood, your adoring Bride, and then we will spend eternity with You in perfect fellowship—even the fellowship you, our Bridegroom, the Eternal Son, has always had with the Father.

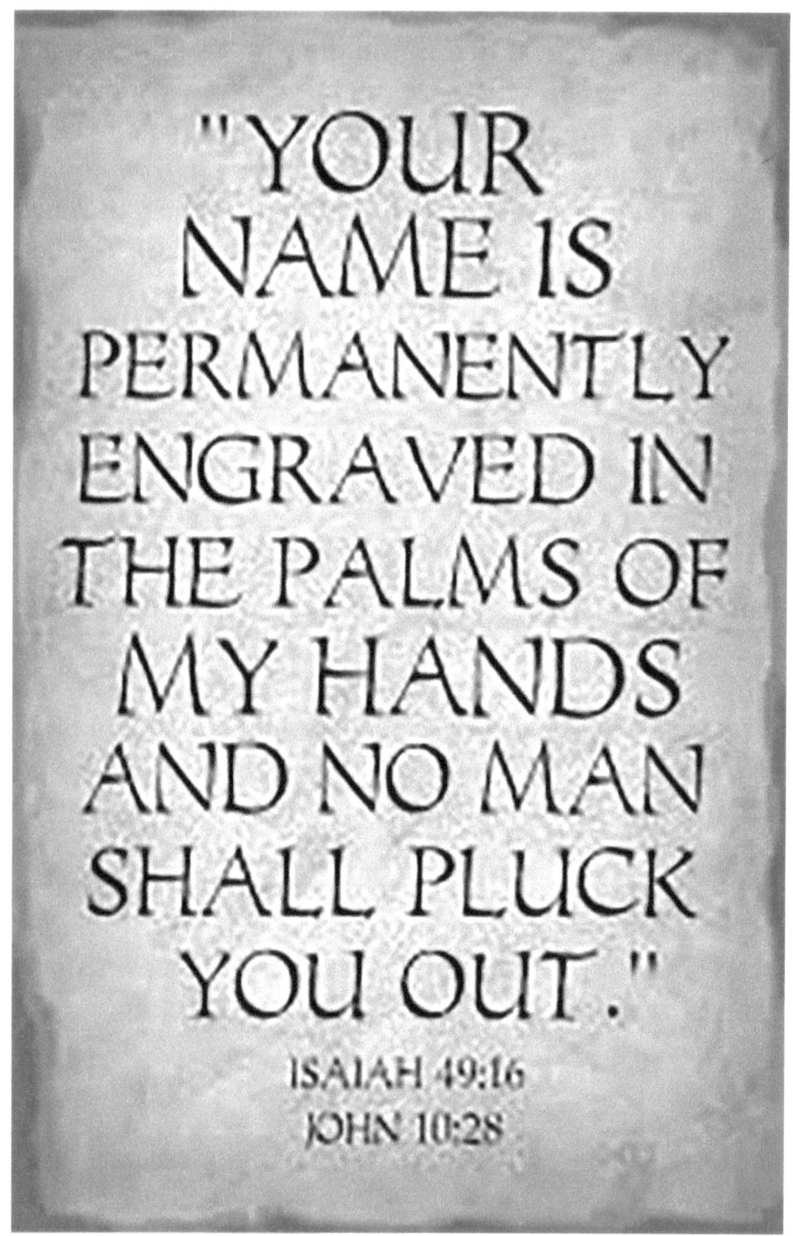

Figure 20 - Isaiah 49:16 - John 10:28

Chapter 10

Called to Be Prophetically Engaged

"And now the LORD says, Who formed Me from the womb to be His Servant, To bring Jacob back to Him, So that Israel is gathered to Him.... Indeed it is too small a thing that you should be My Servant To raise up the tribes of Jacob, And to restore the preserved ones of Israel; I will also give You as a light to the Gentiles, That You should be My salvation to the end of the earth."'

(Isaiah 49:5-6)

IT IS MY FIRM BELIEF THAT IN REFERENCE TO THE MISSION OF THE SERVANT FORESEEN BY ISAIAH 49, AND THE FACT THAT HE WAS FORMED AND FASHIONED TO be a light to the Gentiles, does not belittle nor circumvent His initial and leading role in gathering Jacob back to Himself. Suffice us to look at the modern State of Israel, which, based on the preponderance of Scripture, I conclude to be the fulfillment of Bible Prophecy, the in-gathering of the exiles, a most important stage in their **Holy Pilgrimage**, even in unbelief, who are positioned in their land awaiting the coming of the Messiah whom we, as Christians, affirm to be the glorified Son of Man, the Lord Jesus Christ.

Thus, I strongly trust that we are called to a commitment to bless Israel (*"Blessed is he who blesses you, and cursed is he who curses you"*—Numbers 24:9); while simultaneously affirming the love and concern for all non-Jews, in particular, those peoples throughout the Middle East. There are incredible testimonies of how the Holy Spirit is moving in powerful ways even in the countries surrounding Israel, like Syria, Lebanon, and Jordan just to name a few, let alone Iran where even now a great revival of souls is coming forth to faith in the Lord.

Therefore, in light of these "geographic revivals" and many other places—especially, in the refugee camps in both Jordan and Syria where many are turning to the Messiah, our Lord Jesus Christ—there can be little doubt that in these extremities God Almighty is truly on the move.

Thus, to assert that National Israel (the House of Jacob) is disqualified from the plan of God is a misnomer at best, and a theological aberration at worst. Those who adhere to a Replacement Theology mindset say that today's Israel has no eschatological bearing whatsoever, that it is to be a gathering place for Jacob's trouble, and that the Church is now the new spiritual Israel (in any event), do themselves and Israel a great injustice by not seeing their grafting into the Olive Tree of Salvation called ISRAEL, which still awaits its natural branch to be grafted into the same root that bore the wild branch; namely, the House of Jacob, to be grafted in again. Those pretending to be liberal pundits, unwittingly take part in what is a *Rejection Theology* by considering the Jews theologically irrelevant, but *"God has not rejected His people whom He foreknew"* (Romans 11:2).

We have seen that the solution to the plight of Jacob springs from the Lord, as all acts of righteousness are God ordained. Henry A. Wirkler said it right by claiming:

"... those who understand salvation history as primarily continuous, generally view all Scripture as relevant for the believer today, since they believe there is a basic unity between themselves and believers throughout Old and New Testament history. Dispensationalists in the first half of the 20th century, who saw Salvation history as primarily discontinuous, tended to believe that only the book of Acts and the Church Epistles possessed primary relevance for the Church, since the remainder of Scripture was directed to believers who were under a different biblical economy. Many significant theological issues are affected by the way one resolves this question."[1]

I could not possibly agree more! Likewise, it applies to the relationship in existence between the born-again believer and his/her participation and sharing in the Commonwealth of Israel. One of the voices representing those who are committed to the cause of the Jews through assisting them in their journey to their homeland of Israel is Martin Shoub, who justly says that the

---

[1] Henry A. Wirkler, **Hermeneutics**, Baker Books, 1981

Church must no longer leave Israel and the Jewish people out of the salvation picture by pointing out that Aliyah is central to the Gospel of Jesus Christ and that it is imperative to assist the Jews back to Israel where Yeshua shall be revealed to them as a nation.[2] Sad to say, for many today there seems to be no connection between the modern State of Israel and the people of Israel that is in the Bible; furthermore, no continuity between the ancient people of God and today's Israelis. Those who do not perceive any connections nor continuity are shortsighted in that they cannot discern the significant import that the gathering of the House of Jacob back to the Land has in the prophetic understanding of the end-times. Thus, in disbelief, they are unwittingly putting a stone of stumbling before the way that leads to salvation on behalf of God's ancient people.

The Restoration of All Things

It is the supremacy of the Scripture alone which validates them, the Jews, who have been called to a **Holy Pilgrimage** from the beginning of time. It sets the record straight by declaring the gathering of the exiles, from beginning to end, is in mercy. Isaiah 54:7 says, *"For a mere moment I have forsaken you, but with great mercies I will gather you."* Considering these prophetic promises, I believe responding with certainty to questions like, "Why do you support Israel by helping the House of Jacob reaching their land if afterwards they will have to suffer and die another massacre worse than the Holocaust?" . . . should be answered now. This is because standing with Israel is what makes us prophetically engaged where our current engagements need to go beyond a check box having but superficial understanding of the times with a view toward the final fulfillment.

Therefore, I am all the more persuaded that there is a need for a holistic biblical view between what we teach and do. What

---

[2] Martin Shoub, *To the Jews First*, 2017

is my reasoning behind this comprehensive answer to our critics? Listen, what we do and teach can be better understood by those who observe us in terms of the contribution we give to the significance of the whole. Firstly, this applies when we talk about the *end-times* because I have often observed a natural, if not spontaneous, tendency of keeping the return of Jacob to the land apart from the context in which its biblical truths are found. This has led to misunderstandings, especially in those within the Body of Messiah who are always ready to find faults. In this light, we need to allow the Word of God to convince, instruct, and produce fruit for His purposes on earth. This offers me an opportunity of stressing the importance of the notion of being called to be a *Repairer of the Breach* in Isaiah 58:12, "*And you shall be called the Repairer of the Breach, the Restorer of Streets to dwell in*". If we were to follow the trails of history, we would find that multiple factors concurred in widening the breach between the foundations of our Christian faith and the practices of today's modern Church.

Perhaps the main culprits are to be found in the allegorical method of Bible interpretation which allowed the disintegration of the binding element between its Hebraic context and Church practices leading to Replacement Theology—which to this day claims its adherents in ever growing numbers. In addition, centuries of Gentile practices and traditions have created a breach of titanic proportions between the *Ekklesia's* origins rooted in Judaism and the modern Church which exists today. When non-Jewish Church fathers were no longer feeding on the nourishing sap of the Jewish olive tree and as Greek philosophy infiltrated the Church, the followers of Jesus, mostly Jewish, found themselves as a growing minority as Gentiles flooded into the Assembly. Dr. Garr sums it up by saying that "Constantine outlawed any practice rooted in Judaism transplanting the teaching of Jesus into the foreign soil of human tradition."[3]

---

[3] John Garr, *Our Lost Legacy*, Golden Key Press 1998 – p. 22

Thus, the partition between the Church and Israel was followed by the failure in recognizing that the system of praise and worship and service that was manifest among the Hebrew prophets, kings and sages (Judaism) was a means of God to introduce Himself to the nations of the earth. Concerning this breach, I've heard the messianic pastor of Kehilat HaMaayan of Kfar Saba, Israel, mentioning the split occurred between the Julian and the Jewish calendar, at the time of the Laodicean Council in 336 A.D., when the switch to Sunday keeping was authorized, allowing for the systematic excising of Christianity from its Jewish roots, depriving it of the blessings connected with the Feasts of the Lord, of which Shabbat is the Queen[4] (eighty four times in the New Testament Shabbat is mentioned, either in reference to Jesus and/or the Apostles).

Dr. Bill Hamon has written a book on the masterplan of God for His Eternal Church in which he examines the progressive separation of the Church from its Hebraic roots, expounding upon the transformative transition into a structure rather than keeping its spiritual life properly oriented and in compliance with the "Prophetic Scriptures" which attested to the coming of the Jewish Messiah as the Ekklesia's mediator of the New Covenant—that "root" was cast aside for a more Greco-Roman philosophical accommodation approved by the Roman governance of the day. Thus did the Early Church Fathers succumb to these vain philosophies and traditions of men who despised the "religion of the Jews" and their "histories" (viz. the Bible).

"Christianity became favorable to Constantine because of a supernatural experience he had on the eve of the battle of Milvian Bridge, just outside Rome (October 27, A.D. 312). He saw in the sky, just above the setting sun, a vision of the cross, and above it the words, 'In this Sign Conquer.' He decided to fight under the banner of Christianity, and he won that crucial battle. Constantine made Christianity the religion of his court and encouraged his constituents to become Christians when he made Christianity the

---

4 Tony Sperandeo, *The Feasts of the Lord*, Saturday, September 6, 2015, Evangelical Church in Modena (Italy)

state religion of the Roman Empire. His decree forced all Roman Empire subjects to formally accept Christianity in order to maintain their citizenship, hold office, and carry on business. This was the final blow to the message of repentance, conviction of sin, spiritual rebirth, and the need for a transformed life in order to become a Christian."[5]

When Emperor Constantine provided Christianity the seal of legitimacy as the official religion of the Roman Empire, he offered the churches his protection with intellectual and financial support. Religion endorsed Replacement Theology as it pertained to the Jews by evolving a hermeneutic which claimed Christian triumphalism supplanting the "rejected Jews."

Thus, from that time onward this burgeoning Church-State Matrix completely severed the Church from its Jewish roots. Christian Rome ended the usage of the Jewish festival calendar, including the Jewish Shabbat and feast days which we based upon Jewish Scriptures—all these *"Feasts of the Lord"* were filtered almost exclusively through a Greco-Roman paradigm—*ipso facto* through Paganism. The sword of the state enforced the new laws by Constantine's edict. These horrific laws, requiring separation from the Jews and compelling the Christians to, in essence, despise them, established official state-sponsored anti-Semitic policies.[6] In other words, Christians have been denied a great legacy through centuries of ecclesiastical Judeophobia, anti-Judaism, and anti-Semitism. Mosley teaches:

"The church at Rome was admonished by Paul that the Christian faith was never intended to be a repudiation of its Jewish Roots but rather, the engrafted Gentile Church was actually a branch that grew out of these roots. He also asserted that the Jewish background of the Church was of great benefit because it was out of that Hebrew culture that the oracles of God were given. The essence of these teachings is that without Judaism there would

---

[5] Dr. Bill Hamon, *The Eternal Church* (Destiny Image Publishers, 1991)
[6] Merrill Bolender, *When the Cross Became a Sword*, 2011

be no Christianity."[7]

On this regard, in His sermon at Pentecost the apostle Peter foresaw that prior to the second coming of Jesus there would be a time marked by the restoration of all things when he said:

"Repent, then, and turn to God, so that your sins may be wiped out, that times of refreshing may come from the LORD, and that he may send the Messiah, who has been appointed for you—even Jesus. Heaven must receive him until the time comes for God to restore everything, as he promised long ago through his holy prophets" (Acts 3:19-21 NIV).

Many are those who underestimate these words as they are not concerned with knowing what are the things to be restored prior the coming of Jesus; yet, Peter says plainly that the holy prophets have left a trail of these things in their prophetic writings. There is no doubt the audience was familiar with the promises of God for certain things to be restored. Dr. John A. Looper gives the best response you could ever have on what these promises are:

"The question remains then as to what aspects of the restoration are necessary and relevant to our generation to further prepare the way for Messiah's second advent. There are at least two significant restorations for our generation for which the prophets call. The first is the Aliyah or regathering of the Jewish people from the four corners of the earth to the land of Israel. The second is the full restoration of the church to the roots and faith of its Judeo-Christian heritage."[8]

I believe that this is the answer to the growing opposition which is found even among the most conservative evangelicals to any form of commitment for the cause of Israel. As we have progressed toward the restitution of all things, each generation since the early Church has been given the task of maintaining the faith that was first delivered to the saints and to grow by standing on

---

[7] Ron W. Moseley, Chapter 2 in **Yeshua, A guide to the Real Jesus and the Original Church** (Messianic Jewish Publishers, 1996)

[8] Dr. John A. Looper, *Aliyah. Let us go up to Jerusalem*, in Restore! A Publication of Hebraic Christian Global Community, Vol. 11, No 4.

the shoulders of past generations (as we saw in Chapter 2), until we finally reach the measure of the stature of the fullness of Christ. Yet people repeatedly argue *ad libitum* saying, "You are wasting your time in helping the Jews; just preach the gospel to every creature, this is our mandate after all." This view is consistent with what Isaiah solemnly declares that "**NO ONE SAYS 'RESTORE'**" (Isaiah 42:22); there is no one interested in the prophetic importance of the restoration of the Jewish people to their own land.

I would go one step further. By denying the regathering of the exiles in fulfillment of the prophetic Scriptures, we are, as well, denying "*God is able to graft them in again*" (Romans 11:23), for this is said in the context of this statement: "*. . . how much more will these, who are natural branches, be grafted into their own olive tree?*" (Romans 11:24). And again, within the context: "*And so all Israel will be saved, as it is written: 'The Deliverer will come out of Zion, and He will turn away ungodliness from Jacob'*" (Romans 11:26-27).

Moreover, is not the "Gospel of the grace of God" supplemented with the divine satisfaction whereby we sinners have obtained mercy, spared from the wrath of God due to our sin—our Savior having taken the penalty, justly due, for our sin giving us "*peace with God?*" Yes, He has. But, as well, this gospel wrought peace between hostile peoples through the same "*blood of the cross.*" The best of evangelical preachers seems consumed with the Gospel of Salvation but are they, in the main, oblivious regarding the Gospel of Peace in the making of the ONE NEW MAN, so making peace?

They oft concur with the "Gospel of Peace" then shrug their theological shoulders and spend their remaining days thinking they are preaching the full message of that gospel via discharging their understanding of the Great Commission without further ado to the Almighty's desire in defeating the powers of darkness through the Gospel of Peace: "*And the GOD OF PEACE will crush Satan under your feet shortly*" (Romans

16:20)—said in context of Paul's consummation regarding Romans 9-16 dealing with the Oneness among God's people—the Jews and the Gentiles.

To prevent this cancer's spread I believe we would do a great service fostering a paradigm shift in those in theological opposition if we taught this gathering of the House of Jacob unquestionably falls within a prophetic scenario demanding an appropriate understanding, at least of the sequence of events which are part of it or are to be unfolded wherein the Scriptures have an answer (*"Surely the Lord God does nothing, unless He reveals His secret to His servants the prophets"*—Amos 3:7). Thus, a correct prophetic knowledge could help in defining the role of the various ministries in the Body of Christ (What we do? Where we came from? Where we are? Where are we going?), whilst, the lack of proper comprehension could lead to ignorance and misconception regarding significant prophetic events that will see the Jewish people involved, their return, and the role of nations involved.

For instance, should we believe in the coming of a future Islamic Antichrist, as in fact biblically it is not, and at the same time we would not bother nor be concerned with the coming of a man from the West that would deceive Israel by seemingly assisting her, even forcing her to sign on to a Peace Treaty which would include the rebuilding of the Temple in Jerusalem. Alas! Then, we could end up organizing a conference or write books in praise of the great success the Israeli leadership will have gained through the intervention of this benevolent leader who deign would provide such diplomatic and pragmatic assistance on their behalf.

On the contrary, should we not have the clear understanding on the matter, whereby we would avoid praising the work of such a surreptitious and deceitful figure, known in the prophetic Scriptures as the final Antichrist? Would we not desire to fervently pray for those who would be deceived by dedicating ourselves to further prayer and fasting on behalf of our Jewish compatriots by mourning for them to be delivered from such a satanic scam? Especially, if we live in the time predicted by Daniel, when a body among the people would rise up to tell the truth of the times: *"And they that understand among the people shall instruct many"* (Daniel 11:33).

We should profit by discerning men of God like G. II. Lang, who wrote:

"When this agreement shall have been confirmed, the wise will know that the final seven of years has commenced, that the end days are present, and that the consummation of the age has arrived. They will expect the violation of the covenant after three years and a half, and will not be overwhelmed with surprise, having been told beforehand by this prophecy. Then will it be seen in fullness that the knowledge of prophetic Scripture is simply priceless."[9]

As in all things pertaining to *"rightly dividing the word of truth,"* especially in the matter of prophecy, it is imperative to be reminded of some basic hermeneutical principles to avoid the error of the *"untaught and unstable people"* as found in 2 Peter 3:16 who *"twist the Scriptures to their own destruction."* Here Dr. Hamon comes again to our aid when teaching on prophetic applications when he writes:

"Most prophetic Scriptures have two applications: natural and spiritual; individual and corporate. A prophetic Scripture can apply to natural Israel, the Messiah, and the Church, and not do injustice to the principle of biblical hermeneutics. It can have a natural fulfillment with Israel, personal fulfillment in Jesus, and then a spiritual corporate fulfillment in the Church."[10]

I consider this to be the Golden Ration for interpreting the prophetic Scriptures. At the same time, I cannot more emphatically reiterate that we need to be a people engaged in prophecy as we are approaching a time in which the darkness of hell will be released upon this earth. We are, I believe, that final remnant

---

[9] G. H. Lang, *The Histories and Prophecies of Daniel*, 1942 (out of print)
[10] Dr. Bill Hamon, page 130

who need to be spiritually prepared, as well as psychologically and physically alert and at our peak for the days ahead. We live in a time where many believe Biblical Prophecy is not necessary and that everything will pan-out or that those who will live should just "cool it." "Just preach the gospel," they sincerely or sarcastically entomb, not considering the fact that the announcement of things to come is an integral part of the Gospel's message.

Jesus said, *"But take heed; see, I have told you all things beforehand"* (Mark 13:23). Regarding the *"all things"* Jesus told us beforehand, I believe it is better to take a stand rather than taking a distance, especially when we consider that the Lord is calling out the *"multitudes in the valley of decision."* If the world stands on a precipice, the Church finds herself before a major shift where decisions need to be taken. This is the season in which the old adage applies: "If you do not stand for something, you will fall for everything".

In becoming biblically relevant we must get our priorities straight in these last days. This can only be achieved by being accurate in our elucidations regarding the end of days. Arthur Pink gave the basic principles of hermeneutical prowess:

" . . . the absolute necessity for strictly conforming all our interpretations to the general Analogy of Faith: that each verse is to be explained in full harmony with that system of Truth which God has made known to us: that any exposition is invalid if it clashes with what is taught elsewhere in the Bible."[11]

Incorrect theories need to be answered, now. For example, as stated earlier (in reference to Jacob's Trouble and the aforementioned "three prophetic wars"—the Oracle of Damascus, the Gog-Magog Conflict, and the Armageddon Campaign climaxing in the Wrath of God and the Lamb), one of the most popular questions has to do with the meaning of the 2/3rd cut-off (die or lost) but 1/3rd left in the land to be brought through the fire to be refined

---

[11] Arthur W. Pink, ***Interpretation of Scriptures*** (Sovereign Grace Publishers, Inc – 2002, p. 39)

as silver as revealed in Zechariah 13:8-9. These "prophetic fractions" are closely related to the mission and calling of those ministries who are engaged in supporting Israel—they are used to ridicule their supportive purposes. The narrative of those who oppose anything that is done on behalf of the Jews (especially, by Christians) has as its basis the erroneous belief that the Great Tribulation (or after the *"Abomination of Desolation . . . then there will be great tribulation, such as has not been since beginning of the world until this time, no, nor ever shall be"*—the words of Jesus—Matthew 24:21) will be for "Jews only."

This general second "chamber of horrors" is normally followed by: "So, why are you wasting your time manning the bilge pumps when the Titanic is sinking in any event?" "Your time and talents," they say, "would be much better utilized if you aggressively launch an evangelistic campaign to 'save the Jews' rather than gathering them from ultimate destruction and chastisement!" I know, harsh words, but this is a quite common reaction to our efforts. In this regard, I believe the *Rev. Willem J. J. Glashouwer's* insights offer a thorough explanation as to why we believe that passage in Zechariah does not refer to a future Holocaust for the Jewish people. Here are some of *Glashouwer's* statements for your consideration (January 2017):[12]

> And Israel? After all the slaughters throughout the centuries, there remain only about 15 million Jews in the world. In Israel live about six million Jews, in a land with no oil. Another four to five million live in the USA, about one to two million in the former Soviet Union, and the rest still scattered around the globe.

> Indeed, the prophet Zechariah prophesied about Israel in Zechariah 13:8, *"'In the whole earth,' declares the Lord, 'two-thirds* [of Israel] *will be struck down and perish; yet one-*

---

12 You can access the full article here: https://www.c4israel.org/_teachings/jerusalem-the-un-and-the-times-of-the-gentiles/. Christians For Israel International is the leading ministry in providing educational material on Israel.

third will be left in it.'" And when one adds up all the numbers of Jews who have been massacred throughout the ages, the statistics reveal that in history, two thirds of the Jewish people have been wiped out, and only one third is left. Even if one translates Zechariah 13:8 as "in the whole land," meaning "Eretz Israel," the "land of Israel," this prophecy has been fulfilled as well. At the hands of the Romans in 70 AD and 135 AD, over two million Jews were slaughtered, and the rest, almost totally, were led into captivity — although there have always been Jews living in Israel, also during the last 2000 years!

When we add the numbers of the killing of the Jews over the centuries—with the final slaughter of six million under the Nazi-regime in Germany—the conclusion can be drawn that over the ages, two thirds of the Jews have been wiped out, and only one third is left.

So to think that in the near future, Israel will become "one big Auschwitz" during the "time of Jacob's trouble," the "tribulation," is not necessarily according to Scriptures, *although difficult times for Israel are still to come.* In Jeremiah 30:7 and Daniel 12:1, we read that Israel will be saved in these terrible times, not destroyed—cleansed, but not wiped out. Yes, *the remaining one third will be cleansed by fire, but not destroyed*—cleansed in order that the pure gold will remain (see Zechariah 13:7-9).

The process of redemption has started, not the process of annihilation. The order of events listed in Zechariah 13:7-9 describes the history of the Jewish people in a nutshell. First, the Shepherd Jesus is killed. Then the people of Israel are scattered. Then two thirds perish, even the little ones—1.5 million children were murdered in Auschwitz. *Then the remaining one third in the land will be purified* so that in the end: *"They will call on My Name and I will answer them; I will say, 'They are My people,' and they will say, 'The Lord is our God'"* (Zechariah 13:9b).

In retrospect to the above comments made by Glashouwer, Doug Krieger's perspectives on the 2/3rds vs. 1/3rd add additional possibilities to Glashouwer's perspectives:[13]

"Today's worldwide Jewish population approximates 23.5 million (based upon the Law of Return)[14] with the Jewish population in Eretz Israel approaching 6,900,000 or approximately 75% of the total of nearly 10 million inhabitants in administered areas (Israel proper and the so-called "territories").[15] Since these nearly 7 million Jews in Eretz Israel are roughly 1/3rd of the 23.5 million to 20.7 ("Jewish connected populations"), I find it as a possible explanation of the 2/3rds vs. 1/3rd with the 1/3rd "sealed in Eretz Israel." Also, another explanation may be the account of the 2/3rd vs. 1/3rd found in 2 Kings 1 where King Ahaziah of Israel's Ten Northern Tribes sought healing from Baal-Zebub, the god of Ekron (viz., the Devil himself!); whereupon (but with great apprehension) King Ahaziah sought confirmation of this devilish encounter with the prophet Elijah—prior to Elijah's rapture in the fiery chariot (2 Kings 2).

"The adumbrative language of "final judgment" seems to be envisioned in the King Ahaziah/Elijah exchange where three groups of Israel's soldiers (50 soldiers + 1 captain = 51 * 3 groups = 153 total) are sent to Elijah by King Ahaziah to inquire as to this "healing prospect." The first two contingents are consumed by fire from heaven in Elijah's presence with the final contingent pleading for mercy and receiving it from Elijah (surviving the onslaught); nevertheless, King Ahaziah perishes in his bizarre effort; then Elijah ascends to heaven.

"Furthermore, this "153" could readily signify the "153" in both extremities of the miracles of Jesus recorded in John's Gospel with 153 gallons (15 firkin @ 10.2 gallons each in the six stone

---

[13] Private exchange with Doug Krieger, August 2020.
[14] Source: Wikipedia @ https://en.wikipedia.org/wiki/Jewish_population_by_country (Retrieved on 08.07.2020)
[15] Ibid.

pots equal to 153 gallons)[16] at the Wedding of Cana (John 2:1-12) and the 153 fish caught at the Sea of Galilee in John 21:11—in other words the "153" signifies the ministry of Yeshua—could we therefore extend this "153" into the final judgment where the "wrath of God and the Lamb" are most definitely in view "prior to" Elijah's ministry and ascension/rapture? Even so, the "two number sets" of "42" found in 2 Kings relative to King Jehu's "judgments" (2 Kings 10:12-14) and Elisha's "42 lads" (2 Kings 2:24) killed by female bears, along with the same two number sets found in the Revelation (Rev. 11:12; 13:5) correspond in that the suffering saints in the Revelation are "avenged" when the completion of the "martyrs" beneath of Fifth Seal reaches its conclusion (at the terminus of the Seventieth Week) . . . so, the "153" is related to judgment with "vengeance belongs to the Lord" relative to the "42" (Deut. 32:35; Rom. 12:17-19). Perhaps this sounds like "fanciful commentary" and "eschatological acrobatics"—but I find these numeric juxtapositions found in the testaments most plausible."

The book of James says that God is not tempted by evil nor does He tempt anyone; in other words, He is not the author of evil. This is applicable to the subject of the suffering of the Jewish people as well. On this same theme Dr. Michael Heiser, who in his book ***The Unseen Realm***[17] states that divine foreknowledge does not necessitate divine predestination regarding God foreseeing evil.

"Rather, evil is the perversion of God's gift of free will. It arises from man's choice, not from God's prompting or predestination. God may know and predestine the end, that something is ultimately going to happen, without predestining the means to that end . . . God does not delight in evil and suffering. Nor does he need it for his sovereign plan . . . In other words, it is not necessary at all for the Jews to suffer again prior their salvation . . . His foreknowledge did not require the Holocaust as part of a plan that would give us the

---

[16] The New King James Study Bible submits a chart regarding the 10.2 Gallons and the 15 sets of the same (firkin) equaling to 153 gallons based upon the British Imperial Measuring System.

[17] Michael S. Heiser, ***The Unseen Realm. Recovering the Supernatural view of the Bible*** (Lexham Press, 2015)

kingdom on earth. God does not need evil as a means to accomplish anything."

Yes, God foreknew the Holocaust, but that foreknowledge did not propel the event. Heiser continues his line of thinking:

"Foreknowledge doesn't require predestination," in a sense that "foreknown events that happen may or may not have been predestined," because "God can decree something and then leave the means up to the decisions of other free-will agents."

In other words, God's omniscience (foreknowledge) does not directly or *de facto* predestine evil. I do concur by saying that any sort of suffering of the Jewish people in the future needs to be taken from the biblical text and not from any other theological prejudice.

Conclusion

I have tried to demonstrate that the plan of God for the House of Jacob found to be in exile is likened to a progressive pilgrimage with a glorious end. Likewise, God's purposes, although never changing, are progressively revealed to us, hence it presupposes that we should never be firmly attached to our way of thinking things through—we need to adapt to, distinguish, and recognize His plans. Should the Lord ask us to give ourselves to intercessory prayer for the Jews to be saved, what would be our answer? Will we be willing to give our lives as instruments of travailing for their salvation, thus imploring, "O Lord, *save your people, the remnant of Israel!*" (Jeremiah 31:7)?

My prayer is that all those who have a theologically correct understanding of this masterplan for His people, the Jews, may align their good theoretical thinking with a life that is consistently proved with facts of practical help towards the remnant of Israel--that we truly care about what we say. I would make an appeal by saying, writing only or speaking only, however important it may be, is of little worth unless it is backed up with a concrete willingness to contribute to the reparation of the breach and to the restoration of streets in which to dwell (Isaiah 58:12); when it comes to Israel, a life of balance between proper theology and practical acts is needed.

Throughout these pages we have seen the prominence of a biblically balanced worldview even in the unceasing endeavor and constant work in helping the Jewish people reaching their final destination. By proclaiming the counsel of the Word of God, praying, giving, and practical assistance we have sought to put flesh to the bones of our convictions. These convictions are based upon inalterable scriptural and spiritual principles which allow us to walk the extra mile in order to fulfill our task:

> *God has not rejected His people.*
> *His gifts are without repentance.*
> *He is a Covenant Keeping God.*
> *The Jewish people will be engrafted again*
> *at the unveiling of Yeshua into their own*
> *Olive Tree of Salvation.*
> *This allows us to already see them, by faith, in their future*
> *state of Salvation as they are now (prophetically) part of*
> *the Commonwealth of Israel.*

Consequently, the Aliyah of the Jewish people can be interpreted as a grand march to Zion. We have considered this great homeward march which starts in unbelief but inexorably turns into a Holy Pilgrimage in which, at the end, distance is no barrier and frailty no hindrance. This is indeed a world-wide re-gathering of the House of Jacob from the four corners of the earth and a testimony before the nations of the world that the sight of this great procession is a matter of praise to the One who died for the sins of His people, *"For He was cut off from the land of the living for the transgressions of My people He was stricken"* (Isaiah 53:8).

Most of all, in the articulation of this text we have learned that the concept and doctrine of salvation is rooted in the Exodus motif (Deliverance/Deliverer) and in their visual call to a **Holy Pilgrimage**. For the Jewish people, salvation has been a long process whose completion is at their arrival at the feet of Him who was pierced for them. But the good news is that the pilgrims, if they persist, are assured a safe and joyful arrival at their destination.

I have tried to demonstrate that the overall plan of God comes not from a covenant-breaking God, but that He committed to see it come to pass as the answer of the plight of His people can spring only from Him—*"He who has scattered Israel will gather him"* (Jeremiah 31:10). The Lord has reserved a place in His eternal covenant for the House of Jacob to return to Eretz Israel in their unbelief so that, at the conclusion of the present age, they would be prepared and positioned to receive the Lamb, welcome His return. It is He Who chose to place them in this position wherein there is no way out other than UP!

The Lord never begins what He does not propose to finish. As his name YHVH reveals, the Lord is by nature, the God who brings His people to full salvation unto the day He fulfills all of His promises.

> **"And they shall call them The Holy People,**
> **The Redeemed of the LORD."**
> (Isaiah 62:12)

> **"And it shall come to pass that everyone who is left**
> **of all the nations which came against Jerusalem shall**
> **go up from year to year**
> **to worship the King, the LORD of hosts, and**
> **to keep the Feast of Tabernacles . . .**
> **. . . come up to Jerusalem to worship the King, the**
> **LORD of hosts . . .."**
> (Zechariah 14, excerpts)

THE END . . . and THE BEGINNING!

Bibliography

Barnes, Albert. *Notes on the Old Testament - Isaiah*. Baker Books, 1998.

Barthel, Johannes. *Aliyah. The Miracle of the Jewish Return*. Ebenezer Emergency Fund, 2018.

Beckett, D. Wendy. *God Keeps Covenant*. Wendy D. Beckett, 2006.

Berkowitz, Ariel & D'vorah. *Torah Rediscovered*. Ariel & D'vorah Berkowitz, Fifth Edition 2012.

Bolender, Merrill. *When the Cross became a Sword. The Origin and consequences of Replacement Theology*. Merrill Bolender, 2011.

Davis, David. *The Elijah Legacy*. Bridge Logos, 2009.

Dake, Finis Jennings. *The Dake Annotated Reference Bible*. Dake Publishing, 2013.

Denton, Clifford. *The Covenant People of God*. Tishrei International, 2001

Feinberg, Jeffrey Enoch. *Walk Genesis! A Messianic Jewish Devotional Commentary*. Lederer Books a division of Messianic Jewish Publishers, 1998.

Falk, Gerhard. *The Restoration of Israel. Christian Zionism in Religion, Literature, and Politics*. Peter Lang Publishing, 2006

Garr, John D. *Anti-Israelism. The New Face of Antisemitism*. Golden Key Press, 2018.

Garr, John D. *God and Israel*. Golden Key Press, 2016.

Gallups, Carl. *Gods of the Final Kingdom*. Defender Publishing, 2016.

Gilbert, P. Derek. *The Great Inception*. Defender Publishing, 2017.

Goodman, Paul. *History of the Jews*. Revised and enlarged by Israel Cohen. (E.P. Dutton & Company, INC. New York, 1953)

Greenspoon, J. Leonard. *Next Year in Jerusalem. Exile and Return in Jewish History*. Purdue University Press.

Grudem, Wayne. *Systematic Theology*. Inter-Varsity Press, 1994.

Heiser, S. Michael. *The Unseen Realm*. Lexham Press, 2015

Henry and Scott. *A Commentary Upon The Holy Bible (Isaiah to Malachi)*. London, The Religious Tract Society, 1835.

Horn, R. Thomas. *The Rabbis, Donald Trump, and the top-secret plan to build the Third Temple*. Defender Publishing, 2019.

Horn, R. Thomas and Putnam, Cris. *The Final Roman Emperor, The Islamic Antichrist, and The Vatican Last Crusade*. Defender Publishing, 2016.

Krieger, W. Douglas. *Commonwealth Theology*. Tribnet Publications, 2018.

Krieger, W. Douglas. *Unsealing the End of Days—the Visions, Prophecy & Messianic Scenario of Zechariah*. Tribnet Publications, 2017.

Krieger, W. Douglas. *Signs in the Heavens and On The Earth...Man's Days are Numbered and he is Measured*. Tribnet Publications, 2014.

Krieger, W. Douglas. *The Testimony of Jesus*. Tribnet Publications, 2015.

Krieger, Hamp, Steinle, Finley. *Commonwealth Theology Essentials*. COI Foundation, 2020.

Lake, Michael. *The Sheeriyth Imperative*. Defender Publishing, 2016.

Lifsey, Dalton. *The Controversy of Zion and the Time of Jacob's Trouble*. Dalton Lifsey, 2008.

Merrill, Eugene H. *An Historical Survey of the Old Testament*. Baker Books House, 1991

Motyer, J. Alec. *The Prophecy of Isaiah. An Introduction & Commentary*. Intervarsity Press, 1993.

Nelson Illustrated Bible Dictionary. Thomas Nelson, 2014.

NIV Study Bible. Zondervan Publishing House, 1995.

Pink, W. Arthur. *The Interpretation of Scriptures*. Sovereign Grace Publishers, 2002.

Pawson, David. *Unlocking the Bible. A unique overview of the whole Bible*. Harper Collins Publishers, 2015.

Rubin, David. *God, Israel & Shiloh Returning to the Land*. Shiloh Israel Press, 2011.

Schafer, Chad and Krieger, Douglas W. *The World in the Bondage of Egypt...Under the Triumphal Arch of Titus*, Tribnet Publications, 2017.

Stern H. David. *Jewish New Testament Commentary*. Jewish New Testament Publications, Inc, 1992.

Spangler, Ann; Tverberg, Lois. *Sitting at the Feet of Rabbi Jesus*. Zondervan, 2018

Shoub, Martin. *To the Jew First: The Formation of a New Man*. 2017

Spangler, Ann; Tverberg, Lois. *Sitting at the Feet of Rabbi Jesus*. Zondervan, 2018

The Hebrew-Greek Key Word Study Bible. AGM Publishers International.

The Jewish Annotated New Testament. *New Revised Standard Version*. Oxford University Press, 2017.

The Oxford Dictionary of Jewish Religion. Oxford University Press, 2011.

The Dictionary of Biblical Imagery. Intervarsity Press, 1998.

Unterman, Alan. *Historical Dictionary of the Jews*. The Scarecrow Press, Inc., 2011

Williams, J. Rodman. *Renewal Theology*. Zondervan, 1996.

Wilson, Dr. Marvin. *Our Father Abraham – Jewish roots of the Christian Faith*. Eerdmans Publishing Company, 1989

Young, Edward J. *The Book of Isaiah – Volume III*. Wm. B. Eerdmans Publishing Co, 1972.

Woodley, Nigel. *Holocaust Exposed. The Bible Enigma*. Solid Trust Ministries, New Zealand, 2009.

Subject Index - Exhaustive

A

Aaron (Levite). 79

Abel. 100

Abomination of Desolation. 130 (2x), 158, 164 (3x), 169 (3x)220

Abram, Abraham (Abram), Seed, Abrahamic Covenant. xi (2x), xiv, xvii, xxviii, 233, 25, 26 (2x), 29, 31, 35, 36-37, 39 (2x), 56, 60, 71, 91-91, 94, 106, 122, 127 (5x), 146, 169, 177, 181, 186, 189, 191 (3x), 195 (2x), 200 (4x), 206-207, 228, 273-274, 276

Abraham Accord. 146

Abraham, Ola. 268

Adam. 95

Adar, Month of. 162

Adumbrative, Adumbration. vii, xxii, 115, 117, 120, 121 (3x), 125, 138, 147, 162-163, 222

Africa. 145, 177

Agency, Jewish A. for Israel. 59 (4x)

Agreement with Hell. 136

Ahaziah, King. 221 (2x), 222 (3x)

Akiba ben Josef, Rabbi. xii, 90 (7x), 91

Algeria. 145

Aliyah. vi (2x), vii (2x), xii (2x), xiii (2x), xvii, xxv, xxxi, 5 (5x), 6 (2x), 7 (2x), 8, 11 (4x), 14 (3x), 15, 22, 32 (2x), 33, 39-40, 48, 53 (2x), 54 (2x), 55, 58 (2x), 59 (5x), 60, 63, 65 (3x), 66-67, 71, 78, 80 (2x), 81-82, 91, 114-115, 118, 120 (3x), 130, 134 (3x), 135-136, 140 (8x), 141 (9x), 142 (2x), 143, 150, 151 (2x), 162, 183, 195 (3x), 198, 215 (2x), 224, 227, 273-274

Aliyah Bet. 140 (2x), 141 (5x), 142

All Israel (shall be delivered, saved). ix, 2, 13 (2x), 14, 27, 61-62, 73, 91, 116, 127 (4x), 159, 165 (2x), 167, 172, 191, 193-194, 201, 202 (2x), 216, 271, 274, 276 (2x)

America, Americas, Latin America, American(s), United States of America. iv (2x), xi, xii, xix (2x) xii (4x), xiii, xvii (4x), xxix (2x), xxxi, 23, 26 (2x), 29, 135, 139, 146, 220

Amidah. 67 (2x)

Ammon, Ammonites. 81, 147

Amorites. 81

Analogy of Faith. 22, 219

Annual Sermon on behalf of the London Society for promoting Christianity among the Jews. 19

Antichrist. 48, 121, 129 (2x), 136-138, 147 (2x), 164, 168, 169 (3x), 217 (2x), 227, 236, 240

Anti-Judaism. 214

71 (5x), 72 (2x), 77 (2x), 78 (2x), 80, 119 (2x), 120 (3x), 132 (2x), 142 (5x)

D

Levite, Tribe of Levi. xx, xxii, 75, 78, 81, 95, 156
Lexham Press. 94, 180, 223, 227
Libya, Libyans. 145 (2x), 147
Lifsey, Dalton. 24 (4x), 228 (2x)
Lightle, Steve. 56 (2x), 57 (3x)
Lights, Festival of. xxii, 167
Lion of Judah, Lion of the Tribe of Judah. xxiv, 92, 123, 274, 277
Liverpool, UK. 19
London. 4, 19 (2x), 30, 199, 227
London Society for promoting Christianity among the Jews. 19
Looper, Dr. John. xi, 215 (2x)
Lo-Ammi (lit. "Not My People"). 98
Lo-Ruhamah. 98 (2x)
Lost Ten Tribes. xviii, xx, 8, 34, 36, 53 (2x), 95 (2x), 96 (2x), 97 (2x), 98
     (2x), 99-100, 174, 175 (2x), 176 (2x), 179 (4x), 204, 221, 268 (2x), 270,
     275 (4x)   .
Louisville, KY. 23
Lutterworth Press, The. 31, 47

M

Maccabees. 167
Magog (See Gog-Magog). 148
Maimonides. 68 (2x)
Man of Sin. 137
Manasseh (Tribe of Israel). 55, 177 (2x), 178 (4x)
Mandate, British. 41, 42 (2x), 43, 141 (2x)
Marcion (Heretic). 61, 184
Marriage Supper of the Lamb. 164 (2x)
Mary-le-bone. 19
Masoretic Text. 3, 5, 34, 90-91
Matriarch, Rachel – of Israel. 159-160, 162
Mc'Cheyne, Robert Murray. 25 (3x)
Medians (Medes). 34
Mediterranean Sea. 32
Mediator of the New Covenant. xxiv, 49, 100, 194, 198, 213
Medo-Persian Empire. 53
Megiddo, Plain of. 156
Megilat Ha;'Atzmaut (Israeli Declaration Independence). 7, 41
Megillot (Five Scrolls). 4
Melchizedek or Melchizedec, Order of, High Priest, King of Salem. xxi, xxii
     (2x), 270, 275, 278
Melville, Herman. 26
Memorial, Blackstone. 29

P

Q

R

Syria. 31 (2x), 43, 109, 111, 137 (3x), 145, 209 (2x)
Systematic Theology, by J. Rodman Williams. 124
Systematic Theology, by Wayne Grudem. 227
Szulc, Tad. 140 (2x)

T

Tabernacle of David. viii, 51, 95 (3x), 100, 185, 195 (2x), 196 (4x), 197, 268
Table of Nations. 94
Tabernacles, Feast of. 169, 226
Tachanun Prayer. 67
Talmud. 68, 90, 91 (2x), 93
Tammuz (Month of – Hebrew Sacred Festival Calendar). 162
Tanakh (TaNaKh). xii, 4 (2x), 5, 93, 102, 122
Tarshish, Ships or Merchants of. 13, 145-146
Tattenai. 71
Tel Aviv. 58-59, 101
Telushkin. 68, 123
Temple, First or Solomonic, Solomon's Temple. xviii, xix, xx, xxiv, 66
Temple, Latter Temple, or House – Fourth Temple – Millenarian Temple.
    xix, xx, xxi (7x) xxii (3x), xxiii (3x), xxiv (2x), xxv-xxvi, 27, 120,129,
    145, 162, 168-169, 257 (2x)
Temple, Second. xix (3x), xx (3x), xxii (3x) xxiv, 6, 10, 14 (2x), 35, 53 (2x),
    66, 71, 72(2x) 73, 78 (3x), 79 (2x), 90 (2x), 130, 156, 167 (3x)
Temple, Third (aka "Tribulation Temple"). 145, 151-152, 163-164, 217
Temple, Spiritual. xxiv, xxv, 188
Ten Northern Tribes, Lost Ten Tribes, Ten Adulterous Tribes. xviii, xx, 8, 34,
    36, 53 (2x), 95 (2x), 96 (2x), 97 (2x), 98 (2x), 99-100, 174, 175 (2x), 176
    (2x), 179 (4x), 204, 221, 268 (2x), 270, 275 (4x)
Ten Plagues. 125 (2x)
Tennessee, USA. xi
Tenth Roman Legion. 35
Tents of Jacob. 174
Tents of Judah. 154 (2x), 155
Testimony of Jesus, The, by Douglas W. Krieger. 163, 227
Teshuvah. 7, 68 (2x), 77 (2x)
Tevet (Month of on the Hebrew Festival Calendar). 162
The World in the Bondage of Egypt – Under the Triumphal Arch of Titus, by
    Chad Schafer and Doug Krieger. xiv, 202, 228
Things to Come, by Dwight Pentecost. 145
Thomas, Apostle. 130
Thomas Nelson, Inc. (Publishers). iv, 228 (2x)
Throne of David. xii, 42, 136, 274, 277
Tigris River. 145
Time of Jacob's Trouble. 23-24, 228
Times of the Gentiles. 47, 220

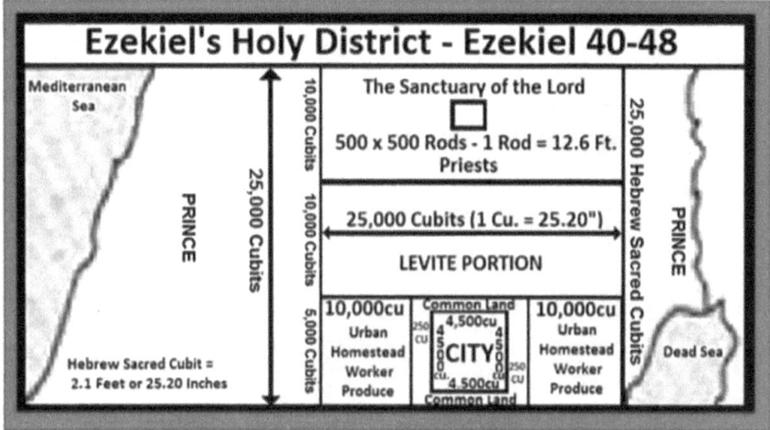

Figure 21 - Ezekiel's Holy District - Ezekiel 40-48

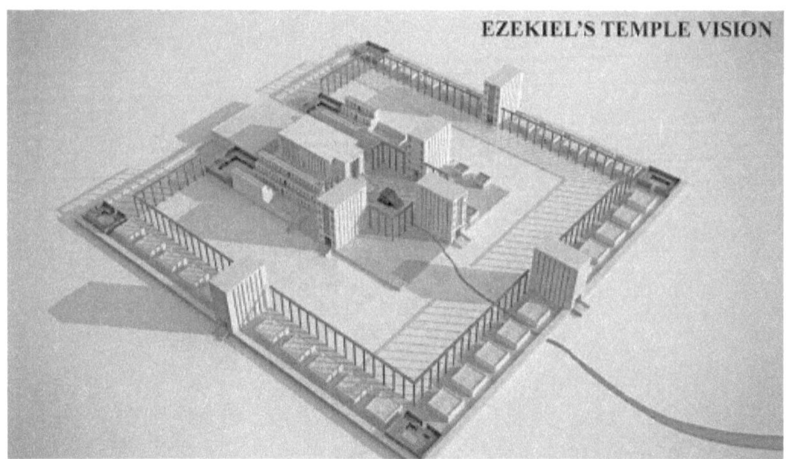

Figure 22 - Ezekiel's Temple Vision

Figure 23 - Ebenezer Operation Exodus - Bringing Them Home

Figure 24 - Isaiah 46:3-4 & John 7:35

Figure 25 - Feast of Tabernacles in Jerusalem

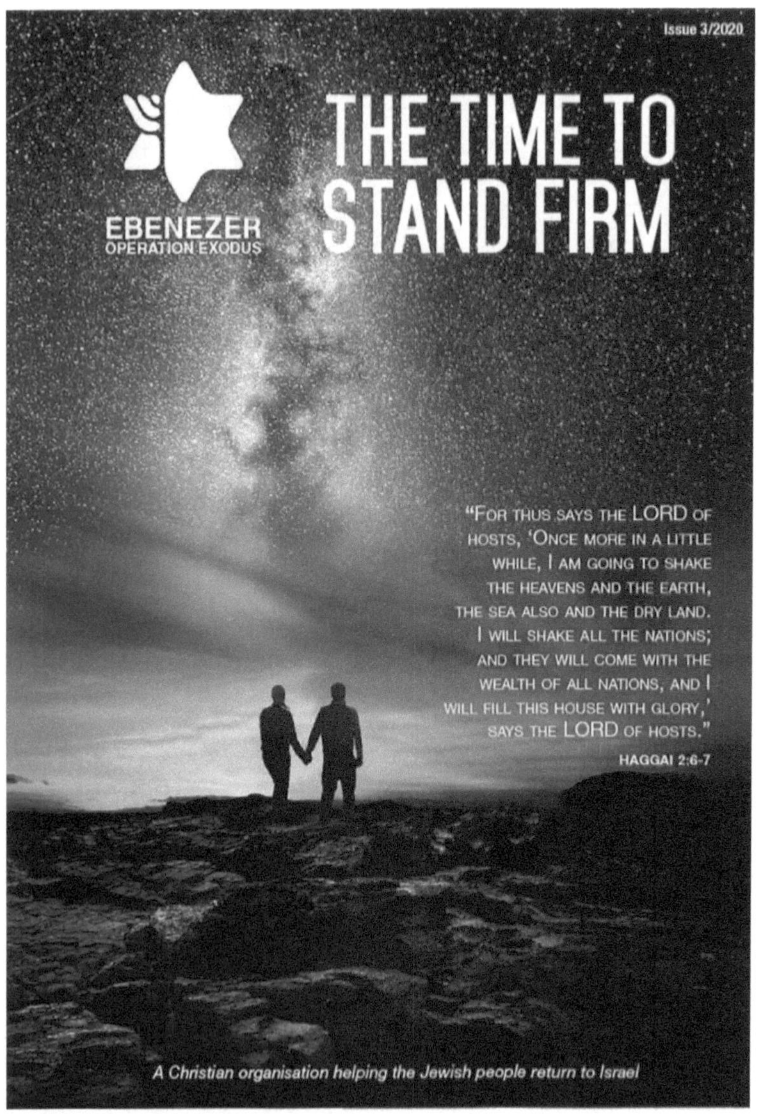

Figure 26 - Ebenezer Operation Exodus—Time to Stand Firm

Scripture Index

<table>
<tr><td>

Genesis

Gen. 3. 91
Gen. 3:14-15. 91
Gen. 3:15. 56
Gen. 10. 94, 139
Gen. 10:8-10. 95
Gen. 11. 139
Gen. 12. 46
Gen. 12:3. xi, 200 (2x)
Gen. 15:7. 6
Gen. 17:8. 20
Gen. 28:13-15. 106
Gen. 28:15. 105
Gen. 44:1-14. 157
Gen. 45:6-10. 157
Gen. 46:3-4. 5
Gen. 46:19. 162
Gen. 48:4. 177-178
Gen. 48:8. 163, 177
Gen. 48:16. 177-178
Gen. 48:19. 179
Gen. 49. 274, 277
Gen. 49:8. 92
Gen. 49:1. 103 (2x)
Gen. 49:10. xxii, 35, 50

Exodus

Ex. 6:4. 7
Ex. 6:6. 6
Ex. 6:7. 6
Ex. 13:17. 5
Ex. 13:18. 6
Ex. 20:2-3. 70

</td><td>

Ex. 20:12. 70
Ex. 30:11. 84
Ex. 34:24. 6

Leviticus

Lev. 7:27. 68
Lev. 26:33. 36

Numbers

Num. 23:19. 52
Num. 24:9. 209

Deuteronomy

Deut. 4:40. 71
Deut. 4:27-31. xxviii
Deut.7:12-11:25. 106-107
Deut. 8:5. 106
Deut. 9:5-6. 106
Deut. 24:1-4. 97
Deut. 28:1. 34
Deut. 30:1-5. 116-117
Deut. 30:1-6. 105-106
Deut. 30:8. 70
Deut. 30:19-20. 71
Deut. 32:8-9. 94
Deut. 32:9. 101
Deut. 32:35. 223
Deut. 34. 87
Deut. 34:34. 87
Deut. 36:26. 153

Ruth

1:16. 46

</td><td>

1 Kings

1 Kings 10:9. 45
1 Kings 11-12. 96
1 Kings 12:10. 175
1 Kings 12:16, 24. 175
1 Kings 12:19. 175
1 Kings 12:20. 175

2 Kings

2 Kings 1. 222
2 Kings 2. 222
2 Kings 10:12-14. 223
2 Kings 2:24. 223
2 Kings. 16:6. 34

1 Chronicles

1 Chron. 17:21, 23. 61
1 Chron. 21:5. 181

2 Chronicles

2 Chron. 7:5. xx
2 Chron. 10. 98
2 Chron. 32:18. 34
2 Chron. 32:20-23. 53
2 Chron. 36:22. 9
2 Chron. 36:22-23. 3

</td></tr>
</table>

Ezra

Ezra 1. 12
Ezra 1:2-3. 12
Ezra 1:3. 53
Ezra 1:4. 13
Ezra 1:6. 14
Ezra 2:2. 54
Ezra 5:13. 72
Ezra 6:3. 72
Ezra 6:9-10. 72
Ezra 6:17. xx
Ezra 7:10. 80
Ezra 7:12-15. 78
Ezra 7:18. 78
Ezra 7:25. 80
Ezra 7:28. 79
Ezra 9:1-2. 81
Ezra 9:8. 81
Ezra 9:10. 81
Ezra 9:15. 82
Ezra 10:6.82

Nehemiah

Neh. 1:8-9. 106
Neh. 7:5. 9
Neh. 9:28-29. 82

Esther

Esther 2:5-6. 34

Job

Job 36:15. 107

Psalms

Psalms 2. 130, 274
Psalms 2:1-12. 140
Psalms 14:7. xxxi, 93
Psalms 24:1-3. 62
Psalms 53:6. v, 115

Psalms 82:6-8. 94
Psalms 102:16. 21
Psalms 102. 60
Psalms 105:11, 44-45: 70
Psalms 122:3-4. 6
Psalms 126. 9
Psalms 147:2. 33

Isaiah

Isa. 1. 83
Isa. 1:15. 83
Isa. 1:16-18. 83
Isa. 2:2-3. xxi
Isa. 10:21. 132
Isa. 11:1, 10. 92
Isa. 11:10-13. 50-51
Isa. 11:13. 182, 186, 198-199
Isa. 14:1. 10, 56
Isa. 16:3-4.143
Isa. 16:4. 143
Isa. 17. 111, 113, 136-138
Isa. 17:1. 137
Isa. 17:4. 137, 144
Isa. 27:9. 93, 154, 159
Isa. 27:12-13. 127
Isa. 28. 138
Isa. 28:15. 136
Isa. 31:5. 40
Isa. 34:4. 166
Isa. 40-66. 132
Isa. 40:1-2. 39
Isa. 40:4. 112
Isa. 41:14. 113
Isa. 42:22. 216

Isa. 43. xxx, 118, (3x)
Isa. 43:5-6. xxix, 118
Isa. 43:13. 142
Isa. 43:14. 119
Isa. 43:21. 124
Isa. 44. 113, 149
Isa. 44:1-2. 113
Isa. 44:2-3. 149
Isa. 44:26-27. 120
Isa. 44:26, 28. 120
Isa. 44:28. 10, 53
Isa. 45. 142
Isa. 45:3. 142
Isa. 45:3-5. 142
Isa. 45:4-5. 10
Isa. 45:13. 142
Isa. 45:6. 33
Isa. 45:17. 85
Isa. 46. xxix
Isa. 46:3-4. 258 (2x)
Isa. 46:9-10. 17
Isa. 46:13. 154
Isa. 48:11. 132
Isa. 48:14-15. 119
Isa. 48:20. 119
Isa. 49-51. 107
Isa. 49:5-6. 209
Isa. 49:6. 132-133, 277
Isa. 49:16. 208
Isa. 49:22. 13, 56, 58
Isa. 49:22, 26. xxiii
Isa. 49:22. xxiii, 13, 56, 58
Isa. 49:26. xxiii

Amos 9:11-12. 95, 100, 182, 197

Matt. 13:52. 22
Matt. 17:11. 73
Matt. 21:13. xxiii, 129
Matt. 23:39. 156, 158
Matt. 24:7-8. xx
Matt. 24:15. 130, 164
Matt. 24:21. 220
Matt. 24:29-31. 126

Mark

Mark 11:17. xxiii, 129
Mark 13:23. 219

Luke

Luke 1:17. 73
Luke 1:31 (2x). 103
Luke 1:67-75. 162
Luke 1:68-75. 122
Luke 9:31. 124
Luke 13:29. 207
Luke 21:20-24. 35
Luke 21:29. 117
Luke 24:39. 130

John

John 1:45. 88
John 1:47-51. xxv
John 1:49-51. 62
John 2:1-12. 223
John 4:22. 35
John 4:23-24. 129
John 5:46. 88
John 7:35. 258 (2x)

Zech. 7:14. 136
Zech. 8:2-8. 136
John 10:16. 179, 204
John 10:22-39. 168
John 10:26. 204
John 10:26, 29, 33. xxiii
John 10:28. 208 (2x)
John 10:33. 168
John 11:47-53. 203
John 11:49-52. 203
John 11:52. xxiv, 202-203
John 17. 270, 277
John 17:20-23. 206
John 20:27. 130
John 21:11. 223

Acts

Acts 3:19-20. 156
Acts 3:19-21. 215
Acts 3:21. 274
Acts 7:38. 184
Acts 15. 196 (2x), 197 (3x), 268
Acts 15:13-17. 100
Acts 15:14. 189
Acts 15:16-17. 182, 196

Romans

Rom. 3:1-2. 131
Rom. 3:31. 132
Rom. 4. 127
Rom. 7. 99
Rom. 7:1-4. 99
Rom. 7:12. 132
Rom. 8:15. 277
Rom. 9-16. 100, 217
Rom. 9:3. 75

Rom. 9:23-26. 204
Rom. 9:23-28. 100
Rom. 9:24. 189, 204
Rom. 9:25-26. 205
Rom. 10:2-3. 131
Rom. 10:4. 134
Rom. 11. 14, 201, 274 (2x)
Rom. 11:1-2. 35
Rom. 11:2. 210
Rom. 11:2-27. 165
Rom. 11:11-12. 53
Rom. 11:13-24. 95
Rom. 11:15-32. 21
Rom. 11:16-24. 29
Rom. 11:23. 116, 216
Rom. 11:24. 216
Rom.11:25. 75, 135, 179
Rom.11:25-26.116, 127
Rom.11:26. xxxi, 154, 159, 202
Rom. 11:26-27. 63, 93, 216
Rom. 11:28. 186
Rom. 11:29. 52
Rom. 11:32. 53, 101
Rom. 12:17-19. 223
Rom. 15:8-10. 52
Rom. 15:12. 92
Rom. 15:27. xxvi, 51
Rom. 16:20. 56, 101, 216
Rom. 16:26. 56, 195, 270

Figure 27 - A New Heaven & A New Earth

Commonwealth of Israel Foundation Literature

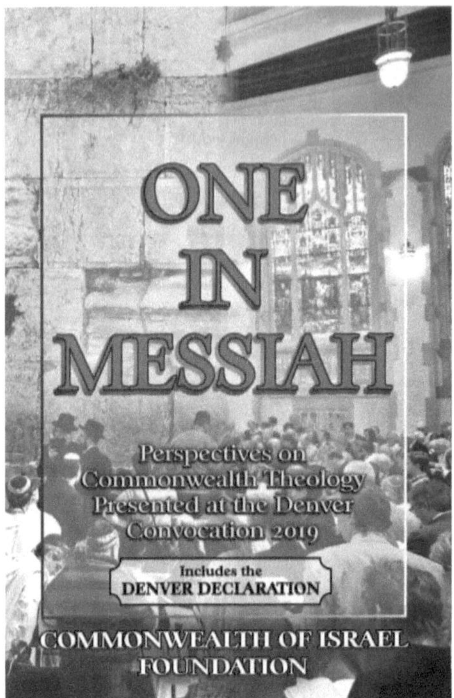

One in Messiah – Perspectives on Commonwealth Theology Presented at the Denver Convocation 2019 . . . Authors: Douglas W. Krieger; Henry Hon, Dr. Douglas Hamp; Jerri Tuck; Pastor Douglas R. Shearer; Patricia Iorillo, M.S.; Ola Abraham; Dr. Gavin W. Finley, MD; Ruel Guerrero; Bob O'Dell; Chad Schafer; Chris Steinle... ONE IN MESSIAH is a compendium of 12 authors out of nearly 20 participants who collaborated at the third annual One in Messiah Convocation. The first such gathering took place in Denver in the summer of 2017; the second took place in Sacramento, California in March 2018 and now this third gathering, again, in Denver, summer of 2019. There is, most definitely, a wide variety of perspective—but they all share something profoundly unique: They all celebrate our Oneness we have in Messiah! Each is coming "at it" in their own unique way—but we all arrive at the "unity of the faith and of the knowledge of the Son of God, unto a Perfect Man, unto the measure of the stature of the fullness of our Messiah" (Ephesians 4:13).

We are all firm believers in the "United Kingdom of David" – i.e., the "Tabernacle of David" which was revealed to the Lord's Ekklesia at the Council in Jerusalem in Acts 15. The Ten Tribes of the Northern Kingdom (the Kingdom of Israel), split off from the Two Tribes of the Southern Kingdom at the "breach of Jeroboam." But now, those "from among the Nations (aka, "the Gentiles") were reunited as the United Kingdom of David through the Gospel of Peace wherein not only was their redemption for all but the "middle wall of separation" between Jew (Judah) and Gentile (the Nations) was broken down by His Cross—the Two were made One!

Commonwealth Theology Essentials - 2020 -Authors: Douglas W. Krieger; Dr. Douglas Hamp; Dr. Gavin Finley, MD; Chris Steinle. Easily the most important advance in Judeo-Christian relations in 100 years, Commonwealth Theology (CT) cuts across denominational divisions to reveal God's plan for the Church and the Jews. CT is based on a more literal interpretation of the Scriptures. Interpretations have, since the 2nd century, been influenced by man's philosophy and politics. Beyond the basics of Christian salvation, mainstream theologies are at odds. Catholic, Reform, and Evangelical interpretations of Bible prophecy do not agree because they have all overlooked the obvious. Is it possible that the truth has been concealed for nearly 2,000 years? The clash of mainline Christian views is, in itself, proof that something has gone wrong. The surprising solution

that will unite God's people has been right there in God's Word all along. In January 2018 Douglas W. Krieger premiered his groundbreaking work: *"Commonwealth Theology: An Introduction."* Joined by Bible researchers, Dr. Douglas Hamp, Dr. Gavin Finley, and Chris Steinle, "Essentials" expands the application of Commonwealth Theology to address even more aspects of biblical theology - areas of theology which have either been ignored or contradicted within mainstream theologies. Indeed, CT reaffirms the truly biblical tenets of both Catholic-Reformed and Dispensational Theology, while resolving Christendom's greatest areas of conflict by examining these heretofore enigmas in the light of Commonwealth Theology. "Essentials" is presented in two main sections: Elements of Commonwealth Theology; and, Commonwealth Eschatology. Following the introduction, which lays out the need and benefits of CT in defining the relationship between the Jews and the Church, the "Elements" section summarizes the core theological basics from Krieger's initial work; as well as covering new insights from all four of the

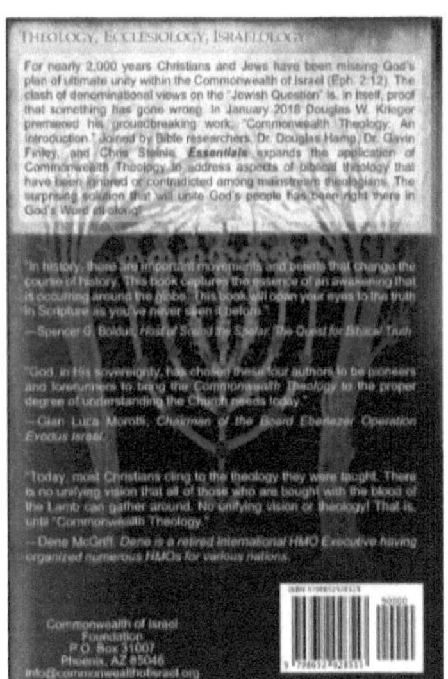

authors. Some of the elements of CT expounded in the first sections include: Krieger's analysis of mainline Christianity's treatment of the Jews in terms of "Distinction" and "Separation," Comparisons of Reformed, Dispensational, and Commonwealth Theology; The peace and unity purchased by Christ with implications for Gentiles and Jews.

The plight of the two houses of Israel and the significance of the scattered Northern Kingdom; The mystery hidden but revealed in the New Testament; The import of the Jerusalem Council; Heresies adopted by the Early Church; False juxtaposition of Law and Grace; The Breach of Jeroboam; The two offices of Melchizedek; and, Israel's divorce and remarriage. Part II: Commonwealth Eschatology contains, among other topics: How to reconcile partially fulfilled Messianic prophecies; The thematic view of Revelation; The Future 70th Week; The Gentile connection to Jacob's Trouble; Analysis of the Resurrection/Rapture; and, What happens on the Day of the Second Coming?

The Denver Declaration is a concise yet dynamic statement on Commonwealth of Israel Theology (Commonwealth Theology). This Summer 2019 edition includes 150 supporting scriptural references. – Excerpt: Introduction to the Denver Declaration: During the course of 2017-2019 a number of believers in Messiah – Jesus – realized from their doctrinal backgrounds that the major theological paradigms now prevalent primarily within evangelical circles were either inherited from Roman Catholicism and Reformational Churches and/or from more modern forms of systematic theology, primarily those with premillenarian/dispensational emphasis. Coupled with these older bodies of doctrinal emphases were eschatologies which emphasized the "disinheritance" of Israel (aka, the Jews) expressed in the corpus of what is considered Replacement/Rejection theology wherein "Israel" is solely the New Israel of God—i.e., the Church; whereas in Dispensational thinking the Ekklesia/Congregation/Church is wholly disconnected from the tribe of Judah (i.e., the Jews) wherein God's plan for both the Church and "Israel" are utterly disconnected, the one from the other. Neither theological extremity sufficed this band of brethren concerning their relationship with what they saw written in the "prophetic Scriptures" (Romans 16:26) – for they saw in the prayer of Jesus in John 17 "that they all may be one" through the work of the cross would not only open up the floodgates of universal redemption but would as well, break down the "middle wall of separation" – making of the two (Jew and Gentile) ONE NEW MAN – SO MAKING PEACE.

Furthermore, neither did the current movements within Messianic Judaism – followers of Yeshua – placate these extremes of profound, even eternal, alienation found in Replacement / Dispensational theologies due to the growing isolationism within far too many of the Messianic confederated organizations – most standing "apart" from their "Gentile" counterparts. Neither were we convinced with most of the "Two-House Theology" during the last hundred years (e.g., British Israelism, Mormonism). Yet, lest we become inflated with "comparing ourselves with ourselves" – we have been greatly blessed by elements within all these branches of Biblical understanding and research. We are keenly aware of both the hostile/superior theologies within Christendom and the isolation among our Messianic brethren; consequently, and as greater fellowship over issues related to the Ekklesia and of the prophetic scriptures related to the Breach of Jeroboam and the true work of the cross in reconciling both the House of Judah and the House of Israel (aka, Ephraim), we set about in developing what we feel is a body of knowledge/truth.

These theological extremes could then be reconciled, while challenging the isolation amongst our Messianic brethren – and, in so doing, build greater understanding and bridges with the House of Judah in preparation for the coming Messianic Era – the Final Redemption.

Thus, since 2017 we have increasingly reached out to a diverse group of leadership—primarily among Christian communities in holding bi-annual convocations, "teaming-up" with other ministries for the "faith of the gospel" and spreading our research through sundry expressions like publications and social media. What you see here within this DENVER DECLARATION is an initial expression of our findings—knowing full-well the insufficiencies of our discoveries; yet, at the same time, introducing these efforts to the greater Body of Messiah because we are persuaded the time has come to take a vibrant stand for the "*Truth of the Gospel*" in proclaiming not only the Gospel of the Grace of God for so great a salvation wrought through our Savior, but embracing the *Gospel of Peace* in bringing His people in both Houses—Judah and Ephraim—to see their prophetic roles at the culmination of this age.

Theology - Israelology - $21.50

Commonwealth Theology--An Introduction--is about 2,000 years overdue. It is fashioned to highlight the RESTORATION of the Two Houses of Israel: Judah and Ephraim--along with Edom, the "rest of mankind." It emphasizes the RECONCILIATION of this One Stick in the hand of YHVH and of the coming Messianic Age. In so doing it unravels the two primary theological systems of our day: Replacement/Rejection Theology and Dispensationalism. It calls for a radical and agonizing reappraisal of why Paul uses Ephraim in Hosea to explain the plan and purpose of the Almighty in displaying His mercy on us ALL, whereby ALL ISRAEL shall be delivered by the DELIVERER Who shall roar out of Zion on that end-time Day. This is not Identity Theology. This is the Awakening! "In the latter days you will consider it" (Jer. 30:24b; Ezk. 37:15-18). This is the Tabernacle of David's United Kingdom!

Doug Krieger is the author of 10 books. He is the publisher of Tribnet Publications - a frequent conference speaker & retired public school administrator.

Commonwealth Theology—An Introduction—is about 2,000 years overdue. It is fashioned to highlight the RESTORATION of the Two Houses of Israel: Judah and Ephraim. It emphasizes the RECONCILIATION of this One Stick in the hand of YHWH and of the coming Messianic Age. In so doing it unravels the two primary theological systems of our day: Replacement/Rejection Theology and Dispensationalism. It calls for a radical and agonizing reappraisal of why Paul uses Ephraim in Hosea to explain the plan and purpose of the Almighty in displaying His mercy on us ALL, whereby ALL ISRAEL shall be delivered by the DELIVERER Who shall roar out of Zion. This is not Identity theology. This is the Awakening! "*In the latter days you will consider it*" (Jeremiah 30:24b; Ezekiel 37:15-28).When we read Ephesians 2:11-22 we understand that the expressions "*without Christ, being aliens from the commonwealth of Israel*" and "*now, therefore, you are no longer strangers and foreigners, but fellow citizens with the saints and members of the household of God*" (vss. 12 and 19) suggests to us that our previous status as "*aliens, strangers, and foreigners.*"

This had everything to do with this *"Commonwealth of Israel."* But now, we who once were *"without Christ"* no longer have those designations, but are now considered as *"fellow citizens with the saints and members of the household of God"* (vss. 12 and 19).To assert that the *"blood of Christ"* (vs. 13) had nothing to do with this inclusion into the Commonwealth of Israel is a jaded reading of the text. There is the pernicious and stultifying tendency in the minds of some to suggest that entry into the Commonwealth of Israel is not at stake here. The notion that the blood of Christ brings us into Christ Jesus Himself—into His *"one body through the cross"* (vs. 16) and that this Is separate and apart from bringing us, as well, into the Commonwealth of Israel, is simply NOT justified by the plain reading of the text.

The context is altogether too clear in that the reference after the mentioning of the *"one body through the cross"* we read: *"Now, therefore, you are no longer strangers and foreigners, but fellow citizens with the saints and members of the household of God"* (vss. 16 and 19). What Paul is emphasizing is abundantly clear: Through the *"blood of Christ"* – *"through the cross"* (vss. 13, 16) we have moved from our previous status as aliens, strangers, and foreigners to full-blown legal citizens of the Commonwealth of Israel and are now within a new polity (state, authority, jurisdiction, administration—the amplified meaning of the word "commonwealth").Once we were *"strangers from the covenants of promise"* – we had *"no hope"* and we were *"without God in the world"* – but now through His blood we *"have been brought near."* "Near" to what? To the Commonwealth of Israel—*"with Christ"* we are included in the Commonwealth of Israel . . . without Christ we once were aliens. NO MORE; through His blood we who once *"were far off have been brought near by the blood of Christ"* (vs. 13).

Many prickly theological issues concerning Israel, the Ekklesia (aka, the Church) and the Nations is carefully laid out; however, the text is decidedly introductory to this most ambitious effort. We delve into the "breaking of the Two Staffs" - Beauty and Bonds or Favor and Unity as found in Zechariah 11 and how these Staffs played out in the Early Church in her relationship with Judah-Israel. An exhaustive commentary is given concerning the Two Witnesses of Revelation 11 - for they are corporate witnesses: Israel (the Two Olives Trees) and the Ekklesia (the Church) as the Two Lampstands. Issues related to the 33-years of deportations of the 10 Northern Tribes and how they were swallowed up of the Nations, by Assyria, and NOT by Judah. Why, at the "last days" the Sticks of Judah and Ephraim shall once again, in the hand of the LORD, be brought together!
PLEASE GO TO: www.commonwealthofisrael.org for purchase or info. These Books or Amazon.com @
https://www.amazon.com/Commonwealth-Theology-Essentials-Douglas-Krieger-ebook/dp/B088X3ZJBR

Book Review by Pete Stucken

Chairman of Ebenezer Emergency Fund International (EEFI)

As the end of the age approaches, and tensions in the Middle East continue to appear in news headlines, Christians across the globe are asking: What lies ahead? Gian Luca Morotti's book *"**Called to a Holy Pilgrimage**"* unwraps a crucial aspect of what we are going to see. With diligent, scholarly research of the Scriptures, he carefully constructs for the reader a doorway into understanding the beauty and completeness of GOD's redemptive plan for His people, purchased at such a high price. Equipped with the authoritative insights which the author gives us, we can be delivered from the "legion of religious spirits swirling around this subject trying to impede the knowledge of truth, placing a gulf of ignorance to serve as a great divide. . . " (Chapter 5, p.93). The truth sets us free!

Covering both the historical calling of Israel as YHVH's covenant people, and their future coming together in the Commonwealth of Israel with the saints from across the nations, the author builds the reader's understanding in an orderly, step-by-step process. Each chapter concludes with a relevant prayer. The return of the scattered exiles to the Land of Israel, their historic homeland, is shown to be indeed a holy pilgrimage, an ascent to Zion, a crucial step in the return of a people to the GOD of Abraham, Isaac and Jacob. A geographical and spiritual positioning to receive a magnificent revelation of their Messiah. A glorious outcome yet with many difficulties ahead.

The book equips the reader with a sturdy platform of faith-building truth from which to walk through difficult times without wavering, and to discharge properly the responsibilities given to all those who are joined to the Commonwealth of Israel. It spans a biblical illumination of history, then includes current events even up to the date of this writing, in order to position us for the future. The author's personal involvement with Israel's modern-day return to their historic homeland provides an added layer of understanding and insight. His analysis of the different historical modes of ***ALIYAH*** will be truly relevant in overcoming the obstructions still to come. The author does not spare us any difficult truths. To be involved with this extraordinary end-of-days restoration by Almighty GOD is to be willing to take a position of costly intercession for the fulfillment of His Kingdom purposes.

Book Review by Dr. Gavin Finley, M.D.

Throughout the Western world, and sadly, in our churches, post-modernism is now supplanting the Western Judeo-Christian ethic of truth and reason. This has had the effect of sidelining the Holy Scriptures. In many ecclesiastical quarters the foundations of our faith are being severely eroded. As we approach the end-time drama, we see the beginnings of the general apostasy spoken of by our apostle Paul. In vision, the prophet Daniel was also told of *"the time of the end"*, when *"truth was thrown to the ground."* In Psalms 2 King David wrote a song in which the question is asked, *"why do the nations rage?"* He is then shown that the raging is very specifically directed against the coming Messiah.

It is against the backdrop of this general confusion, and the moral and cultural declension, that Gian Luca Morotti, presents his book, *"Called to a Holy Pilgrimage, the Gathering and Salvation of the House of Jacob."* It is a faithful biblical guide, opening up many inspiring new leads and showing just how everything ties together in a beautiful unity at the end of this age. In the pages of this book we see the much-needed expanded scope of full restoration of *"all Israel"* (Rom. 11), that will come through Messiah, *"whom heaven must receive until the restoration of all things"* (Acts 3:21).

The author presents a scholarly Biblical exegesis of the progressive regatherings that have been occurring, and those that are yet to occur in a climactic way, in times to come. His presentation of the restoration goes out beyond the usual well-worn dispensationalist discussions of the political restoration of a nation of Israel in 1948. These returns to the Holy Land, or Aliyah, have been wonderful fulfillments of Bible prophecy in their time. But they do not exhaust the prophecy of the full *"restoration of all things."* The returns we have seen so far primarily involve the royal Jewish House of Judah. This indeed is the national tribe of Israel that brings us the Son of David, the Lion of the tribe of Judah, who is destined to return as King of kings. He is to be seated upon the Throne of David as the Shiloh of Genesis 49, the promised Messiah, the One to whom the royal scepter of sovereign rule truly belongs.

However, the prophesied restoration, involving all of the 12 tribes of Israel, is still up ahead. This is spoken of by the prophets of old, and specifically by the apostle Paul in Romans 11. But there is more! Outsiders from the nations are grafted into Israel by a spiritual adoption, through Israel's Messiah. Those who are *"in Christ, are Abraham's Seed, and heirs according to the promise"* (Galatians 3:29). These are just some of the neglected themes of restoration and regathering the author brings to our attention.

In this book we see the full story of the Breach of Jeroboam laid out clearly, along with its aftermath with the division of Israel into two kingdoms. We see the subsequent deep idolatry, then God's divorce of the House of Israel, and their subsequent scatterings into the nations. But the prophetic scriptures are clear. Holy history will see the return of both houses of Israel at the end of the saga. Just how that will play out, and just what awesome revelations lie up ahead, remains to be seen. These are just a few of the many mysteries yet to be revealed.

Within the narrative we are also shown the law vs. grace dichotomy. This theological favoritism in matters of law vs. grace goes back into Israel's earlier history. But it is on full display now in each of the two houses. The bias of each party in their groupthink, with one favoring God's righteous Law and the other favoring His Grace and mercy comes out of the general cultural neglect of the New Covenant. The reconciliation of the two divine initiatives comes with the indwelling Messiah. Within the hearts He establishes both His throne, and His altar. Both of them are there in the dual Office of Melchizedek as King and High Priest. This is why the Greco-Roman rationalistic religious arguments persist, fall short, and continue to feed the family feud. When a continuing unsound theology becomes politicized it can, and it does, spawn new upwellings of antisemitism, along with their attendant sad histories. This book is important. It is presenting the indwelling Messiah as the Prince of Peace. As such, He is central to ultimate World Peace. His great salvation is the only real Peace Process that this world will ever see.

The author spotlights the rebellion of the ten tribes and subsequent divorce of the Northern Kingdom. He traces the story of the rebelling Northern Kingdom as it went into captivity, then disappeared into the mists of history as the lost House of Israel. We also read of the scatterings of the ten tribes into the nations and their national amnesia as to their origins. The perennial jealousy of the House of Israel and their bitter resentment of Judah is also now understandable. Their inner angst and grief are over the national identity they lost, when after the death of King Solomon, they walked out on the royal Jewish house.

Here we come to understand the reason for the zealous crusading undertaken by western Christendom, and their pilgrimages back to the Holy Land. They continue to return to the Holy City, even as salmon unwittingly and instinctively return from the seas and up the streams to the place of their birth. We go on to see the promised redemption of both houses, noticing in Zechariah 12 that the epic future collective wave of salvation is set to sweep across the Jewish House of Judah quite late, even as the armies of the nations surround Jerusalem. Nevertheless, as the story ends, we are shown that both houses, indeed all

12 tribes, will be there, bringing with them their many companions, as described in Ezekiel 37. These are some of the neglected and untold biblical clues that help to fill out the "rest of the story" of Israel's promised restoration.

The author firmly establishes the theological basis for the reconciliation and the eventual glorious reunion of the two estranged and feuding houses of Israel. This is shown to become a reality in the very personal New Covenant spoken of in Jeremiah 31:31 wherein the law of God is not just policed externally, as by a schoolmaster, but is now written in the hearts. This is a promise given to both the House of Israel and the Jewish House of Judah. The prophet Jeremiah declares, *"In His days, Judah will be saved, and Israel will dwell securely"* (Jeremiah 23:6).

The author also points to the affirmation given to those who are *"repairers of the breach"* (Isaiah 58:12). He also refers to the two sticks of Ezekiel 37, with both Judah and Joseph/Ephraim coming together as one in the hand of Messiah. These are scriptures that open up new understandings. Full salvation in the hearts and deliverance at Jerusalem will both be undertaken by the Holy One of Israel, *"for Zion's sake."* The author makes a special point of describing the Greek Gnosticism that even now, in both companies, is limiting our present understanding the full restoration of Israel. This "us and them" groupthink is apparent in both the replacement theology of the older denominations, the dispensational theology of the evangelicals, and the rabbinical theologies in the House of Judah. All of them are inclined to focus on bloodlines. The evangelicals also focus on a generic "Church" as some sort of a "spiritual Israel," and just a heavenly home. They are vague about their part in the future physical restoration of the land of Israel or the New Jerusalem. All of the factions foster a party spirit. Sadly, both houses still suffer from the "partial blindness" that tries to keep them from seeing the complete view of the "all Israel" that God is calling to Himself in Messiah. The relevant scriptures brought to bear establishing the complete restoration of Israel are seen throughout the pages of the Old Testament and in the Pauline epistles.

The restoration of all Israel as the myriad starry company that Abraham was shown, goes beyond race and DNA. The ultimate destiny of Israel is not just a royal nation, (Jewish Israel), and a holy priesthood, (the Church). Both Moses and the apostle Peter describe a cross-linked, royal priesthood and a holy nation. This is destined to be established and brought to completion in the atoning blood of Christ in the New Covenant. Out of this swelling spiritual house will come Israel's full physical return as a nation of 12 tribes, restored to the land, Eretz Israel. The two houses of Israel will be reunited, bringing with them their companions from among all the nations.

Very early on, Israel was destined to reach out to the nations, even given a mandate for outreach, a great commission of sorts. In Isaiah 49:6 we see that the 12 tribes are not just brought back and restored for their own benefit. They are actually regathered and called to a divine purpose. They belong to Messiah, Israel's Servant. In Him, they are commissioned to become a *"light to the nations."* These are just some of the wonderful Biblical themes that open up to the reader, giving an expanded understanding of the full end-time agenda of God.

As the author describes, the Holy Scriptures only speak of just one Elect. The full company of the Redeemed are destined to be gathered as one united company. As we see in Ezekiel 37, they are to be gathered under the combined stick of Joseph and Judah. Out of Judah comes the Son of David, who sits upon the Throne of David. He is the Prince of Peace, the sovereign Head over the Kingdom of Messiah. He is the promised Shiloh to whom the scepter of Genesis 49 belongs, the Lion of the Tribe of Judah. All, these unfolding wonders will fulfill the prayer of Jesus in John 17, *"That they may be one, as we are One."*

The author points to the long-neglected truth that there is, and always has been, a means by which a person from any nation may enter into Israel by adoption. There are many examples of this. Our apostle Paul affirms, *"Ye have received the Spirit of adoption wherein we cry, 'Abba, Father!'"* (Romans 8:15) All are redeemed the same way, by grace, through faith, in the atoning blood of Israel's promised Sacrificial Lamb. In this blood we find the basis for the national identity, the Commonwealth, and the citizenship in Israel. This is part of the hidden treasure imputed to all blood-bought believers. It is very hard for Christian believers in the "Church and State," "God and king" ethic to embrace this vital truth. But this is stated very clearly to us by the apostle Paul in Ephesians 2:11-14. This then becomes the basis for a second passport, of sorts. This could become precious to many hard-pressed saints in times to come who might otherwise consider themselves a people without a nation, and persona-non-grata.

The author describes the various stages of the gathering and the eventual final harvest at the end. We also see that the remnant that returns is a huge company. They are the glorified saints from both sides of Calvary, the living and the dead, raised incorruptible. As John saw in vision, and described in Revelation 7, all of the redeemed and glorified saints are numbered among the 12 tribes of Israel, even a company of saints from every nation, race, and tribe. They are all there, gathered around the throne of God.

Gian Luca Morotti brings a plethora of Scriptures to bear to establish the full story of the pilgrimage home. There is also a full compendium of references for further study. Through the telling of the story the reader can sense a spirit of encouragement, of exhortation, and of cheer for the pilgrims in passage, even as they prepare to embark upon that difficult last leg of their journey, their pilgrimage home to the Holy City.

How precious this is for the saints of the Latter Days! They have been given a roadmap laying out the full plan of God. With it comes the promise in Joel 2 of the Holy Spirit outpouring, even the true and genuine Latter Rain. How wonderful for them to realize that there is a dual anointing by the Holy Spirit in the Order of Melchizedek for both salvation and for righteousness. This is the true "double anointing." Under the auspices of the Shepherd-King the pilgrims in passage will be given this divine provision. Their God will be with them, even as they make their journey through the Valley of Decision, out of the present morass, and up onto the highway of holiness. There, the great vistas will be seen, even visions of splendor that beggar description.

Through all the pages of this book the grand theme remains the same. We are shown a God who wants to save as many people as He can. He is healing the family feud and repairing the Breach of Jeroboam. And even as He does so, He is drawing people from all nations to Himself, even to Israel's Messiah, Yeshua HaMashiach, our Lord Jesus Christ.

Dr. Gavin Finley, M.D.
Biblical Commentator, Endtime Pilgrim (Blog), RET. Medical Doctor
Commonwealth of Israel Foundation, Board Member
Pensacola, Florida – USA

9 789898 551766 8